Modern Language Association of America

Approaches to Teaching
World Literature

Joseph Gibaldi, Series Editor

Approaches to

Teaching the

Arthurian Tradition

Edited by
Maureen Fries
and
Jeanie Watson

The Modern Language Association of America
New York   1992

Library of Congress Cataloging-in-Publication Data

Approaches to teaching the Arthurian tradition / edited by Maureen
Fries and Jeanie Watson.
    p. cm. — (Approaches to teaching world literature ; 40)
  Includes bibliographical references and index.
  ISBN 0-87352-701-1 (cloth) ISBN 0-87352-702-X (pbk.)
  1. Arthurian romances—Study and teaching. 2. Arthurian romances—
Adaptations—Study and teaching. I. Fries, Maureen. II. Watson,
Jeanie, 1943– . III. Series.
PN57.A6A67 1992
809'.93351—dc20   91-31090

Cover art for the paperback edition: Illustration by Dorothea Brady, from
Sir Gawain and the Green Knight (London: Golden Cockerel Press,
1952). Reproduced with permission of the Rare Books and Manuscripts
Division, The New York Public Library, Astor, Lenox and Tilden
Foundations.

Published by The Modern Language Association of America
10 Astor Place, New York, New York 10003-6981

CONTENTS

PREFACE TO THE SERIES

In *The Art of Teaching* Gilbert Highet wrote, "Bad teaching wastes a great deal of effort, and spoils many lives which might have been full of energy and happiness." All too many teachers have failed in their work, Highet argued, simply "because they have not thought about it." We hope that the Approaches to Teaching World Literature series, sponsored by the Modern Language Association's Publications Committee, will not only improve the craft—as well as the art—of teaching but also encourage serious and continuing discussion of the aims and methods of teaching literature.

The principal objective of the series is to collect within each volume different points of view on teaching a specific literary work, a literary tradition, or a writer widely taught at the undergraduate level. The preparation of each volume begins with a wide-ranging survey of instructors, thus enabling us to include in the volume the philosophies and approaches, thoughts and methods of scores of experienced teachers. The result is a sourcebook of material, information, and ideas on teaching the subject of the volume to undergraduates.

The series is intended to serve nonspecialists as well as specialists, inexperienced as well as experienced teachers, graduate students who wish to learn effective ways of teaching as well as senior professors who wish to compare their own approaches with the approaches of colleagues in other schools. Of course, no volume in the series can ever substitute for erudition, intelligence, creativity, and sensitivity in teaching. We hope merely that each book will point readers in useful directions; at most each will offer only a first step in the long journey to successful teaching.

Joseph Gibaldi
Series Editor

PREFACE TO THE VOLUME

Beginning with sometimes contradictory and confused accounts from historians and pseudohistorians in the early Middle Ages, the Arthurian tradition in literature continues in the late twentieth century to show amazing longevity and continuing vitality. Whether there ever was a historical King Arthur—and if there was, whether he was the *dux bellorum*, or battle leader, who defended his Celtic homeland against the invading Germanic tribes of Anglo-Saxons and others and (historically, though not in legend) was defeated by them—his literary namesake and those legendary followers associated with, and sometimes newly invented for, him are alive and well in our own time. They are, moreover, the subject of an ever-increasing number of courses in Arthurian literature in milieus ranging from high school classrooms through two- and four-year college courses to university graduate seminars. Unlike its companion medieval Matters of France and of Rome the Great, the Matter of Britain maintains its appeal to our students because of its attention to universal problems in human relations, its unflagging idealism, and its affirmation of the triumph of the spirit over dilemmas unsolvable at the earthly level, and even—in the figure of the king himself—over death.

But such a complex and many-faceted tradition presents a plethora of problems to its practitioners, whether the specialist in Arthurian literature, the generalist who chooses to teach it, or (especially) the neophyte who approaches it for the first time. Where does one begin a course that embraces the most important continuous thread of the tapestry of British (and, latterly, American) literary history? Which works from which literary periods should one choose? What about texts in languages other than English? What translations are available, and how good are they? Should the course embrace only medieval works or include modern ones as well? And, if both, what kind of mix is most desirable? Are there discrete Arthurian traditions, and—if so— what are they and which works best exemplify them? What kinds of backgrounds in history and chronicle, romance and epic, mythology and Celtic tradition are most helpful? Who or what are the major Arthurian authors or works? What is the place of archaeology and history in such a course or courses? What about music, art, film? Or audience adaptation—for example, children? These and other pedagogical dilemmas require expert advice.

To investigate such expertise, the Modern Language Association distributed questionnaires on the teaching of Arthurian literature to members of the International Arthurian Society and to a selected group of its own membership. Almost a hundred responses were received, from high schools as well as from every postsecondary level, from all regions of the United States as well as from Australia, Canada, France, and Spain. The resulting data offer a fascinating panorama of approaches and techniques for teaching the Arthurian tradition in literature.

In its composition as well as in the materials and approaches described, the volume offered here reflects the needs and desiderata apparent from these responses. Unfortunately, both the format of this series and the page limitations of the volume itself prevent our providing either "an Arthurian canon" (we wonder if there is such a thing) or an essay on "the present state of Arthurian studies," as requested by one respondent each. Other recently published tools, such as *The Arthurian Encyclopedia* (ed. Lacy et al.) and *King Arthur through the Ages* (ed. Lagorio and Day), as well as the recently merged journal *Arthurian Interpretations* and newsletter *Quondam et Futurus*, should be useful for these purposes.

As is usual in the series format, the volume consists of two major sections. Part 1, "Materials," which contains specific information for teaching the tradition, is divided into a section on medieval and modern works and on anthologies and a section on readings and other teaching aids. Part 2, "Approaches," commences with an extensive survey of the actual teaching of Arthuriana and continues into five groups of essays that naturally suggested themselves in an overview of responses to the questionnaire: backgrounds, the "hoole" tradition (Malory's word), major authors, various levels of instruction, and specific approaches. Twenty-four essays represent the refreshing range and variety teachers of the Arthurian tradition bring to their chosen subject, and we regret that considerations of space prevented our commissioning the number of other approaches our respondents described so attractively. A list of contributors and survey participants, a list of works cited, and an index round out the volume; all bibliographic references in the text are keyed to full citations in the list of works cited.

Several contributors to *Approaches to Teaching the Arthurian Tradition* delivered their essays at two sessions sponsored by TEAMS (Consortium for the Teaching of the Middle Ages) at the 1987 International Conference on Medieval Studies (Medieval Inst., Western Michigan Univ., Kalamazoo, MI). Entitled "Symposium on Pedagogy and Curricular Resources: Teaching the Arthurian Tradition in Literature," these sessions featured the essays by Beverly Taylor, Kevin J. Harty, and Mary Alice Grellner (session 1); and Mary L. Beaudry, Sally K. Slocum, and Maureen Fries (session 2).

This volume was undertaken and brought to completion without the "help from many sources" usually cited. But we did receive crucial aid from a few people at critical junctures, and to these we owe heartfelt thanks. Joanne Martonis, as part of her studies for a master's degree in English at Fredonia State University College, was responsible for the bulk of the material in Works Cited, which she heroically organized from the often fragmentary references supplied by our questionnaire respondents. At a later stage, Margaret Pabst, associate librarian at Fredonia, called on her own personal network of librarians to help circumvent steep charges placed on interlibrary computer services by the budget freeze in the State University of New York. Gary Barber and Richard Hart are other librarians whose dedicated work in the final days of checking references should not go unmentioned. Cecilia Filopkowski, my graduate assistant for the 1991 spring term, also cheerfully shared in that labor. Most important, Richard S. Jarvis, former vice president at Fredonia and now vice provost for academic programs and research of the State University of New York, provided, through his institution of the Office of Research Services, the assistance of a skilled professional to complete finished copy for the "Materials" and the first part of the "Approaches" sections. That professional, Joanne Foeller, through her talents with machines, her considerable editorial expertise, and, above all, her enthusiastic cooperation, made a contribution to this book impossible to overestimate.

Our most enduring thanks, of course, go to the many colleagues who took time out of busy lives not only to answer our questionnaire but to send and to speak words of invaluable encouragement—often at times when we most needed it. Our contributors, who with equanimity and patience responded to the demands of the various stages of this volume, also deserve our gratitude, as do the Modern Language Association and the members of its Publications Committee for its sponsorship of this series. Joe Gibaldi, general editor of the series, offered patience and support throughout the preparation of the manuscript, and the anonymous reviewers, both of the original proposal and of the completed book, provided guidance and useful suggestions. Finally, without all those authors, living but mostly dead, who created, continued, and are sustaining the wonderful tradition that inspired this collection, we would have lacked such a fruitful subject. We are grateful for what they wrote and are writing, and we are proud to be their interpreters.

In their names and in my own, I dedicate this book to Professor Valerie Marie Lagorio, "Auntie Val" to so many of us and superb guide through the perilous forest of Arthurian studies.

MF

Part One

MATERIALS

Texts for Teaching

Teachers of the Arthurian tradition in literature choose textbooks and other resources for a variety of reasons: design of the course, availability, and cost all play a necessary role. Because Arthurian literature extends over a longer period of time and contains more works than perhaps any other tradition except the Bible, course design is highly individual. Instructors may choose to include one Arthurian work or more in a general literature course, such as a literature survey; or in a specialized class, such as medieval literature; or in a study of mode or genre, such as the epic or romance. Or they may teach only such works in an Arthurian course proper. For some of these courses, additional considerations are necessary. First, in what language and out of what culture (national or international) will the teacher conduct the class? While an overwhelming number of respondents to the Arthurian survey are teachers of English or American literature, using texts in English, a majority use at least one text from another literature, in translation. A sizable minority—about one-sixth—of the respondents are teachers of French (professors of German and of Spanish and Portuguese count for only one response each, and there are none for other literatures containing Arthurian works). Second, will the course use the original language (Middle English or Old French, for instance) or a modern translation in the same language or in English? Third, will the course feature works only from the seminal medieval period, only from the modern period (mostly the nineteenth and twentieth centuries), or from both? Fourth, will an anthology or individual texts or a combination of the two best serve student needs? Fifth, at what level will the course be taught (a question that bears on all the previous ones)? Respondents to the questionnaire on which our textual data are based teach at all levels, from high school to college undergraduate to university graduate programs, although most of them teach at the undergraduate level at which this volume is primarily aimed.

But course-design considerations are only the first of several limitations in planning Arthurian or parti-Arthurian syllabi. Availability of text is an all-important factor. Texts come into and go out of print with dizzying frequency. Anthologies in particular have not been very numerous in Arthurian studies, and often only one is available at any one time; yet because of the desire of many instructors to provide thorough coverage of the field and the cost and bulk of individual texts, anthologies are often a painful necessity. Many who have used them, however, would agree with Donald L. Hoffman: "I have found no anthology that really works." Use of nonanthologized texts, such as one or more of the over two hundred novels that have appeared in the last century, also depends on whether the books are in print—and, regrettably but understandably, many of the dozens from which choices might be made are not.

Cost is another important factor, especially in these days of inflation and a wider but poorer pool of students who must do the buying. Particularly in a comprehensive, medieval-cum-modern, all-Arthurian course, the costs of books can run to a student-staggering total. Some publishers have shown admirable initiative, however, in issuing (sometimes numerous) cheap but quality editions of Arthurian works—or, in the words of Stanley Kahrl, "Without Penguin we'd be dead." Themes of cost (cheapest) or availability (what's still in print) or both echo repeatedly throughout the answers to our questionnaire.

Medieval Works

Arthurian Chronicles

Among those instructors who teach the earliest Arthurian literature, none teach the Latin chronicles in their original language—not surprising, given our students' widespread ignorance of that tongue. The most popular of these chronicles is Geoffrey of Monmouth's *Historia regum Britanniae* (c. 1136), of which the section on the Arthurian matter forms the most prominent part. The definitive English translation is that of Lewis Thorpe, which has a full introduction and accurately reproduces its original. Other translations used are abbreviated versions. Parts of Sebastian Evans's rendering as revised by Charles W. Dunn—in a more stilted and less colloquial English than Thorpe's—appear in Richard L. Brengle's now out-of-print anthology, *Arthur King of Britain*. And a new and even more curtailed translation, by Richard M. Loomis, is part of James J. Wilhelm and Laila Zamuelis Gross's collection, *The Romance of Arthur*. A few teachers also use some of the pre- and post-Galfridian chroniclers, of whom selections from Gildas (c. 540), Bede (731), Nennius (c. 800), the *Annales Cambriae* (c. 950), William of Malmesbury (c. 1125), Giraldus Cambrensis (c. 1195), and Ralph Higden (c. 1327) may be found in Brengle. The latter has translated all these except for Giraldus, which has been rendered into English by H. E. Butler, and Higden, modernized from the edition of Joseph Rawson Lumby. Brief excerpts from Gildas, Bede, Nennius, the *Annales*, *The Legend of St. Goeznovius* (c. 1019), and William also appear in *Romance*, translated by Wilhelm.

All these readable translations are based on the Latin texts edited by
E. K. Chambers in *Arthur of Britain.*

A few instructors also teach the Galfridian-inspired chroniclers Wace
(Old French) and Layamon (Middle English), late twelfth and early
thirteenth century, respectively, although rather more teachers mention them briefly in lectures. Selections are available in competent
translations (no one reports using the originals except in the occasional
photocopied sample) in Brengle (abridged from Eugene Mason, whose
translation *Arthurian Chronicles [Represented by Wace and Layamon]*
is also cited separately) and in Wilhelm, editor and translator, *The
Romance of Arthur II.* J. A. W. Bennett and G. W. Smithers's *Early
Middle English Verse and Prose* also contains Layamon.

Celtic Literature

Many instructors use at least one of the Arthurian tales of the so-called
Mabinogion or *Mabinogi* (late eleventh century). As James Dean puts it,
the medieval Welsh tales aid in introducing "the Celtic background of
the Arthurian story in myth and folktale." By far the most popular
choice among these stories is "Culhwch and Olwen," but "The Dream
of Rhonabwy" and the three Welsh romances allied to the work of
Chrétien de Troyes—"Geraint and Enid," "Owain," and "Peredur"
(all from thirteenth-century mss.)—are also sometimes singled out. As
with the Latin chronicles, no respondent teaches the Celtic originals,
but a number of translations are available. "Culhwch," "Rhonabwy,"
and all the romances appear in *The Mabinogion*, edited and translated
by Jeffrey Gantz; "Culhwch" in *The Mabinogi and Other Medieval
Welsh Tales*, edited and translated by Patrick K. Ford, and in Brengle,
translated by Gwyn Jones and Thomas Jones, as well as in *Romance*,
translated by Richard M. Loomis; "Peredur" in *Romance II*, translated
by John K. Bollard; and "Rhonabwy" in Brengle, translated by Jones
and Jones. (Both translations by the Joneses are from the old
Everyman's Library *Mabinogion*, 1949; revised edition, 1974.) All
these are fairly literal translations, with minor differences largely
depending on taste. Gantz's translation tends to be both the most frank
and the most colloquial in its English. For example, compare these
parallel passages describing Culhwch's conception:

> After his [Cilydd's] stay with her the country went to prayers
> whether they might have offspring. . . .   (Jones and Jones)

> After his wedding feast with her, the country went to prayer to
> see whether they would have an heir.   (Ford)

> After he lodged with her, the country went to prayers that they
> might have an heir.   (Loomis)

> After he had slept with her the country went to pray for the
> couple to have children. . . .   (Gantz)

Besides individual stories, teachers also mention using "early Welsh
tradition" or, in the words of Sally Mussetter, "early evidential
snippets." Some of these, including selections from *The Gododdin, The
Book of Taliesin, The Stanzas of [on] the Graves*, and other poems from
The Black Book of Carmarthen, and *The Triads of the Isle of Britain*, all
found in thirteenth-century manuscripts, are conveniently collected in
"Arthur in the Early Welsh Tradition," translated by John K. Bollard,
in *Romance*. They include texts both heroic and comic, the exact
compositional dates of which are hotly debated, on such subjects as the
praise of Arthur and his (sometimes only eventual) warriors, and
material that may have contributed to the stories of Guinevere's
abduction and the Holy Grail.

French Literature

Like other works from this early period, French Arthurian literature is
taught overwhelmingly in translation, even by French instructors, who
teach it in modern French or even English versions. Only two
respondents to our survey said they used Old French originals except
in the occasional illustrative photocopy, and those for specialized
upper-division courses. But French works are taught by almost all
instructors who teach either a medieval or a mixed modern and
medieval Arthurian course. And they include representative texts from
almost every stage and facet of this exceptionally vital and long-lived
part of the tradition, necessary for "a comprehensive view of Arthurian
literature" (Harvey L. Sharrer).

The originator of the French romance tradition, the highly imaginative poet Chrétien de Troyes (fl. 1160–80), is the most popular French
author for teachers of every language allegiance. James Dean has
stated his influence well:

> Chrétien is crucial for the early development of Arthurian
> romance. He grapples with issues that occur again and again in

the tradition: Can love exist between married people? Can a knight fulfill himself both as a soldier and as a lover? Can true joy exist in love? Must a lover suffer? How far should lovers go in proving their love? Is love a kind of madness? Chrétien, with his concern with psychological problems and with meaning, provides an excellent contrast to the mythic tales in *The Mabinogi*, and his works help define the romance as a genre, especially against *The Mabinogi* and Geoffrey's historical work.

Of Chrétien's works the most popular is the *Lancelot (Le Chevalier de la Charrete)*, but his other works—*Yvain (Le chevalier au lion)*, *Erec et Enide*, *Perceval (Le conte du Graal)*, and even the only marginally Arthurian *Cligés*—are also taught. Standard editions in the original Old French have been those of Mario Roques for the *Lancelot*, *Yvain*, and *Erec*; Felix Lecoy, *Perceval*; and Alexandre Micha, *Cligés*. French instructors mainly report, however, that they use the modern French translations of Chrétien by Andre Mary, Claude Buridant and Jean Trotin, and Jean Frappier in their classes. New editions with *en face* English renderings have also recently been published: the *Lancelot* and *Yvain*, edited and translated by William W. Kibler; and *Erec et Enide*, edited and translated by Carleton W. Carroll. Both these works, in English translation alone, appeared as Penguin paperbacks in 1991. The *Perceval* has been freshly translated by Ruth Harwood Cline, although several instructors report continued use of Roger Sherman Loomis and Laura Hibbard Loomis's out-of-print *Perceval*, in *Medieval Romances*, and one uses Nigel Bryant's version.

The W. W. Comfort English translation of four of Chrétien's romances (all except the *Perceval*), the standard named most often by respondents in all fields, has been newly revised by D. D. R. Owen, but the sprightly new versions by Kibler are gaining in popularity. "Lancelot: Or, The Knight of the Cart" is conveniently available in *Romance*, and "Yvain: Or, The Knight with the Lion" in *Romance II*, as well as in their Garland Press originals. Jeanne T. Mathewson expresses the view of those who have tried the Kibler: it is "far superior to the Comfort translation," which has remained in print and been sought after mainly for its cheapness and availability.

Here is a comparison of the two translations as they render an early passage of the *Lancelot*, in which the Otherworld abductor Meleagant challenges the court. Comfort has:

King Arthur, I hold in captivity knights, ladies and damsels who belong to thy dominion and household; but it is not because of any intention to restore them to thee that I make reference to them here; rather do I wish to proclaim and serve thee notice that thou has not the strength or the resources to enable thee to secure them again. And be assured that thou shalt die before thou canst ever succour them.   (270)

But Kibler gives us this:

King Arthur, I hold imprisoned Knights, ladies and maidens from your land and household. I do not bring you news of them because I intend to return them to you; rather, I want to inform you that you have neither wealth nor power enough to ensure their release. And know you well that you will die before you are able to come to their aid.   (90)

Kibler's version, as even this small selection indicates, has a number of virtues: it is both less pompous and more economical than Comfort's; it does away with the second person singular address of Meleagant to the king, a calculated insult the linguistic subtlety of which we can understand but that is as off-putting to our students as would be (to most of them) the original languages of all this early material; and it exhibits a colloquialism and grace closer to the original's than its predecessor does. Kibler has put the case for the virtues and limitations of his, or any, rendering of the poetry in his *Romance II* introduction to *Yvain:* "One cannot hope to capture Chrétien's technical virtuosity in a translation, and much of what was original with Chrétien may appear to us eight centuries later as unexceptional, or even naive," but "perhaps this translation will help us realize that he also could tell a very good story."

Besides Chrétien, instructors (mainly French but in other languages as well) teach a number of other works, which often followed from and in some cases were inspired by his example. Some of the most popular are *Les lais* of Marie de France (1170), particularly the Arthurian "Lanval" and the "Ch[i]evrefeuille," which is based on the Tristan matter that was shortly to be drawn permanently into the Arthurian corpus. Respondents cite the Pierre Jonin modern French translation and the English renderings by Joan Ferrante and Robert Hanning and by Patricia Terry. The editions of J. Rychner and of Jeanne Lods and Mario Roques are also useful. "Ch[i]evrefeuille," translated by Russell Weingartner, is available in *Romance II*. Perhaps the new Penguin version of Marie's *Lais* by Glyn S. Burgess and Keith Busby will be as popular as other Penguin paperbacks in Arthurian literature have been.

A number of other texts from Old French are regularly taught. Other Tristan romances are those of Thomas (1175), edited by Bartina H. Wind, and included in modern French in the Bédier edition as well as those of Andre Mary, Pierre Jonin, and Brian Stone, and conveniently translated into English, along with Gottfried's version, by A. T. Hatto; and Béroul (1191), edited by Ernest Muret and translated by Alan S. Fedrick. Alternatives to these are the anthologized complete Béroul, translated by Norris J. Lacy, and the final section of the Thomas, translated by James J. Wilhelm, both in *Romance II. Tristan* is also taught in its English translation by Hilaire Belloc, available in Bédier. While the central book of the Prose Vulgate (1215–35), the *Lancelot*, is far too long for assignment in class, two other seminal works from that immense compilation make tidy additions to an Arthurian course; and thus a number of teachers use either *The Quest of the Holy Grail*, translated by P. M. Matarasso, or *The Death of King Arthur*, translated by James Cable, or both. Miscellaneous French Arthurian romances a few instructors choose include Robert Biket's "Lay of the Horn," translated by Isabel Butler, in Brengle, and the *Perlesvaus*, edited by William A. Nitze and T. A. Jenkins. Also available are "The Lay of Graelent," translated by Russell Weingartner, and "Episodes from the Prose Merlin and the Suite de Merlin," translated by Samuel M. Rosenberg, both in *Romance II*. One teacher uses the selections from Morris Bishop's *Survey of French Literature*, volume 1, which includes Joseph Bédier's version of the "Philtre" and "Mort" episodes from his modernization of the conflated *Tristan*.

German Literature

As with the works from Old French, Middle High German texts are taught mainly in translation, but at least one is included in English by a majority of those who teach medieval Arthurian works only and a sizable number who also teach modern works. Only one instructor, Arthur Groos, reports using a work by the earliest German Arthurian author, Hartmann von Aue (c. 1200), but he is emphatic about its value to his Introduction to Middle High German course: "I *always* use *Iwein*, because it's crucial for all the later romances of the thirteenth century." *Iwein* appears in a recent edition and translation by Patrick M. McConeghy. More popular, probably in part because of their readily available Penguin translations, are the works of Wolfram von Eschenbach and Gottfried von Strassburg (both c. 1210). Gottfried's *Tristan und Isold* appears in a German edition by Friedrich Ranke, and in English translation by A. T. Hatto; Wolfram's *Parzival*, in a German edition by Albert Leitzmann and Wilhelm Deinert, and in English translation by Hatto as well as by Helen M. Mustard and Charles E. Passage. Harvey L. Sharrer, comparing the last two, says that the Hatto "seems superior." Some instructors, however, still choose the abridged Jessie L. Weston version of *Tristan*, in Loomis and Loomis's *Medieval Romances*.

Other Continental Literatures

Harvey Sharrer's complete and detailed response to our questionnaire also indicates his use of the Icelandic *Saga of Tristram and Isond* (c. 1400), translated by Paul Schach. Additionally, in a survey of medieval Portuguese literature, he uses the following: *The Portuguese Book of Joseph of Arimathea*, edited by Henry Hare Carter (selections are in somewhat modernized form—that is, with word and paragraph divisions and punctuation); "La version galaïco-portugaise de la *Suite de Merlin*," transcribed by Amadeu-J. Soberanas (handout with text); the *Demanda do Graal*, edited by Maria Leonor Carvalhao Buescu (with additional selections from the full edition by Augusto Magne); and the *Fragmento de un "Livro de Tristan" galaïco-portuges*, edited by José Luis Pensado Tomé (handout with text).

English Literature

Works from the Middle English Arthurian tradition appear on the syllabi of almost all our respondents—the only time they do not is in specialized foreign language courses in which only one or two Arthurian works are taught. By far the largest number of mentions accrue to Sir Thomas Malory's *Morte d'Arthur* (1469 or 1470), which is used in a number of versions. The most popular is Eugène Vinaver's one-volume edition of the whole work, available in paper. Vinaver's *King Arthur and His Knights: Selected Tales by Sir Thomas Malory* is also popular, perhaps not least because its modernized spelling is combined with fidelity to the original text. As Vinaver says in his introduction to the 1977 edition:

> Of the innumerable previous printings of Malory's works in modern orthography not a single one preserves the text as written by him; in all without exception obsolete words are removed or replaced by their modern equivalents in spite of the claim of some editors [to the contrary].

That Vinaver's does preserve the actual vocabulary makes it a teaching tool superior to all others. But the old Everyman edition of John Rhys is also popular, as are Michael Senior's, Keith Baines's, Sanders and

Ward's, and Janet Cowen's. Anthologized possibilities include the Rhys version in Brengle, and Laila Zamuelis Gross's in *Romance*. The Derek Brewer edition of the last two books of Malory (of the eight-part division suggested first by Vinaver) is useful but is apparently now out of print. Two complete hardcover editions, Vinaver's three-volume *Works of Sir Thomas Malory* and the James W. Spisak and William Matthews two-volume version of what was until several decades ago the standard redaction—*Caxton's Malory: Le Morte d'Arthur*—both with handsome critical apparatus, are too bulky and expensive for regular student use, but do nicely for reserve shelves.

For most teachers, in the words of David C. Fowler, "Malory is *the* text," and it often determines what other works are taught: "The first half of the course is devoted to earlier works for their own sake and as a background to Malory," Fowler adds. The most popular Middle English work next to the *Morte d'Arthur* is *Sir Gawain and the Green Knight* (before 1400), which numerous instructors, whether teachers of English or of other languages, choose. As is evident also from a previous MLA volume, *Approaches to Teaching* Sir Gawain and the Green Knight (ed. Miller and Chance), the most sought-after edition is the modern poetic translation of Marie Borroff, which drew as many superlatives in our responses as in the previous survey. Mark Allen states his reasons for this choice as succinctly as anyone: "the quality of the poetry." That Borroff's translation is available in *The Norton Anthology of English Literature*, volume 1 (ed. Abrams et al.), as well as in a separate edition, only adds to its enthusiastic adoption. Other editions used—not nearly as popular as Borroff's—are those of Brian Stone, James L. Rosenberg, A. C. Cawley, J. A. Burrow, Burton Raffel, and John Gardner. A verse translation by Wilhelm is available in *Romance*. One mention of W. R. J. Barron's *en face* edition with the original bolstered by a modern prosification presents another possibility. But this too shares the "when available" caveat, and a recent attempt to choose a translation (spring 1988) revealed that only Raffel's (not by any means most people's first choice) and the anthologized versions by Borroff and Wilhelm could be had. Fewer than a handful of respondents seem to teach *Gawain* in the original, but among these the only edition mentioned was the definitive one of J. R. R. Tolkien, E. V. Gordon, and Norman Davis.

Besides *Sir Gawain and the Green Knight*, several related Middle English poems are taught by a few instructors. The most popular is Geoffrey Chaucer's Wife of Bath's Tale (c. 1390s), taught mainly by those who assign the *Norton Anthology* as their main text. This also is (or was) available in a Bellerophon illustrated coloring-book version of the original text, which I used some years ago with roaring success.

Like other shorter works, it is sometimes duplicated on ditto and presented as a handout. Not many instructors mention the other English Gawain romances, but for those who teach them, a convenient collection is Louis B. Hall's *Knightly Tales of Sir Gawain*, which contains prose translations of the following, primarily from the late fifteenth and early sixteenth centuries: "Sir Gawain and the Carl of Carlisle," "The Green Knight," "The Adventures at Tarn Wadling," "Golagros and Gawain," "An Adventure of Sir Gawain," "The Avowing of King Arthur, Sir Gawain, Sir Kay, and Sir Baldwin of Britain," and "The Wedding of Sir Gawain and Dame Ragnell." Selections from *Arthur and Merlin* (1265), translated by Jessie L. Weston, and *The Prose "Merlin"* (c. 1450), modernized by Brengle from the Henry B. Wheatley Early English Text Society (EETS) version, appear in Brengle.

Brengle's anthology also contains selections from the two final Middle English Arthurian poems taught with any regularity, the *Stanzaic Morte Arthur* (mid-fourteenth century) and the *Alliterative Morte Arthure* (before 1400). These two appear on syllabi both in their own right and as known English sources for Malory. Selections from the *Alliterative Morte* are also anthologized in *Romance*, in the modernized text of Valerie Krishna; her poetic version of the original and her translation are also available separately. Brengle uses the translation of Roger Sherman Loomis and Rudolph Willard, *Medieval English Verse and Prose*, for the alliterative poem, and his own modernization of James Douglas Bruce's EETS edition of the stanzaic one; both are in prose. The best teaching edition of these poems in the original language, slightly modernized and well glossed—and with useful critical apparatus—is that of Larry D. Benson.

Modern Works

While Arthurian works have continued to be written in several languages other than English from the fifteenth century until the present, only the Anglophone tradition has proved a viable one. No respondent to our survey, including teachers of French, German, and Spanish and Portuguese, uses works from the modern era except English or American ones, no matter in which course. Within this era, moreover, only a couple of authors are ever taught outside the nineteenth and twentieth centuries; and more twentieth-century texts appear on syllabi than for all previous centuries combined—appropriate to the avalanche of materials that has issued forth from modern writers.

Renaissance through Eighteenth Century

Only two works of recognized genius from this period are named. A few respondents teach Edmund Spenser's *Faerie Queene* (1590, 1596), for which Arthurian characters and themes provide some of the frame. But of its six books, only the first and sometimes the second and third appear on just a few text lists. The standard edition is that of Edwin A. Greenlaw, Charles Grosvener Osgood, et al., but instructors mostly use the *Norton Anthology* excerpts in class. The other text, cited by only one instructor, is the Arthurian-inspired *Don Quixote* (1605, 1615) of Miguel de Cervantes Saavedra, with its parodies of Arthurian quest and courtly love; it is available in numerous paperback editions.

Nineteenth Century

Almost one-half of our respondents teach the works of the major writer of Arthurian literature in the nineteenth century, Alfred, Lord Tennyson. *Idylls of the King* (1833–86) is taught in whole or in part by several non-Victorian specialists and is the cornerstone of the course for two respondents who teach Victorian literature alone. Linda K. Hughes puts the case for the *Idylls* well: "After Malory, it is the next full-length work devoted to Arthur in English, and . . . marked the full renaissance of the Arthurian tradition in the nineteenth century, coming as it did on the heels of Southey's and another edition of Malory." It also shows, Hughes says, "how two authors can take many of the same stories and yet create a fundamentally different" work of art—in Tennyson's case, "a story of faith and doubt as well as of kingship." J. M. Gray's is the definitive edition; a variety of paperbacks have been available, and the anthology *Victorian Poetry and Poetics*, edited by Walter Edwards Houghton and G. Robert Strange, contains selected *Idylls* as well as "The Lady of Shalott," "Morte d'Arthur," and "Sir Galahad," which are taught by a few instructors.

Next most popular (with about one-third of our respondents) is Mark Twain's *Connecticut Yankee in King Arthur's Court* (1889), usually taught in paperback.

Three other British Victorians, poets all, are the choice of a few teachers. To Matthew Arnold belongs the first modernization in English of the Tristan story, "Tristram and Isolde" (1852), available in *Poetical Works*, edited by C. B. Tinker and H. F. Lowry, and in *Victorian Poetry*. William Morris's first and most commended book of poetry, *The Defence of Guenevere and Other Poems* (1858), contains— besides the title poem—"King Arthur's Tomb," "Near Avalon," and "A Good Knight in Prison"; "The Defence of Guenevere" also appears in *Victorian Poetry* as well as the edition of Carole Silver. Algernon

Charles Swinburne's "Tristram of Lyonesse" (1882) may be found in the *Complete Works*, edited by Edmund Gosse and T. J. Wise.

Twentieth Century

Numerous instructors use twentieth-century Arthurian works with a special emphasis on the novel, which has become the preeminent form in the last fifty years. Of the more than two hundred novels published in the last century, however, only a few appear as texts of choice on syllabi. As with so many other materials under discussion here, much depends on availability, although the books most in demand can almost always be found in print. A distinct advantage is that such novels are widely and cheaply available in paperback.

The most widely mentioned twentieth-century novel is T. H. White's *Once and Future King*, taught by half of our respondents. Phillip C. Boardman says, "I always use White's *Once and Future King* (I start the course with it)." Kevin J. Harty chooses instead White's less frequently read *Book of Merlyn*: "I teach only *Merlyn* rather than all of *The Once and Future King*; the latter is too long, given the other reading requirements of the course, and *Merlyn* represents materials not previously seen."

Next to White's book, the most popular novels are those of Mary Stewart, including her Merlin trilogy *The Crystal Cave*, *The Hollow Hills*, *The Last Enchantment*; and *The Wicked Day*, whose central character is Mordred. Several instructors indicate they teach (in the words of one) "anything by Mary Stewart." Linda K. Hughes best expresses the rationale: "to expose students to the approach of historical reconstruction, especially useful because the Roman or Latin element is likely to have been forgotten after the students' focus on Malory, Tennyson, and White."

About one-tenth of our respondents teach Thomas Berger's *Arthur Rex: A Legendary Novel*. Its appeal is obvious—as Raymond H. Thompson says, "Like Twain, Berger has a keen eye for the ridiculousness inherent in so many romance conventions"—but I have discovered both in conversations with students and exchanges with other teachers that Berger's is perhaps the most controversial of modern Arthurian novels.

Among the remaining Arthurian novels instructors mentioned the following, one or two times each: Marion Zimmer Bradley, *The Mists of Avalon*; Gillian Bradshaw, *Hawk of May*, *Kingdom of Summer*, *In Winter's Shadow*; Catherine Christian, *The Pendragon*; Susan Cooper, *The Dark Is Rising*; Parke Godwin, *Firelord*, *Beloved Exile*, *The Last Rainbow*; C. S. Lewis, *That Hideous Strength: A Modern Fairy-Tale for*

(1945)

(1952)

Grown-ups; Bernard Malamud, *The Natural*; Richard Monaco, *Parsival: Or, A Knight's Tale, The Grail War, The Final Quest*; Andre Norton, *Merlin's Mirror*; Walker Percy, *Lancelot*; John Steinbeck, *Tortilla Flat* and *The Acts of King Arthur and His Noble Knights, from the Winchester MSS of Thomas Malory and Other Sources*; Rosemary
1963 —Sutcliff, *Sword at Sunset*; Charles Williams, *War in Heaven.* (1930)

Williams is also one of only three twentieth-century poets taught: his *Taliesin through Logres* and *The Region of the Summer Stars* earn a couple of mentions, while his prose work *The Figure of Arthur*, edited by C. S. Lewis in *Arthurian Torso*, earns one. The other two poets are T. S. Eliot, *The Waste Land*, mentioned twice, and Edwin Arlington Robinson, whose "Merlin" and *Tristram* are the choice of one instructor.

Although Arthurian drama had a vogue around the turn of the century, only two (musical) dramas occur on our respondents' syllabi. They are *Camelot*, by Alan Jay Lerner and Friedrich Loewe, mentioned a handful of times, and the operas of Richard Wagner, mentioned twice.

Anthologies

While the cry "I refuse to anthologize!" resounds through our instructor responses, the prohibitive cost of separate texts for most of the courses in which Arthurian literature is taught makes an anthology necessarily a frequent choice. Three collections mentioned often above, where their contents are detailed, are made up entirely of Arthurian selections. Richard L. Brengle's *Arthur King of Britain* and ←
James J. Wilhelm and Laila Zamuelis Gross's *Romance of Arthur* emphasize mostly British texts, while Wilhelm's *Romance of Arthur II*) OK
concentrates on the French tradition. Wilhelm's *Romance of Arthur III* includes works from the rest of Europe. More specialized is Peter Goodrich's *Romance of Merlin*.

Although the Brengle volume is out of print, it has its enthusiastic adherents. Sally K. Slocum likes it so much that she keeps a number of copies for her successive classes. Michael Rewa notes of Brengle, "I'm sorry it's out of print. I like its suggestive variety and its third section of critical materials." A number of teachers either keep it as a supplementary, often reserve, text or consult its selections on their own.

Reaction to the *Romance* volumes varies far more widely, as we discovered in a separate and supplementary query, to which about one-third of our original respondents replied. Of these, about two-thirds had taught from one or both volumes. On the one hand, some teachers are enthusiastic about the series. Joseph McClatchey says, "I

am very pleased with these volumes," while George R. Keiser notes of
Romance, "This is a very good anthology, and I would probably use it if
I were to reorganize the structure of my undergrad and grad Arthurian
literature course"; he is one of several instructors who indicate
possible future use of the book(s). On the other hand, a number of
caveats arise, particularly over the questions of cost, translation, and
general suitability of both volumes.

"Yes, I have used *Romance of Arthur* in both a sophomore Arthurian
survey and in a graduate seminar in the past," says Phillip C.
Boardman, and "this semester . . . I am using *both* volumes, . . .
although like most Garland books they are expensive for classroom
use." Delmar C. Homan adds that Garland "gave such a low discount
that our bookstore charged students over three dollars more than list
price for the book." Translations of texts in the *Romance* volumes also
elicit controversial opinions. Douglas J. McMillan states, "I find the
translations in the Garland volumes excellent—they speak directly to
our modern students without distorting the medieval culture and
content. The illustrations and maps are also helpful in presenting the
material." Not all instructors agree, at least about all the translations.
Finding Kibler's translation of Chrétien's *Knight of the Cart* "far
superior . . . especially in retaining some of the suspense of the story
and also in ease of style," Kathryn L. Lynch "did not like the
translation of *Sir Gawain and the Green Knight* as well as Marie
Borroff's, especially its rendering of the last few lines, which I think
removes some of their tantalizing ambiguity." She adds, "My other
quibble is with the advisability of using so heavily abbreviated a text of
Geoffrey of Monmouth or of Malory," but notes "on the positive side
. . . this anthology picked out just the texts that are most central on
my, and I think other teachers', reading lists." A further opinion is that
of Michael Rewa: "I've found chapter 1 of *Romance* no easy or
substantial pleasure to deal with. . . . The quoted texts seem almost
buried. I think I'd rather read a straightforward introduction, followed
by a chapter with excerpts from the historians prominently offered,
preceded or followed by a substantial commentary on the nature of the
source (what are the works the quotations come from like?)." Praising
some other chapters and "the intelligence shown in most of the
prefactory materials," he nevertheless adds: "Ultimately, I'm not sure
I'll want to use the text again."

Other instructors comment on the advisability of using two anthologies in one course, and particularly on the utility of *Romance II*.
Raymond H. Thompson says that he has used volume 1 (*Romance*) in a
graduate course on Arthurian literature in the Middle Ages and will
use it again; but, while he will consider using volume 2, he "would be

more inclined to spend time on Malory." Delmar Homan adds, "The second volume is good, but probably the first stands alone better for an introductory course. . . . In a course such as mine with more modern materials also used, the two volumes would probably provide too much material." Another all-Arthurian anthology cited by a few respondents is Richard W. Barber's *Arthurian Legends*, which contains selections from the *Annales Cambriae*, Nennius, *The Life of St. Carannog*, Geoffrey of Monmouth's *Historia* (Thorpe translation), Wace and Layamon (Paton translation), a "Death of Arthur" from a north Welsh manuscript, Gwyn Jones and Thomas Jones's "Culhwch and Olwen," Mason's "Sir Launfal," Comfort's "Yvain," Hatto's *Tristan*, Mustard and Passage's *Parzival*, Matarasso's *Quest*, Stone's *Sir Gawain and the Green Knight*, Vinaver's Malory, and Cable's *Death of King Arthur*.

Some objections raised (to the *Romance*, Barber, and Brengle volumes) apply to anthologies in general. Alan T. Gaylord says, "I use individual volumes and do not work out of anthologies." And Donald L. Hoffman says he does not intend to use either *Romance* volume:

> The problem is that there are too many things I like to teach that are not in the book and too many things that, if they are in the book, are in such itsy-bitsy pieces that they are all but useless. The volume (*Romance*) has undertaken to fulfill a real need, but it does not fulfill it satisfactorily. It might, in fact, be final evidence that Arthurian courses are so individual and so complex that no anthology can be entirely satisfactory, perhaps not even reasonably useful.

Even only partially Arthurian anthologies nevertheless continue in use, especially for survey and other only parti-Arthurian courses. Most popular of these are the Norton series. The *Norton Anthology of English Literature*, volume 1 (ed. Abrams et al.), contains Chaucer's Wife of Bath's Tale, *Sir Gawain and the Green Knight* (Borroff translation), *The Faerie Queene*, books 1 and 3 (selections, including the "Visit to Merlin"); the *Norton Anthology of English Literature*, volume 2, Tennyson's "Lady of Shallot" and "The Epic [Morte d'Arthur]" as well as (from the *Idylls*) "Pelleas and Ettarre" and "The Passing of Arthur"; and the *Norton Major Authors*, the Wife of Bath's Tale, *Sir Gawain and the Green Knight*, *The Faerie Queene*, book 1, "Lady of Shalott" and "The Passing of Arthur," and Eliot's *Waste Land*.

A few instructors also teach Arthurian matter from anthologies of medieval literature, although most of these works now seem to be out of print. Loomis and Willard's *Medieval English Verse and Prose in Modernized Versions* includes selections from Layamon, the *Allitera-*

tive Morte Arthure, and Malory as well as Theodore Howard Banks's translation of *Sir Gawain and the Green Knight*. Loomis and Loomis's *Medieval Romances* offers Chrétien's *Perceval*, Gottfried's *Tristan*, Malory's "Book of Balin," and Florence Ridley's prose *Sir Gawain and the Green Knight*. Lewis J. Owen and Nancy H. Owen's *Middle English Poetry: An Anthology* contains selections from Layamon and the *Alliterative Morte* as well as all of *The Auntirs of Arthure at the Terne Wathelyn*. D. W. Robertson's *Literature of Medieval England* has selections from Gildas, Bede, and Malory, "Culhwch and Olwen," Marie de France's "Lanval" and "The Woodbine" ("Ch[i]evrefeuille"), the Wife of Bath's Tale, and *Sir Gawain and the Green Knight*. In *Middle English Verse Romances*, Donald B. Sands provides "Sir Launfal," "The Wedding of Sir Gawain and Dame Ragnell," and *Sir Gawain and the Carl of Carlisle*. Thomas J. Garbáty, in *Medieval English Literature*, offers *Sir Gawain and the Green Knight* in Middle English.

Contents of *Victorian Poetry and Poetics*, used by a couple of teachers, are detailed above. Alone among our respondents, Carol Harding uses *The Oxford Anthology of English Literature*, general editors Frank Kermode and John Hollander, medieval editor J. B. Trapp (vol. 1), which she cites as "well chosen and well glossed" and as having a "decent price." It contains Stone's translation of *Sir Gawain and the Green Knight*, as well as The Wife of Bath's Tale and selections from Malory and Spenser, in volume 1; Tennyson's "Lady of Shalott," "Morte d'Arthur," and selections from the *Idylls*, in volume 2, which also has an Arthurian excerpt, "King Pellam's Launde," from David Jones's *In Parenthesis* (1937). Finally, *Sir Gawain and the Green Knight* appears in John Gardner's *Complete Works of the Gawain-Poet*.

Readings for Students and Instructors

Respondents to our survey, asked to suggest background, reference, and critical texts with which teachers of the Arthurian tradition ought to be conversant as well as outside reading required of or recommended to students, provided lists that were not only similar for both purposes but were surprisingly (or perhaps not surprisingly) uniform in their selections. Almost all the instructors furnished such out-of-class material, and a few supplied extensive bibliographies—those of David Fowler and Don Kennedy were especially impressive.

It has not been possible to include here all the scholarship on the abundantly documented Arthurian tradition. Even the bibliographies listed below are not exhaustive or infallible. By piecing the various bibliographical sources together, however, teachers can achieve a fairly complete coverage, and we therefore urge readers to consult them. In the essays in this volume, contributors suggest specialized lists of works of great interest and utility; and their own bibliographies, along with the books and articles cited in this prefatory section, are available in the list of works cited at the end of the book. The sections that follow discuss the most frequently alluded-to works: what instructors have found most helpful both for their own and their students' guidance through the long and mazelike Arthurian tradition and the various cultures in which it has flourished.

Reference Works

Teachers of Arthurian literature are fortunate in having a rich trove of reference sources available. Chief among them in the past was *Arthurian Literature in the Middle Ages*, edited by Roger Sherman Loomis. A "collaborative history" of its subject, with essays of strikingly uneven utility and with no bibliography except in its useful footnotes, it was nevertheless the beloved and indispensable *ALMA* for generations of Arthurian scholars. It will undoubtedly now be replaced by three books. *The Arthurian Encyclopedia*, general editor Norris J. Lacy, contains over 1,200 entries by 130 contributors, who provide a comprehensive descriptive and critical treatment of Arthurian authors, works, and subjects; each topic offers a brief bibliography. Ranging from short entries to substantial articles on single works and authors to discussions of themes and a number of long surveys on such topics as the literature, the art, and the scholarship of the various national traditions, and extending in time from the Arthurian beginnings to the present, the new second edition of this encyclopedia offers even more complete coverage than the previous edition. Lacy has also, along with Geoffrey Ashe, written *The Arthurian Handbook*,

> a critical survey of the Arthurian legend [that] deals with all periods from the fifth and sixth centuries through the Middle Ages and to the present, examining Arthurian origins, the development of the legend in chronicles and other sources, the interpretation of Arthurian themes in literature and their treat-ment in the other arts.   (x)

A glossary and brief bibliography are also included. A successor proper to *ALMA, King Arthur through the Ages*, edited by Valerie M. Lagorio and Mildred Leake Day, was published in 1990; it contains annotated descriptive and critical articles not only on early and modern literature but also on such specialized areas as comics and film.

While Arthurian bibliographies have been numerous in the last few years, they have also been widely available throughout the twentieth century. A pioneer was James Douglas Bruce, whose listings in *The Evolution of Arthurian Romance from the Beginnings down to the Year 1300* are valid to 1922. Successor bibliographies include John J. Parry's (1922–29) and Parry and Margaret Schlauch's (1930–35), as well as those in *Modern Language Quarterly* (1940–63; 1940 listings cover 1936–39). Since 1949, a staple has been the *Bibliographical Bulletin of the International Arthurian Society* (also listed as the *Bulletin Bibliographique de la Société Internationale Arthurienne*), a handsome annual. References to listings in *BBIAS* and to various reviews form the principal and by no means complete annotation to *The Arthurian Bibliography*, edited in several volumes by Cedric E. Pickford, Rex Last, and C. R. Barker between 1981 and 1987. Other annotated bibliographies include those of Clark S. Northrup and John J. Parry (with its supplement by Parry and Paul A. Brown); of Edmund E. Reiss, Louise Horner Reiss, and Beverly Taylor (vol. 1 covering the Middle Ages, vol. 2 the Renaissance to the present); and, for twentieth-century material, of Mary Wildman. Annotated bibliographies of new books and articles have appeared in *Quondam et Futurus*, edited by Mildred Leake Day, since 1980. The annual MLA *International Bibliography*, the MHRA *Annual Bibliography of English Language and Literature*, *The Year's Work in English Studies*, and general bibliographies on medieval literature (such as William Matthews's *Old and Middle English Literature* and John H. Fisher's *The Medieval Literature of Western Europe*) are also possible if often outdated sources.

Among research bibliographies and checklists for individual authors and periods are Glyn S. Burgess, *Marie de France*; Douglas Kelly, *Chrétien de Troyes*; Harvey L. Sharrer, *A Critical Bibliography of Hispanic Arthurian Materials*; and David J. Shirt, *The Old French Tristan Poems*. (Robert Adams's *Tristan Bibliography* is, unfortunately, almost half a century out of date.) To implement onomastic searches, there are Robert W. Ackerman, *An Index of the Arthurian Names in Middle English*, and G. D. West, *French Arthurian Prose Romances: An Index of Proper Names* and *French Arthurian Verse Romances, 1150–1300: An Index of Proper Names*. For manuscript data and plot summary, Helaine Newstead, "Arthurian Legends," is widely cited. A unique source is Tomomi Kato, *A Concordance to the Works of Sir Thomas Malory*. Miscellaneous tools include Phyllis A. Karr, *The King Arthur Companion*, and Charles Moorman and Ruth Moorman, *An Arthurian Dictionary*.

Among general reference sources cited are the *Dictionary of the Middle Ages* and the *Encyclopedia of the Middle Ages*. Albert C. Baugh's *Literary History of England* is popular, as are E. K. Chambers's *English Literature at the Close of the Middle Ages* and (a good student choice) *The Oxford Companion to English Literature*, edited by Paul Harvey. Teachers of French works cite Georges Grente et al., *Dictionnaire des lettres françaises: Le Moyen Age*; Pierre Le Gentil, *Littérature française du Moyen Age*; John Fox, *A Literary History of France*; and Jean Frappier and Reinhold R. Grimm, *Le roman jusqu'à la fin du xiiie siècle*. For German, there is Karl Bertau's *Deutsche Literatur im europäieschen Mittelalter*. A good brief survey of Western European literature as a whole from the seventh to the sixteenth century is W. T. H. Jackson's *Medieval Literature: A History and a Guide*. For general themes applicable to Arthurian works, respondents mentioned Stith Thompson's *Motif Index of Folk Literature* and Gerald Bordman's *Motif-Index of the English Metrical Romances*.

Primary Sources

While the list of non-Arthurian primary source material is not extensive, it is important—especially for students—for an understanding of the wellsprings from which medieval thought and literature in general, and Arthurian literature in particular, flowed. The Vulgate version of the Bible is crucial, for instance, to the comprehension of such varied matters as the concept of Arthur as Christ figure and the matching of Arthurian with biblical events in Geoffrey of Monmouth's *Historia*. Boethius's *Consolation of Philosophy* provides not only a general ideological background but the specific motif of the Wheel of Fortune on which so often the peripety of medieval Arthurian works turns. Saint Augustine's *On Christian Doctrine* illuminates the mind-set of the (mainly clerical) medieval Arthurian writers and (sometimes) their modern successors. Gildas's *De excidio et conquestu Britanniae*, [Nennius's?] *Historia Brittonum*, and the Venerable Bede's *Ecclesiastical History of the English Nation* offer early historical allusions, and one respondent also cites the *Anglo-Saxon Chronicle*. Dante's *Letter to Can Grande* is a general rationale for the vernacular(s) in which Arthurian literature triumphed, and the scene in the *Inferno*, book 5, in which Paolo and Francesca's sin follows on their reading of the Prose *Lancelot* is a specific one. Amatory complications that move Arthurian plots have paradigms in Ovid's *Art of Love* and *Metamorphoses*, Andreas Capellanus's *Art of Courtly Love*, and Guillaume de Lorris and Jean de Meun's *Roman de la rose*. Analogues in classical literature that inform Arthurian motifs—such as, for instance, the disguised Uther's conception of Arthur on Ygerne, or the white sails–black sails theme in the Tristan story—are so numerous as to defy enumeration and to require specific study.

Studies of the Arthurian Literary Tradition

Respondents cited many works that covered all or part, or special aspects, of the long and rich Arthurian tradition. Most popular, besides his *ALMA*, was Roger Sherman Loomis's *Development of Arthurian Romance*, which deals with the medieval period. Like E. K. Chambers's *Arthur of Britain: The Story of King Arthur in History and Legend*, which also includes early texts, it has withstood the years well. Two other well-received works that emphasize the early period are Jean Frappier's *Le roman breton. Introduction: Des origines à Chrétien de Troyes* and James Douglas Bruce's *Evolution of Arthurian Romance from the Beginnings down to the Year 1300*, the bibliography of which has already been cited.

Among surveys that move from medieval to modern, G. H. Maynardier's *Arthur of the English Poets* still has wide appeal after almost nine decades. Also mainly on English literature is Margaret J. C. Reid's *Arthurian Legend: Comparison of Treatment in Modern and Medieval Literature*. Richard W. Barber, prolific author of popular texts in the field (a few respondents suggested they would use "anything by Richard Barber"), discusses material from historical origins to the nineteenth century in *Arthur of Albion: An Introduction to the Arthurian Literature and Legends of England*. Elizabeth Jenkins's *Mystery of King Arthur* is a misleadingly titled study of the influence of Arthurian matter on (also mainly English) literature from the Middle Ages to our own century. Useful, too, is *King Arthur and the Grail: The Arthurian Legends and Their Meaning*, by Richard Cavendish.

Emphasis on Celtic origins appears in some further works mentioned. John Rhys's *Studies in the Arthurian Legend*, a century old, is still helpful on sources and analogues from Celtic legend. Lucy Allen Paton's *Studies in the Fairy Mythology of Arthurian Romance* investigates the origins, in a goddess figure, of the story's magic females— Morgan and the various Ladies of the Lake. In *Celtic Myth and Arthurian Romance*, Roger Sherman Loomis looks at the possible and subsequently controversial roots of heroic action and the Grail, a concern he expands on in the ten essays of his *Wales and the Arthurian Legend*. And Jessie L. Weston's *From Ritual to Romance* traces the "Grail problem" from ancient anthropological roots to a Welsh flowering.

Treatments of well-defined segments of the Arthurian story are also available. The early chronicle tradition is the subject of *La légende arthurienne*, by Edmond Faral, which includes documents as well as studies, as it is of Robert W. Hanning's *Vision of History in Early Britain: From Gildas to Geoffrey of Monmouth*. J. S. P. Tatlock's *Legendary History of Britain: Geoffrey of Monmouth's* Historia regum Britanniae *and Its Early Vernacular Versions* offers a comprehensive examination of Geoffrey and his influence on Wace and Layamon. Robert Huntington Fletcher's *Arthurian Material in the Chronicles, Especially Those of Great Britain and France* covers the entire corpus of chronicles from the sixth to the sixteenth century. Even the period of greatest neglect of Arthurian matter has been anatomized, in James Douglas Merriman's *Flower of Kings: A Study of the Arthurian Legend in England between 1485 and 1835*. Beverly Taylor and Elisabeth Brewer's *Return of King Arthur: British and American Arthurian Literature since 1900* [misprint for 1800] deals more thoroughly with the nineteenth than the twentieth century. But two other books help to remedy that gap: Nathan Comfort Starr's *King Arthur Today: The Arthurian Legend in English and American Literature, 1901-1953* and Raymond H. Thompson's *Return from Avalon: A Study of the Arthurian Legend in Modern Fiction*.

Studies of medieval interdisciplinary topics include Rosemary Morris, *The Character of King Arthur in Medieval Literature*; Joan Ferrante, *The Conflict of Love and Honor: The Medieval Tristan Legend in France, Germany, and Italy*; and Madeline Pelner Cosman, *The Education of the Hero in Arthurian Romance* (especially Tristan, Lancelot, and Perceval); and Helaine Newstead, "Arthurian Legends."

Studies of Individual Authors

So numerous are the articles and books on individual writers that it is possible here only to cite books and collections, and only those mentioned most prominently. Of the many studies of Chrétien de Troyes's entire corpus, the most influential is Frappier, *Chrétien de Troyes: L'homme et l'oeuvre*, which has been translated into English by Raymond Cormier. Other frequently cited works are Lacy, *The Craft of Chrétien de Troyes: An Essay in Narrative Technique*; L. T. Topsfield, *Chrétien de Troyes: A Study of the Arthurian Romances*; Roger Sherman Loomis, *Arthurian Tradition and Chrétien de Troyes*; and Urban Tigner Holmes, *Chrétien de Troyes*. On Marie de France, respondents mention Emmanuel J. Mickel, *Marie de France*, and Edgar Sienaert, *Les lais de Marie de France: Du conte merveilleux à la nouvelle psychologie*.

Cited for German authors are a number of studies. Respondents mention Joachim Bumke, *Wolfram von Eschenbach*; on Gottfried von Strassburg, W. T. H. Jackson, *The Anatomy of Love: The Tristan of Gottfried von Strassburg*, and Winfried Christ, *Rhetorik und Roman: Untersuchungen zu Gottfrieds von Strassburg "Tristan und Isold"*; on Wolfram and Hartmann von Aue, Herbert E. Wiegand, *Studien zur Minne und Ehe in Wolframs* Parzival *und Hartmanns Artusepik*. Works devoted to several authors include Hugo Kuhn, *Tristan, Niebelungenlied, Artusstruktur*, and—especially useful—James A. Schultz, *The Shape of the Round Table: Structures of Middle High German Arthurian Romance*, which has an appendix of summaries of all of the romances in question.

By far the most popular resource for teaching *Sir Gawain and the Green Knight* is Larry D. Benson, *Art and Tradition in* Sir Gawain and the Green Knight, and A. C. Spearing, *The Gawain-Poet: A Critical Study*, is a close second. Several collections of essays frequently mentioned are Sir Gawain *and* Pearl: *Critical Essays*, edited by Robert J. Blanch; *Twentieth Century Interpretations of* Sir Gawain and the Green Knight: *A Collection of Critical Essays*, edited by Denton J. Fox; and *Critical Studies of* Sir Gawain and the Green Knight, edited by Donald R. Howard and Christian Zacher. For this poem and the other Gawain poems of its time, *The Alliterative Tradition of the Fourteenth Century*, edited by Bernard S. Levy and Paul E. Szarmach, is often cited.

Probably the most frequent recourse for critical and scholarly information on Malory is to the various works of Vinaver, including the introduction and notes to his three-volume edition of the *Works*, and his *Malory*. Next most often mentioned is Benson, *Malory's* Morte Darthur. Other popular monographs are those of Beverly Kennedy, *Knighthood in Malory's* Morte Darthur; Mark Lambert, *Style and Vision in "Le Morte Darthur"*; Elizabeth T. Pochoda, *Arthurian Propaganda: "Le Morte Darthur" as an Historical Ideal of Life*; Sandra Ness Ihle, *Malory's Grail Quest: Invention and Adaptation in Medieval Prose Romance*; and Muriel Whitaker, *Arthur's Kingdom of Adventure: The World of Malory's "Morte Darthur."*

Among collections of articles on Malory, the most often mentioned is *Studies in Malory*, edited by James W. Spisak; *Aspects of Malory*, edited by Toshiyuki Takamiya and Derek Brewer, is also popular. Teachers and students may trace the decades-ago argument over whether the *Morte d'Arthur* is a unified work or a collection of tales, in *Malory's Originality: A Critical Study of* La Morte Darthur, edited by Robert M. Lumiansky, and (intended at least partly as a reply to the previously published essays of Lumiansky and his adherents) *Essays on Malory*, edited by J. A. W. Bennett.

Fewer works on individual authors are mentioned for the modern period. Most frequent resources are those for Tennyson, including J. Phillip Eggers, *King Arthur's Laureate*; John R. Reed, *Perception and Design in Tennyson's* Idylls; John D. Rosenberg, *The Fall of Camelot: A Study of Tennyson's* Idylls of the King; and David Staines, *Tennyson's Camelot:* The Idylls of the King *and Its Medieval Sources*. For *A Connecticut Yankee at King Arthur's Court*, there is Henry Nash Smith, *Mark Twain's Fable of Progress*. For the twentieth century, Charles Moorman, *Arthurian Triptych: Mythic Materials in Charles Williams, C. S. Lewis, and T. S. Eliot*, is cited. *The Figure of Merlin in the Nineteenth and Twentieth Centuries*, edited by Jeanie Watson and Maureen Fries, contains essays on a number of important works from the last hundred years.

Literary Contexts

Perhaps because there are so many works available on the Arthurian tradition proper, the number of general works recommended is fairly small. It nevertheless includes texts of which every student should be aware. Joseph Campbell, *The Hero with a Thousand Faces*, provides an overview of heroic archetypes that are characteristic of many cultures worldwide. Erich Auerbach, *Mimesis: The Representation of Reality in Western Literature*, concentrates on passages of crucial significance in a number of works from the European tradition. Specifically medieval in focus are several other background studies: Henry Osborne Taylor, *The Medieval Mind*; Henry Adams, *Mont St. Michel and Chartres*; C. S. Lewis, *The Discarded Image*; and E. K. Chambers, *English Literature at the Close of the Middle Ages*. C. N. Manlove, *Impulse of Fantasy Literature*, is a newer work one respondent finds helpful. Georges Dumézil, *Mythe et épopée*, and Joel Grisward, *L'archéologie de l'épopée médiévale*, are also useful. Among older theoretical works most frequently cited is T. S. Eliot's "Tradition and the Individual Talent," while Jacques Derrida, *Disseminator* and *The Post Card*, are among the newer.

Northrop Frye's *Anatomy of Criticism* contains, among other useful features, a famous discussion of romance, and works on romance and allied genres are understandably of wide interest. W. P. Ker's *Epic and Romance* has not lost its classic status, nor has Ezra Pound's *Spirit of Romance*. Vinaver's *Rise of Romance* is an encyclopedic condensed discussion of its subject, as is his "Shaping Spirit in Medieval Verse and Prose." Works found especially useful for the study of Middle English romance are John Spiers, *Medieval English Poetry: The Non-Chaucerian Tradition*, an extreme mythological reading; Dieter Mehl, *The Middle English Romances of the Thirteenth and Fourteenth Centuries*, which concentrates on genre; John Ganim, *Style and Consciousness in Middle English Narrative*, a study of time, space, and audience; and Anne Wilson, *Traditional Romance and Tale*, focusing on the English Arthurian romances. Lillian Hornstein's "Middle English Romance" is a useful survey of scholarship and criticism, now unfortunately almost twenty years out of date.

For French romance, respondents cite Paul Zumthor, *Essai de poétique médiévale*; Karl D. Uitti, *Story, Myth, and Celebration in Old French Narrative Poetry*; Hanning, *The Individual in Twelfth Century Romance*; and M. Domenica Legge, *Anglo-Norman Literature and Its Background*. John Stevens's *Medieval Romance* surveys themes from Chrétien de Troyes to Malory, and Dennis H. Green's *Irony in the Medieval Romance* looks at French, German, and English exemplars. The titles of Erich Köhler's *Ideal und Wirklichkeit in der höfischen Epik: Studien zur Form der furhen Artus- und Graldichtung* and William W. Ryding's *Structure in Medieval Narrative* indicate their focus. A more comprehensive book is Denis de Rougemont's *Love in the Western World*, an analysis of the Tristan legend and its influence on literature and culture.

Courtly love, the focus of de Rougemont's work, is the subject of a number of reliable resources. C. S. Lewis's controversial but perdurable *Allegory of Love* is a favorite, as are the largely skeptical essays in *The Meaning of Courtly Love*, edited by F. X. Newman. D. D. R. Owen's *Noble Lovers*, John C. Moore's *Love in Twelfth-Century France*, and Frappier's collection of articles *Amour courtois et table ronde* are also cited. Roger Boase's *Origin and Meaning of Courtly Love: A Critical Study of European Scholarship* surveys previous approaches.

Allied to courtly love is the topic of chivalry, the subject of a number of essays in *Chivalric Literature: Essays on Relations between Literature and Life in the Later Middle Ages*, edited by Larry D. Benson and John Leyerle. Charles Moorman, *A Knyght There Was*, discusses its subject from the twelfth century to the Renaissance. Among Richard W. Barber's books, *The Knight and Chivalry* and *The Reign of Chivalry* are popular, as is an old favorite, Sidney Painter's *French Chivalry: Chivalric Ideas and Practices in Mediaeval France*.

History, Archaeology, Anthropology

Especially important because of the possible existence of a historical Arthur and the mention of actual, possible, and probable geographical sites in Arthurian literature are books on history and archaeology. Among general historical studies the most frequently cited are Winston Churchill, *A History of the English-Speaking Peoples*; R. W. Southern,

The Making of the Middle Ages; A. D. Deyermond, *The Middle Ages*; and Christopher Brooke, *The Structure of Medieval Society*. Studies focusing on specific periods are Doris Stenton, *English Society in the Early Middle Ages*, and Alec R. Myers, *England in the Late Middle Ages (1307–1536)*; Colin Morris, *The Discovery of the Individual, 1050–1200*; Dorothy Whitelock, *The Beginnings of English Society*; and Olive G. Tomkieff, *Life in Norman England*. Of particular interest for early origins are Anne Ross, *Pagan Celts*; Jean Markale, *King Arthur: King of Kings* (originally published in French as *Le roi Arthur et la société celtique*); and Peter H. Blair, *Roman Britain and Early England*. Aimed at a wide audience is Jack Lindsay, *Arthur and His Times: Britain in the Dark Ages*, while John Morris, *The Age of Arthur: A History of the British Isles from 350–650*, takes the king's reign as a focus for its period.

One of the leading proponents of a historical Arthur who unites geographical with cultural considerations is Leslie Alcock, whose *Arthur's Britain: History and Archaeology A.D. 367–634* and *Was This Camelot?* are frequently cited. Even more widely used are the works of Geoffrey Ashe, including *Camelot and the Vision of Albion*, *King Arthur's Avalon: The Story of Glastonbury*, and *The Quest for Arthur's Britain*. Also mentioned is R. F. Treharne, *The Glastonbury Legends: Joseph of Arimathea, The Holy Grail and King Arthur*. Colin Wilson, *The Search for the Real Arthur*, and Christopher Hibbert, *The Search for King Arthur*, are other investigations into origins, which Barber's *Figure of Arthur* proposes to find in Scots-Irish sources—while Nikolai Tolstoy seeks to prove the shaman origin of Arthur's seer in *The Quest for Merlin*. *British Heritage* magazine's *King Arthur Special Issue* (ed. Huganir) offers a variety of specially commissioned articles on Arthurian Britain.

Serial Publications

Arthurians are fortunate in the number and variety of periodicals in their field and allied areas. The *Bibliographical Bulletin of the International Arthurian Society* offers a yearly account of scholarship, criticism, and book reviews organized under the rubrics of the numerous national branches of the society and in articles in the section "Research and Criticism." *Quondam et Futurus: Quarterly for Arthurian Studies*, edited by Mildred Leake Day, had articles, book reviews, brief notices, and lists of current publications, and *Arthurian Interpretations*, edited by Henry Hall Peyton III, contained articles and book reviews. As of 1991, these two publications have merged to become *Quondam et Futurus: A Journal of Arthurian Interpretations*. *Encomia:*

Bibliographical Bulletin of the International Courtly Literature Society, edited by Maria Dobozy, includes yearly bibliography organized by national branches. *Avalon to Camelot*, published by Freya Reeves Lambides, was an attractive quarterly with Arthurian columns, departments, and articles for the lay reader as well as the specialist, but it ceased publication in 1991. *Tristania*, edited by Pedro Campa, publishes articles and book reviews associated with the figure of Tristan. News of calls for papers, conferences, publications and works in progress, and other business appears in the *International Arthurian Society North American Branch Newsletter*, edited by Hans R. Runte.

Aids to Teaching

Most of the survey respondents report the use of various kinds of teaching aids in whatever course they teach. As Mary P. Richards notes, "Audiovisual aids are unusually effective in teaching the Arthurian legend because such a wealth of archaeological and art historical evidence remains to document its growth and popularity." Such aids range from postcards and slides or facsimiles of manuscript and book illustrations, through videotapes and a complete telecourse, to one or more of the almost three dozen films on Arthurian subjects— and even include dramatized reenactments of often quasi-Arthurian events by students themselves.

One of the most thoroughly documented of the latter is Camelot Consciousness Day, the culmination to the Arthurian unit taught by Debi S. Graham, who sent along with her response a recipe for the castle cake that tops the students' display. Her pupils assume medieval characters for the day and arrive in costume; entertainment includes juggling, music on instruments of medieval origin, and recitals by class "scops"; crafts include baking, weaving, and handcrafting of wooden shields, stained glass windows, and architectural diagrams; and the authentic medieval feast that follows is climaxed by the performance of jesters. After the performance, the participants give their impressions in what Graham calls a "bittersweet discussion." Recipes for medieval feasts are available in Cosman's *Fabulous Feasts: Medieval Cookery and Ceremony* and Constance B. Hieatt and Sharon Butler's *Pleyn Delit: Medieval Cookery for Modern Cooks*. A prime source for such reenactments in the past was the Society for Creative Anachronism, but only one respondent, Margaret Grimes, reports currently using this resource.

Perhaps the most frequent recourse reflected in our survey is to pictorial Arthuriana of various sorts. Some teachers merely pass around books with illustrations; others offer postcards purchased or slides taken by themselves or others abroad (most frequently in England); still others exhibit elaborate professional slide carousels or videotapes. One may combine a variety of these—Mary Richards, for example, supplements her own slide presentation and script relating to the Arthurian sites in Britain with a twenty-minute archaeological video-tape, *King Arthur*, from the University of Toronto Media Centre (which also has other useful materials) and professional slides pro-duced by the Bodleian Library, Oxford. Besides such depictions of actual sites, slides of illustrations from Arthurian books are popular. Alan Lupack draws on his personal collection of over two thousand Arthurian books. He finds, for instance, that "slides of the Dan Beard illustrations for the first edition of *Connecticut Yankee* not only suggest the various levels of meaning in the book but also help to show how the book comments on the social-economic-cultural conditions of the late nineteenth century." Beverly Taylor uses slides of drawings and paintings by the Pre-Raphaelites in both a Victorian and a more general humanities course, especially for teaching Tennyson and Twain.

Recordings also have appeal as teaching tools. In Taylor's class, students may hear Richard Wagner's *Tristan und Isolde*; Mary Alice Grellner plays Claire Bloom's reading of Joseph Bédier's moderniza-tion of medieval texts, *Tristan and Isolde*. Michael Rewa makes extensive use of "matter-related songs" from the 1960s and 1970s: as examples he offers Moody Blues's "Are You Sitting Comfortably," which "refers to Merlin and Camelot"; Rich Wakeman's album "Myths and Legends of King Arthur"; and Crosby, Stills, and Nash's, and also Donovan's, "Guinevere." Information on recordings, videotapes, and other teaching aids is available from a variety of sources, not always current. Frederick E. Danker, "Teaching Medieval Literature: Texts, Recordings, and Techniques" is, unfortunately, two decades out of date, but the *Schwann Record and Tape Guide*—issued every month—can be of some help. So can the catalogs of the University of Toronto Media Centre, whose extensive series of videotapes may be rented or purchased from the Distribution Office, 121 Saint George Street, Toronto, Ontario M5S 1A1, Canada. References to possible sources for slide reproduction or other classroom display appear both in *The Arthurian Encyclopedia*, under numerous relevant articles, and in *The Arthurian Handbook*, in the chapter "Arthur in the Arts."

Also in the *Encyclopedia* are articles on films as a group and on individual examples, usually listed under the name of the director. Film is a popular, although by no means universally utilized, resource for the teacher of Arthurian matter. There have been almost three dozen such films, not including television series (mostly aimed at children), to date, of varied provenance and quality. The most popular movies for the classroom are *Camelot* (1967), *Excalibur* (1981), and *Monty Python and the Holy Grail* (1975)—the last two cult films with large followings among students. Also mentioned are the third movie version of *A Connecticut Yankee in King Arthur's Court* (1949) and three other productions from Hollywood's golden years, *Knights of the Round Table* (1953) and *The Black Knight* and *Prince Valiant* (both 1954). Among Continental versions of the legend, much praise goes to Robert Bresson's *Lancelot du Lac* (1974) and Eric Rohmer's *Perceval le Gallois* (1978). While many teachers show such films as adjuncts to or illustrations of literary texts, Bruce A. Beatie has described in a recent article, "Arthurian Films and Arthurian Texts: Problems of Reception and Comprehension," his planning and teaching of a course, Faces of Camelot, in which the active watching and discussing of seven films occupied equal time with the written material.

Identification, suitability, and availability of Arthurian films remain problems. Kevin Harty, whose "Cinema Arthuriana: Translations of the Arthurian Legend to the Screen" is another useful article for the teacher who is interested in movie portrayals, excludes from his discussion any of the latter that treat Arthurian characters only in passing or "Arthurian themes only indirectly or analogously" (95; his example here is *The Natural*). In a more recent book on Arthurian films, Harty lists thirty-five; Beatie, in an appendix to his article, lists twenty-nine. The lists largely overlap, but some titles are unique to each—and certainly, if Beatie finds Disney's *Sword in the Stone* (1963) "too childish to be of use in a college-level course" (71), few who have seen another Disney entry, *The Spaceman and King Arthur* (called by its other title, *The Unidentified Flying Oddball*, in Harty's list, 1979), would waste class time on it. Beatie found that a four-month waiting period allowed "no opportunity for pre-screening or for detailed research on . . . quality" and says some films are inaccessible "except, perhaps . . . with a videocassette recorder and a sharp eye on the late-night movie schedule" (66, 71). Nevertheless, for the interested instructor who wants to plan ahead, there are—besides the *Encyclopedia* entries and the Beatie and Harty articles, and the *Arthurian Handbook* section "Film"—standard film reference works: Gene Brown, *The New York Times Encyclopedia of Film*; Leslie Halliwell, *The Filmgoer's Companion* and *Halliwell's Film Guide*; and *Leonard Maltin's TV Movies and Video Guide*, as well as Roger Manvell, *The International Encyclopedia of Film*. Harty's "Cinema Arthuriana" contains valuable periodical references.

Part Two

APPROACHES

INTRODUCTION

The Labyrinthine Ways:
Teaching the Arthurian Tradition

Maureen Fries

The student in my Chaucer class came to me two weeks into the semester to say that, although she had been reluctant to take the course, she liked it and planned to stay in it. "What I really wanted," she said, "was Arthurian literature. But the chairperson said that it wouldn't be offered until next year, and I will have graduated by then." Her face brightened. "Maybe I can come back and take it from you anyway."

Why do this student and others like her—often numerous others—show such interest in a tradition older than Chaucer, as old as the Old English most of them will never take? Is it the appeal of an ideal society, the Round Table that, while never realizing completely its own goals, went down valiantly in their defense? Is it the lure of the love story of Lancelot and Guinevere, with its conflict between duty and passion? Is it the mysterious supernatural aura surrounding characters such as Morgan le Fay and Merlin and objects such as the Holy Grail? Is it the supposed survival of Arthur himself, dozing in Avalon until Great Britain (and by analogy, the world) should need him again? Or is it the contemporary media hype that uses, and sometimes abuses, all these elements, in films such as *Excalibur* and comic books such as *Camelot 3000* and novels such as *The Mists of Avalon?*

The media hype may draw them to the Matter of Britain, but students stay to absorb themselves in the pseudohistorian Geoffrey of Monmouth, who first pulled the tradition together; the master romancer Chrétien de Troyes, who infused it with its interest in love; the grand synthesizer Thomas Malory, whose *Morte d'Arthur* gave enduring form to the French prose tradition that preceded him. Whether they study one or all of these works or the postmedieval versions of the story that accumulated (and are accumulating still) in such surprising numbers, pupils at every level from high school to graduate school respond to The Legend (as some of them call it, as if there were no other) with awe and delight. This volume seeks to capture, through investigation of the backgrounds to and teaching of the tradition, "the sense of wonder" (in the words of one respondent, Kevin J. Harty) "that runs through all of Arthuriana" and makes both its teaching and its learning such a joy. "Your volume should raise the question 'Why Arthur?' and suggest a whole range of possible answers," Harty goes on. It "should show, with apologies to Chaucer, that it is in Arthuriana that one finds God's plenty."

Plenty there is, as this introduction demonstrates, in the replies we received from the respondents to the questionnaire on teaching the Arthurian tradition in literature sent them by the Modern Language Association. This survey offers a fascinating glimpse of what teachers are doing and how students are responding to that tradition in classrooms ranging from the high school through the junior college, four-year college and graduate levels, mostly in the United States (although we received one reply from Canada and one from Australia). Here I offer the reader an overview of the survey and the essays commissioned from some of its respondents that follow. Section 1 details the kinds of courses in which Arthurian literature is taught; section 2 concentrates on the classroom ramifications of this teaching; section 3 describes papers and projects used to implement and test student learning; and section 4 contains a brief summary of the essays on individual approaches generated by this study.

1. Teaching the Arthurian Tradition

While almost all respondents taught Arthurian literature in courses at the undergraduate level, a few (about one-tenth) taught it at the graduate level and some fewer in mixed undergraduate and graduate courses, and about one-twentieth in high school classes. Somewhat over one-tenth of all participants taught the works in French, one in German, and one in Spanish and Portuguese; the rest taught in English. By far the most frequent type of setting—mentioned by three-quarters of the instructors—was the undergraduate survey, twice as likely to be upper- rather than lower-division. Such surveys bore a dizzying array of titles and provenances: world literature, medieval literature, English or British literature, comparative literature, humanities, medieval culture, fantasy, romance, and Victorian literature by no means exhaust their names. A little over ten percent taught purely Arthurian courses, but others confessed to tailoring a standard survey—say, in medieval literature—to such a use. In the area of special topics, besides courses bearing that name there were such titles as King Arthur Today, Arthur in Literature and Film, Love and Duty in the Twelfth Century, Malory and Medieval Romance (a graduate seminar, as we might expect), and even a course called Camelot. Freshman courses, too, served as vehicles for Arthurian texts.

One of the fullest responses on course variety came from Arthur Groos, who told us, "Arthurian literature is taught in many forms at Cornell, and I can only report on a few that I'm involved in." These include a freshman seminar, "composition course with 'content,'" formerly entitled King Arthur and His Knights (since retitled Literature of Chivalry); Comparative Literature 343, an epic-romance course that includes Chrétien, Wolfram's *Parzival*, (the German) *Gawan*, and Malory; and German Literature 405–406, Introduction to Middle High German, which contains *Iwein*, *Parzival*, and *Tristan*. Groos also teaches a graduate, comparative survey of Arthuriana.

While most of the respondents have had no chance to engage in such a wide variety of across-the-board course offerings, they display imagination and ingenuity in their use of Arthurian materials. Not the least impressive of these efforts are those of interested high school teachers.

High School Courses

Replies in this category indicate that high school teachers use Arthurian materials mostly at the upper level (in junior- or senior-year courses). David W. Pitre incorporates versions of the legend into his year-long survey of British literature. Elizabeth Fishbach finds that her introduction to the matter "as an ongoing literary cycle," in which she employs both translations and modern works as well as films, works with "upper termers" of all abilities. Ernest Gabrielson gives his junior-year students a three-week unit based on selections from high school texts. The most complete description of a course offering came from Debi S. Graham, who uses Arthuriana as a unit in her senior writing workshop for college-bound students: her comprehensive selections run from Andreas Capellanus through medieval materials and Tennyson. Graham chooses the Keith Baines edition of Malory because she likes it, but has typed up an "easier" version for her students "so they can understand Arthur's beginnings as a young man and king. . . . I do not want them to struggle for meaning until later in the unit."

But because of time constraints and course requirements, high school teachers are limited in what they can offer. Greater freedom of design is often available to instructors of undergraduate college courses, even when Arthurian materials must be included in general surveys. Such courses appear at every level of instruction, including the junior college.

Junior College Courses

Opportunities for teaching Arthuriana at this level are aptly described by Mary L. Beaudry:

> Courses in which I have incorporated Arthurian studies include Survey of English Literature and Drama Appreciation. Arthurian material can, of course, be appropriately included in several other general education, liberal arts, or humanities courses that at the two-year college level are often expected to provide a broad background of cultural understanding to students, many of whom do not plan to earn a baccalaureate degree.

Even at a two-year school, a special-topics Arthurian course is possible. Beverly Kennedy teaches to Canadian grades 12 and 13 a three-credit course in Malory's *Morte d'Arthur*, "in the 'Great Works' category. We read the entire work—Everyman edition." Kennedy explains:

> I teach Malory's entire work on the grounds that (1) this is the seminal work for the Arthurian tradition in English literature and (2) it is not possible to appreciate Malory's achievement by reading an abridged version or by reading only the post-Grail narrative, which is all that can be accommodated in a survey course, whether medieval lit only, or medieval to modern.

But, as with high school, most community college settings do not allow for this much specialization. It is at the four-year college and university that Arthurian materials assume their most prominent place in the curriculum.

College and University Undergraduate Courses

Lower-Division Courses. Most freshman- and sophomore-level classes in which Arthurian materials appear are concerned primarily with literature, but—and this came as a surprise—some are writing courses. The freshman writing seminar cited by Arthur Groos as a "composition course with 'content,'" Medieval Studies 102, is assigned to teaching assistants and usually progresses from Marie de France, Chrétien, Wolfram or Gottfried, Malory or *Gawan* to a "modern" Arthurian work, such as *Connecticut Yankee,* although instructors are "free to play with this program within reason." Groos enclosed several syllabi showing options perhaps not available at schools where freshman writing courses are more general or more uniform.

Teachers of general literature courses at the freshman and sophomore levels can also often incorporate Arthurian works into their syllabi. Raymond H. Thompson usually includes some Arthurian literature in his sections of first-year survey courses. Julian Wasserman confesses, "I tend to sneak Arthurian lit into all of my courses," including a freshman literature offering called Emerging Self and a sophomore survey. Lorie Roth organizes her freshman introduction to literature and sophomore humanities courses so that they include such works as the Vinaver selection of Malory's *Tales, Sir Gawain and the Green Knight,* the Wife of Bath's Tale, and some Tennyson, as well as *The Natural,* by Bernard Malamud. In both of her humanities courses, Margaret Grimes includes Chrétien, *Sir Gawain and the Green Knight,* and parts of Malory. Robert Merrill fits not only these but Gottfried, Wolfram, and a translation of *The Quest of the Holy Grail* into his general British literature and comparative literature surveys. While fantasy courses are usually found in upper divisions, George R. Keiser teaches a lower-division offering called Fable and Fantasy:

> Here I use pairs of works, one ancient or medieval and the other modern—the Arthurian portion of Geoffrey's *Historia* in conjunction with Mary Stewart's *Crystal Cave* or Vinaver's little anthology of selections from Malory, in conjunction with T. H. White's *Once and Future King . . .* to make students aware of the tradition that is behind the modern works they read (and the modern world in which they live).

At the opposite extreme from such widely inclusive options is the necessary narrowness of choice for Delmar C. Homan, who teaches in his course Western World Literature, mostly for sophomores, only *Sir Gawain and the Green Knight* because it is the only Arthurian work in

the *Norton Anthology*. As with writing courses, lower-division literature courses face constraints—in this case, of textbook, not a small
consideration in view of rising costs. Yet some teachers at this level can
design their offerings as all-Arthurian, using paperbacks. Thus Phillip
C. Boardman teaches a general literature course, King Arthur and His
Knights, including both medieval and modern works, and Mark Allen
lists Arthurian Literature under Popular Topics in Literature.

These courses are representative of English offerings at the freshman
and sophomore levels, but only a handful of professors in languages
other than English teach Arthurian works in lower-division contexts,
and some of these works are taught in translation (either in moderniza-
tions of the original or in English). Lenora D. Wolfgang teaches
medieval literature in modern French "with selected photocopies of
the original editions" and lectures on "the evolution of the Arthurian
stories" and on works in the tradition not assigned for class. The
former group includes some Chrétien and the Bédier modernization of
Tristan; the latter, the chronicles and the prose romances. Heather
Arden offers for majors a first-term survey, in modern French, of the
Middle Ages and the Renaissance, including Marie, Chrétien's *Lancelot*
and *Yvain*, and excerpts from *Tristan*; for nonmajors, Arthurian
Romance, in English. Jeff Rider teaches Arthurian Literature in the
Middle Ages for freshmen and King Arthur through the Ages "for
everyone" in English. No respondents in other languages (German,
Spanish, Portuguese) indicated any lower-division offerings. Such a
pattern of mainly English instruction persists in upper-division undergraduate courses, where by far the greatest number of listings appear.

Upper-Division Courses.   Not only in numbers but also in variety of
course type and nomenclature, upper-division Arthurian offerings defy
easy classification. What follows is an attempt to tame the dozens of
titles and descriptions submitted into some recognizable—if not
always conventional or canonical—shape.

As with their lower-division counterparts, teachers at this level most
frequently use Arthurian literature in survey courses of every type,
from the broadest—world literature—through areas of increasing
specialization, such as medieval literature, British literature, and
Victorian literature. Arthurian works lend themselves especially well
to comparative and interdisciplinary courses, where they are usually
taught in translation. Malory (often with modernized spelling) is the
great exception to this rule, and the most frequently taught work is his
Morte, with *Sir Gawain and the Green Knight* the runner-up for the
medieval period and White's *Once and Future King* for the modern. Of
the Continental authors, Chrétien is the most likely to be cited, and

Chaucer's Wife of Bath's Tale also makes frequent appearances. Along with freshman and sophomore courses, these junior and senior offerings are often tailored to Arthurian or mostly Arthurian content by afficionados of the tradition.

Special-topics courses are other likely homes for the Matter of Britain. These may be grouped around a theme (Love and Duty in the Twelfth Century, for instance, which cries out for a tale by Chrétien), a genre (romance is the most frequent choice—it is sometimes grouped with epic), or a mode (fantasy, sometimes coupled with another term, such as "legend" or "reality"). A philosophy professor, Douglas Carmichael teaches a winter-term course at various levels that he calls King Arthur in Romance and Reality. "My emphasis is historical," he says, "with no literature except Malory and *early* Welsh," but he also uses his own novel, *Pendragon*. Mark Allen's Theory of Romance course utilizes *Sir Gawain and the Green Knight*, Gottfried's *Tristan*, and Wolfram's *Parzival* (both in their short versions). David Fowler sent us his entire syllabus for Medieval Romance, which he still uses although he no longer teaches it as the television course in which it originated; it is primarily Arthurian. The several people who teach the material in fantasy courses have a wide choice of modern materials to combine with medieval ones if they wish to construct—as Myra Hinman and Raymond Thompson have done—a completely Arthurian syllabus.

All-Arthurian courses enable even broader choices between medieval and modern, or the use of each separately. About one-seventh of our respondents teach such courses under the rubric proper (as opposed to the enthusiasts who have tailored courses with broader names to this purpose) at the upper undergraduate level. David Fowler teaches a senior course called Arthurian Legends, in which he uses English works in the original and others in translation:

> The first half of the course is devoted to earlier works for their own sake and as a background to Malory. Important authors read in translation are Geoffrey of Monmouth, Marie de France, Chrétien, etc. Students may choose still other works as focus of study in outside papers. A main purpose is to enable students to grasp the evolution of the tradition.

Fowler's course is all medieval, but the several Arthurian courses Don Kennedy teaches combine medieval and modern materials. In his senior honors seminar, for instance, he uses Layamon, two Chrétien romances, Gottfried and Wolfram, the Vulgate *Quest*, Malory, Tennyson, Twain, and White. Most such all-Arthurian courses are mixed medieval and modern in content, with the ratio often depending on the instructor's literary specialty. Linda K. Hughes, for instance, says of her King Arthur in Legend and Literature:

> As I am not a medievalist but a Victorianist, I spend less time on strictly medieval sources than some might. Instead, my selection principle is to choose major works from at least three different centuries to introduce students to an ongoing and still living tradition, to examine the connection between a given age and a work produced in that age, and to discover at once the continuity and variability of Arthurian tradition. I therefore assign Malory (selections, but broad selections rather than snippets), the *Idylls* (entire), T. H. White (*Once and Future King*), and, if the course permits, additional twentieth-century examples.

Interdisciplinary Arthurian courses are extremely popular—indeed, the nature of Arthurian literature makes such an approach more feasible than with almost any other subject. Sometimes an interdisciplinary course utilizes two language traditions, such as that taught by Thomas Kelly (French) and Thomas Ohlgren (English) at Purdue University. But the most frequent second discipline invoked is film. While some of our respondents reject the teaching of anything but literature, most people who teach all-Arthurian courses make use of from one to a wide selection of the films available.

Of single-author courses there was very little mention. Malory and Tennyson, as might be expected, dominate here. Linda K. Hughes teaches, for instance, a Tennyson seminar to English majors in which she includes the *Idylls*. A few people teach *Sir Gawain and the Green Knight*, a natural companion to the Wife of Bath's Tale, in their Chaucer courses.

Non-English teachers surveyed did not mention anything similar— there was, for example, no course devoted solely to Chrétien. But medieval French courses especially make use of the Matter. As Theodore Rupp observes, "Much of medieval French literature is, of course, Arthurian." Usual choices are in the main line of development: Marie de France, Chrétien, the *Tristans*, the *Mort Artu*, sometimes Andreas Capellanus and Geoffrey of Monmouth. In German Literature 405–406, Arthur Groos teaches Hartmann's *Iwein* as well as *Parzival* and *Tristan*; in his comparative literature course, besides *Parzival* and *Gawan*, Chrétien and Malory. Harvey L. Sharrer uses, in his comparative literature course in medieval literature, various Arthurian topics, the Tristan and Iseult legend, and the Grail theme; readings are in English translation and in the original for students with sufficient language background. All students read a sample passage of each work in the original language and discuss the "difficulties and pitfalls of translations." Sharrer also teaches a survey of medieval Portuguese literature, with selections from Arthurian romances read in the original Galician-Portuguese and Portuguese.

Both Sharrer's Portuguese survey and Groos's German literature accommodate graduate as well as upperclass students; they constitute two of a handful of instructors who teach dual-level undergraduate-graduate courses.

Dual-Level Courses. Obviously dual-level courses, apparently increasingly common, require careful handling to be successful. George Keiser makes the differing requirements by level clear on the syllabus for his dual course:

> Undergraduates write a short paper every month, in which they discuss their most recent readings and, where possible, draw comparisons and contrasts with their previous readings. For example, in the third paper they were asked to write about the fact that *Sir Gawain and the Green Knight* ends with the hero discovering and having to accept his imperfections, while the heroes of *Ywain* and *Parzival* face their imperfections early in the work and then undertake a series of adventures in which they find some absolution for their sins. The graduate students devote a great part of their time to becoming acquainted with historical and literary studies of fourteenth- and fifteenth-century England, as these relate to the particular Middle English romance they have chosen to treat in their term papers, and they meet with me for a half-hour tutorial every week during the first half of the semester to discuss their readings.

Finally, a few teachers offer courses either wholly or partially Arthurian at the graduate level.

Graduate Courses. All the choices at the other levels also obtain here, except for an understandably greater degree of specialization. Linda T. Holley, in her medieval literature course excluding Chaucer, teaches selections from the chronicles, Wolfram and Gottfried, Chrétien and the Gawain Poet, Malory and Spenser. Don Kennedy adds to these in his graduate Arthurian course the *Mabinogion*, Marie de France, Robert de Boron and the *Alliterative Morte*, and the Vulgate *Quest* and *Mort*. Mary Alice Grellner offers a graduate seminar, the Arthurian

Tradition, that follows a chronological approach and focuses on works written in English.

2. Classroom Aspects of Teaching the Arthurian Tradition

With such a wide variety of courses at a number of levels, the allocation of class time and the integration of individual works into the tradition are the chief concerns of all teachers from high school to college graduate provenance.

Apportionment of Class Time

In general courses at whatever level, the average time spent on the Arthurian tradition is about three weeks; in such courses—medieval literature, for instance, or the British literature survey—when tailored to an Arthurian measure, from one half to almost all (sometimes all); and in Arthurian courses proper, naturally, the entire span. Other considerations obviously include the length of the instruction period. As Stanley Kahrl notes, "On a quarter system you're always out of time. I mix lectures (early in the week) with discussion of particular scenes. . . . Works get about one week, with two for Malory." While half-year courses allow for more time, usually two weeks per work, allocation of time may depend on purpose. Says Phillip C. Boardman, "I prefer the survey approach with as many works as possible, so I rarely spend more than three class meetings on a work."

As with everything else, teaching methods vary widely, but the favorite mode is lecture and discussion. Again, the nature of the class—and the level of students enrolled—help to determine the proportion of these. Many instructors would agree with Donald L. Hoffman that the material requires so much background that "mainly lecture" is required. Others not only allow for more discussion but set aside time for the reading of student papers and reports—a method obviously more suited to the specialized advanced or graduate than the general introductory class. Almost universal as a beginning are the background lectures the Matter of Britain requires. For courses that use film—as so many do—time must be found for showing movies either in class or out. Slides and other reproductions, and recordings, also require time. Finally, the number of works chosen and the emphasis—medieval or modern, or both—is a key determinant.

Many teachers have experimented with various arrangements of works. An articulate discussion of this process is that of Sr. Frances Gussenhoven:

Some years we have read Malory first and then have gone back to the tradition Malory inherited, beginning with Gildas and Nennius and moving on to a reading of parts of Geoffrey of Monmouth, followed by Wolfram and Gottfried, and ending with *Sir Gawain and the Green Knight.* This approach highlights Malory's contribution to the Arthurian legend in English literature and also capitalizes on the students' energy and enthusiasm in dealing with difficult material in Middle English during the beginning days of a new semester. Malory becomes the focal point of our ensuing readings and the springboard for critical papers.

Other years I have begun with Gildas, Nennius, and Geoffrey and have ended with Malory. By the time the students get to Malory, they have learned how to read, and what to expect, from romance as a genre, and, although they have some trouble with the language (we use the Oxford University Press paperback edited by Vinaver with the original spelling), on the whole they manage well. This arrangement makes possible an overview and sequential treatment of themes and characterization. The disadvantage is that we haven't finished reading Malory by the time their papers are due, and, consequently, most of the students choose some other work for critical analysis.

Gussenhoven's time allotment in her all-medieval class contrasts with the allocation of materials Mary P. Richards uses in her medieval and modern course:

The first week of the course is spent on an overview of the Arthurian tradition from the perspectives of history and legend. I have developed my own slide presentation and script relating to the Arthurian sites in Britain, which have been extremely successful in giving students essential background and geographical information. I apportion time relatively equally . . . among the various international strands of the Arthurian tradition in the Middle Ages, before moving to Malory, whom I regard as the centerpiece of the course. The last twenty-five percent of the course focuses on the Arthurian legend after Malory, with special emphasis on Tennyson, T. H. White, and Mary Stewart.

A common complaint from many respondents was that, however much time they had, there was never enough time to teach the tradition as thoroughly as they would have liked, even in all-Arthurian contexts.

Integration of Individual Works into the Tradition

For both general and specialized courses, class discussions and syllabi indicate that the two main approaches are chronological, in which the emphasis is on comparison and contrast, and achronological, in which students first read an important work (often Malory) and then move— sometimes backward, sometimes forward, sometimes more freely around—through other works that illuminate it. Saul N. Brody remarks, "Integration is achieved by my returning again and again to certain themes: the conflict between courtly love and political-social needs, the idea of the king, the role of women," and others. In her class Mary Richards compares, for each work, the treatment of major characters, themes, and symbols with those in other works studied. The students then explore the significance of the differences they find. Throughout the course, the focus is on "the meaning of the Arthurian legend to writers from varying cultures and periods."

The course itself, of course, often mandates a particular focus, as Mark Allen demonstrates for more general syllabi:

> In medieval surveys and theory of romance class, I use Arthurian materials for as much as half of the semester as a means to exemplify the growth and development of "story"—how motifs, characters, and episodes accumulate and shift. The popularity of Arthur makes the material apprehendable, giving the students touchstones whereby they can recall both that literary forms change and how they do. Tracking the Lancelot-Guinevere story from Chrétien to Malory to Tennyson to White is a fine exercise for Theory of Romance. In my survey of medieval literature, I track the narrowing of the chastity motif from Biket to the lyrics and ballads; this contrasts nicely with the development of romance from Geoffrey to Layamon to the *Alliterative Morte* to Malory.

Sometimes juxtaposition of Arthurian with other works is a deciding factor. Witness Linda T. Holley's testimony:

> My job is to choose specific works that establish, react to, exploit, transcend, satirize, represent, or otherwise articulate the genre. For example, Malory (like Cervantes) is the crucial point for the development of the romance. He collects, synthesizes elements of epic and romance; in vocabulary, style, narrative pattern, sensibility, and expressions of moral obligation he "chronicles"

romance and clears the field for new corn. (Cervantes, of course, recommends moving to new ground.)

For the all-Arthurian, medieval and modern course, Jay Ruud's treatment is typical: allotting one half of the time to the earlier and one half to the later versions, he integrates "very deliberately" as the class considers changes in the characters of Arthur, Lancelot, and Guinevere. Another method is that of Douglas J. McMillan: "I use the Christian (often allegorical) and/or courtly love elements in the works to integrate."

But Paul E. Szarmach asked us, "What tradition? In English, there is Malory and beyond, but I try to suggest variety in the matter of Britain before Malory." And Delmar C. Homan confesses, "I'm afraid I don't integrate works into the entire tradition. Right now I am trying an interdisciplinary approach to show the interconnectedness of art and literature in a society."

Similar time apportionment and methods of integration obtain in classes taught by non-English instructors. Harvey L. Sharrer tells us:

> In the comparative literature courses I devote approximately three class sessions to background material: the question of the historical Arthur, a rapid overview of the development of the legend across the centuries, including different literary forms (pseudohistory and chronicle, romances in verse and prose, ballads, and so on). With each text to be studied, additional background is provided in the first class session (historical and biographical information, literary form and style, themes and motifs). A combination of lecture and discussion is then used in studying the work in detail. Additional discussion takes place after the close reading, as we compare and contrast the works with others in the tradition.

3. Projects, Papers, and Creative Assignments

Asked to respond to this area of instruction, teachers of the Arthurian tradition indicated that they almost always use papers and projects of various types in addition to examinations, and some instead of examinations. What sort of work was required—length, scope, and depth—depended generally on two things: level of instruction and type of course—that is, whether all- or only parti-Arthurian. But beyond that, amazingly similar sorts of projects, papers, and creative assignments appeared at every step of instruction, from high school through graduate school.

Projects

These included oral reports and class presentations, book reviews, and even class-read research papers, as well as journals. Most frequently mentioned topics related to structural elements of the literature: theme (mentioned most often), character, motif, plot, and so forth. For her junior college, not exclusively Arthurian, classes, Mary L. Beaudry uses focused book reports, critiques, and class presentations of research papers. Antony Annunziata asks students in a survey "to trace the development of a character or theme from Celtic sources through the later medieval British tradition." In David Fowler's senior-level Arthurian legends course, students choose a topic that emerges from the reading, class discussion, or private conferences. Students, Fowler says, are "encouraged to discuss research problems with each other and in class." In another all-Arthurian course, Henry Hall Peyton III uses periods of literary history to foster student interest. Here is the account of his method he sent us:

> The most successful Arthurian studies course I have taught is the senior honors seminar. At the beginning of the semester (for about one month) students study Malory with the specific purpose of deciding which major Arthurian figure they wish to do research on during the remainder of the term. If the class is small enough (it usually is), one student chooses Arthur, one Gawain, one Lancelot, one Guinevere, and so on. Should the class be large, a group of three or four can devote attention to one character. Research periods are four: the beginnings to 1500, 1500–1700, 1700–1800, 1800 to the present. When there is little or no interest in matters Arthurian in one of the research periods (for example, in the eighteenth century), the student or students must consider why interest is high in one period of history but not in another. Within these convenient time limits, all types of Arthurian materials are studied. In the early period, comparative studies of romances and pseudohistories are important. In the sixteenth and seventeenth centuries, literary concerns include Spenser and Milton, along with the music of Hans Sachs and Purcell. In the nineteenth century, painting, Chausson, and Wagner become centers of interest, while in the twentieth century, students look into T. H. White, comic books, Broadway musicals, the comic strip "Prince Valiant," Disney, Monty Python. Underlying these studies, the objectives are to postulate how Arthur first captured the artistic imagination and why fascination with the Knights of the Round Table survives and

continues to be reinterpreted. The class also attempts to determine how and why changes in characters come about within time periods. Students have discovered an amazing number of prominent and obscure works, including novels, plays, poems, operas, tone poems, comic books, popular songs, television programs, and anecdotes. Through this interdisciplinary approach, they can better understand how and why Arthur continues to be a prominent force in diverse imaginative literary, pictorial, performance, and theatrical works.

Delmar C. Homan has his students in a general course keep journals to record their analyses and responses to the work. This approach apparently is appropriate for advanced courses as well, as Mark Allen indicates: "I have found critical notebooks or journals a convenient way to encourage students to explore and begin to control the vast field of criticism and scholarship."

Papers

Again, types of papers, their length, whether they were critical or research, and their relation to (often) semester-long projects depended on all the variables we have seen as constants. Teachers of the lower-level or general courses were more inclined to assign shorter papers, with a critical rather than a research orientation, and those teachers usually failed to cite specific topics—"critical papers" or "short papers" or just, in the words of Phillip C. Boardman, "the usual papers" were a common response. But teachers of more specialized courses were often quite specific about and justly proud of their constructs.

A frequent assignment for all- or mostly Arthurian classes was to discuss a modern work as it relates to the whole tradition; another, to place an individual work in historical context; a third, often growing out of the projects described above, to trace a character, theme, motif, image, or the like throughout the literature. Among the most individualistic assignments were several provocative ones. Margaret Grimes regularly uses a short research assignment on the meaning of the Grail, in which she has a special interest. Linda T. Holley says: "I like the students to deal with the language of the romance: Wife of Bath's Tale, Sir Gawain, and Malory *together* offer a good chance to see the variety of vocabulary, syntax, tone, imagery, and style of the English Arthurian romance." Referring to his course Epic and Romance, Stanley Kahrl says: "I have used with great success an assignment suggested by McRorie. I ask the students to take an

incident in their own life and describe it and then use it to understand
an aspect of the text."

Creative Assignments

Creative projects include the purely literary, creative writing, artistic
work of various kinds, on-site investigation, and role-playing. Here the
instructor's inventiveness is not bound by student level. As part of her
Camelot Consciousness Day, for instance, Debi S. Graham allows the
choice of character portrayal: "A student dresses up as a knight; those
at the medieval feast have to guess, from the 'knight's' behavior, who
in fact he is." Such role-playing has its literary extension in the paper
described above, in which Stanley Kahrl invites connections between
literary and real character. Among the creative writing assignments,
teachers in high school, including Elizabeth Fishbach, assign the
writing of original stories, as do teachers in college—Marilyn Nellis
has her students write or illustrate an original fantasy, while Mary
Alice Grellner, in a more specialized course, also encourages "something original." For her introductory course in literature, Lorie Roth
asks students "to create romances of their own, following the
conventions of the genre." The re-creation of armor, castles, and,
especially, food projects overlaps language and age boundaries: for her
course for adults, Heather Arden, a French teacher, has had students
prepare medieval dishes for the final class, while an English professor,
Raymond H. Thompson, confesses to having "great success doing
medieval banquets, but they are exhausting!" Finally, along with a few
others, Joseph McClatchey uses his Wheaton College course, when he
teaches it in England, to take the students to see Arthurian sites.

4. Individual Approaches to the Arthurian Tradition

The preceding parts of this introduction represent an outline of the
practices of the respondents to our questionnaire, which should in
itself be helpful to other teachers of the Arthurian tradition interested
in pedagogical matters. Those respondents, asked what they would
most like included in a sourcebook on the tradition, also requested
kinds of information that we used, when feasible, as a guide for the
assignment of essays among their number. A caveat: we had, of course,
to be faithful to the guidelines of the series for which this volume is
intended. We therefore could not really produce "an Arthurian
canon," as one teacher asked (will such a canon ever be possible or
even desirable?), or a "section on the Grail [alone]," as another
wanted. But we were able to provide information on media other than

literature, for instance, as a number of people requested, and "consideration of structural elements, historical development, and background" (the words of one respondent that speak for many others), as well as other teaching ideas that seem sorely needed.

A frequent request was for a variety of background essays, and the first three pieces, under the heading "Backgrounds," speak to this need. Here the reader will find discussions of the historical and chronicle Arthur (Norris J. Lacy), Arthur and the Green World (Alan T. Gaylord), and modern visions and revisions of the Matter of Britain (Raymond H. Thompson).

In the remaining essays, which focus on classroom teaching proper, writers explore, through descriptions of their own, often highly individual courses, a wide range of contexts in which the tradition is taught. Both the whole tradition and parts of it, such as medieval and modern on the one hand, and major authors on the other, are considered. Levels of instruction covered range from high school through graduate school and include interdisciplinary courses as well. Among specific approaches to contexts not strictly literary are those especially relevant to Arthurians' attention.

Included in the section on the "hoole" tradition (the title alludes to Malory's "hoole boke") are essays on teaching the interdisciplinary course (Kathryn T. Lynch), individual characters and motifs (Joseph McClatchey), parallel passages (Jay Ruud), more than one culture (Thomas Kelly and Thomas Ohlgren), and the moderns (Phillip C. Boardman).

The next section begins with an essay on translating Chrétien de Troyes and *Sir Gawain and the Green Knight* for the classroom (Burton Raffel). Then appear discussions of teaching major authors: Gottfried von Strassburg and Wolfram von Eschenbach (James A. Schultz), Malory (Robert L. Kindrick), Alfred, Lord Tennyson (Linda K. Hughes), and three twentieth-century novelists (Harold J. Herman).

Problems and suggested solutions for various levels of instruction identified by our respondents are explored in the fourth section: secondary school (Ruth E. Hamilton), the two-year college (Mary L. Beaudry), the dual-level (Sally K. Slocum), and the graduate (George R. Keiser). Since the single-level undergraduate course is the focus of most of the essays in other sections, we thought it unnecessary to include a separate piece on it here.

The last section of the book presents information on specific approaches involving not strictly literary considerations that bear in a practical way on the Arthurian course: archaeology (Paul E. Szarmach), music—here, Wagner (Martin B. Shichtman), the visual arts (Beverly Taylor), film (Kevin J. Harty), children's needs (Muriel Whitaker), the position of women (Maureen Fries), and popular culture (Mary Alice Grellner).

The essays as a whole reflect our intention to provide not only practical guidance for both beginners at Arthurian teaching and generalists who regularly use (or who would like to use) the Matter but also new ideas for experienced Arthurians who might welcome some fresh or stimulating suggestions for their courses at whatever level.

We offer this volume as an interim report on teaching the Arthurian tradition in full consciousness that, as a living entity, it is impossible to pin down. As I have been revising this introduction, a number of new novels have appeared—two of them by major novelists, Robertson Davies's *Lyre of Orpheus* and Anthony Burgess's *Any Old Iron*. The recent film *Indiana Jones and the Last Crusade* makes use of the Grail motif—somewhat distorted to a purist, but then Arthurian literature has always, from the beginning to now, been subject to deconstruction. If our survey and this collection of essays both reflect Arthurian teaching and heighten such continuing interest in the tradition, we will feel we have not labored in vain.

TEACHING THE BACKGROUNDS

Teaching the King Arthur of History and Chronicle

Norris J. Lacy

Teaching the Arthur of history and chronicle is a challenging and potentially frustrating enterprise. That this should be so is ironic, since the first question students traditionally ask about Arthur concerns his historicity. Yet the reason for this difficulty is obvious: while students may express curiosity about the historical existence of an Arthur, the Arthur they have in mind is invariably the product of centuries of literary and legendary elaboration. A good part of our teaching may thus consist in undoing the received ideas students bring to the course.

The problem is compounded by the fact that the majority of Arthurian courses are evidently given by teachers and scholars of literature, who may be inadequately equipped to deal with the complexities of post-Roman British history, with the background for the scant documentary evidence pointing to a "historical" Arthur, and perhaps even with the chronicle tradition.

In the initial design of an Arthurian course, one of the instructor's most crucial decisions concerns the amount of time to be given to history and chronicle. Some may decide to dispose of historical matters quickly, giving the barest introduction in a single lecture. If the course is specifically devoted to literature, that is, of course, a defensible approach; in such a course, history may legitimately be presented as prefatory. In a broader Arthurian course, history and chronicle should be presented as more than a perfunctory introduction: they should constitute a serious intellectual and pedagogical concern, and the instructor should devote enough time and attention to such matters to allow students to develop some real (however incomplete) command of them.

The Arthur of history and the Arthur of chronicle are two overlapping but nonetheless quite distinct subjects—just as the Arthur of romance is again a different matter—and we should make the distinction clear to students. Once we arrive at true Arthurian chronicles, the Arthurian "fact" (assuming there is one) is obscured by time, as well as by the absence of contemporary references to any "King Arthur." The required first step in the effective treatment of the historical question is therefore some substantial consideration of the Arthurian period: the history, political situation, geography, and archaeology of Britain during the Roman and post-Roman periods. If possible, teachers of literature should enlist the aid of historians on the faculty who deal with those periods and who can offer guest lectures. Materials are available, however, that offer an adequate introduction to the period (John Morris; Ashe, *Discovery* 40–59; Clayton).

Since writers and filmmakers have routinely updated the Arthurian legend (often to the High Middle Ages), many students will bring to a course an image of Arthurian knights living in sumptuous castles, dressing in plate armor, and indulging in tourneys and courtly love. Thus many will be surprised and perhaps vaguely disappointed to learn, for example, that during the Arthurian period a "castle" (such as Cadbury Castle) was a fortified hill rather than the elaborate chateau popularly associated with the very name of King Arthur. It is therefore advisable to give not only a notion of political and historical developments of the Arthurian period but an indication of customs and costumes, of institutions and buildings. The careful replacement of preconceptions with solid facts can provide a useful point of departure for a consideration of the way the skeletal Arthurian "fact" developed into a full-blown legend involving hundreds of characters and a complete society. Again, materials are not in short supply; the volumes cited above should suffice, as will Ashe's *Quest for Arthur's Britain*, a concise and convenient source of information about life—dress, institutions, and art—in post-Roman Britain (see esp. ch. 9, "Life in the Arthurian Age").

Most courses that deal with history, chronicle, and romance doubtless do so in that order, considering the question of Arthur's origin and identity and then progressing to the King Arthur of romance. That order, of course, is logical; it may not, however, be the most effective pedagogical approach, for most students will find the historical background interesting to the extent that they know something of the legends that grew out of it—and that "something" needs to be more than their vague impressions of Arthur. The instructor should therefore consider reversing at least the presentation of history and chronicles, to follow the early development of the idea of Arthur (from Nennius to Geoffrey or Wace, for example) before turning to a study of the origin of that idea. An alternative beginning, which I have found particularly effective, is to study one full romance, such as Chrétien de Troyes's *Lancelot*, before introducing historical matters.

The instructor's most difficult task will doubtless be the discussion of the historical "Arthur" (which is to say the personage or, conceivably, personages around whom the legend crystallized and grew). The identifications that have been proposed and the theories that have been developed vary widely in plausibility and scholarly reliability, from the solid to the highly speculative to the entirely fanciful; none has completely and finally settled the question. Perhaps none ever will.

Accordingly, the instructor should present in some detail a number of hypotheses concerning Arthur's identity. The presentation should include at least the theories of R. G. Collingwood (concerning an Arthur who led cavalry against the Saxons) and Kenneth Jackson (who, by identifying possible locations of Arthur's battles, posited him as a leader, probably real, of forces in southern Britain); the "Sarmatian connection" (involving an Artorius, leader against the Picts of an army that included mounted forces imported from Pannonia); the contributions made by archaeological excavations (particularly at Cadbury Castle); and the Riothamus theory of Geoffrey Ashe.[1]

While the arguments in favor of some of these theories can be persuasive, most responsible scholars (even if they are ardent advocates of a particular hypothesis) will admit that the subject of Arthur's historicity and identity is not closed. Accordingly, skepticism is good pedagogy. Surely students should be warned against those who, all too frequently, have presented theories virtually as revealed truth. In the light of students' probable difficulties in dealing with the historical evidence, however, it may be not only permissible but advisable for the instructor to express a preference for a particular theory—but without introducing a theory as incontrovertible fact and, above all, without excluding any intelligent approach to the question.

As we move from history, and the historical setting, into chronicle,[2] the instructor should refer to works (by Nennius, Gildas, and others) that either develop the background against which the legend of Arthur will evolve or devote short passages to the monarch. Thereafter, the attention given to chronicles will vary greatly from course to course, again depending on whether the emphasis is to be heavily literary. The chronicle material may be reduced to the essentials, but the essentials should not be limited, as they too often are, to Geoffrey of Monmouth. Obviously, any course must devote significant time to Geoffrey's *Historia regum Britanniae* (c. 1136), the most important of the chronicles and one of the most influential books of the Middle Ages. Yet, at the very least, teachers should include also some consideration of Wace's adaptation of Geoffrey, if for no other reason than that the Round Table first appears in Wace's *Brut*, and of Layamon, whose *Brut* represents the first appearance of the Arthurian story in English.[3]

At this point, having dealt with the chronicles that made the most substantial contribution to the legend, most courses will move on to medieval romance. Such an approach is understandable and most often inevitable, but regrettable nonetheless: the most effective way to dramatize the mystery of Arthur's existence and identity is to show how the chroniclers themselves regularly questioned legend and each other and debated the truth or falsity of earlier views, including especially Geoffrey's. The logical approach to teaching additional chronicles in the classroom, if time and the syllabus permit, is thus a focus on the question that brought most of the students into the course: Did Arthur exist? In other words, did the chroniclers *think* he existed? and why or why not?

The instructor may point out that, even before Geoffrey, William of Malmesbury (c. 1125) lamented the grafting of fictional details onto the reality of Arthur and that a good many later writers (for example, John Major, fifteenth century) would accept Arthur's historicity but reject parts of the legend, such as the notion that Arthur survived his apparent death and would one day return. And although most chroniclers who followed Geoffrey accepted his account in the main, a certain number (including Giraldus Cambrensis, c. 1195) remained skeptical or even concluded (as did William of Newburgh, c. 1197) that Geoffrey's Arthur was simply a fiction.

In many ways the reasoning of the chroniclers is as interesting and important as their conclusions. Some argued that the scope and persistence of the legend offered proof of a reality behind it. Others, like William of Newburgh, objected that if Arthur *had* lived, Bede and other writers should certainly have known and presumably written of him.

In addition to discussing the reliability of chronicles and the historicity of Arthur, instructors should deal with the relation between chronicle and romance—that is, with the fact that a good many romances adopted a chronicle-like structure, while even the very early chronicles regularly included material (such as characters' thoughts, emotions, and reactions) that clearly belongs to the domain of imaginative literature. Students are often fascinated by the intrusion of the imaginative (such as the details of Arthur's conception) into texts they expect to be factual, and the instructor can exploit this interest to provide a natural transition to the study of Arthurian literature.

In short, a study of the Arthurian chronicle tradition and of the historical background often follows a strange path. Students will most likely come to the course expecting to learn all about Arthur's origins. Once they discover that the answers are not easy (and perhaps not even available), that history and chronicles do as much to confuse the issue as to clarify it, and that the problems are bound up with the complexities of Roman and post-Roman Britain, their interest is likely to wane. However, the teacher who allows sufficient time for such subjects and who anticipates the students' reactions can help students understand that the "problems" of Arthurian history and chronicles can be fully as exciting as the romances themselves.

NOTES

[1]A brief account of these theories (and others) is provided by Ashe (*Discovery* 75–77, 80–83, 114–15, 158–159, 184–85). For more detail, see Collingwood and Myres; Jackson (in R. S. Loomis, *Arthurian Literature* 1–19); Littleton and Thomas. Ashe's Riothamus theory is itself developed in detail in *Discovery* but also in "A Certain Very Ancient Book."

[2]Concerning the chronicles, see Fletcher; R. S. Loomis, *Arthurian Literature* (chs. 1 and 8–10); Lacy, *Arthurian Encyclopedia* entries "Chronicles, Arthur in," "Chronicles in English," "Scottish Arthurian Chronicles," and entries devoted to individual authors and works.

[3]Significant Arthurian excerpts, along with introductory material and bibliographical information, are available in Wilhelm and Gross (for Latin chronicles and Geoffrey of Monmouth) and Wilhelm (for Wace and Layamon).

Arthur and the Green World

Alan T. Gaylord

In the teaching of Arthurian story, the Celtic question must surely be basic, yet it is not at all clear whether that question gets properly asked. Most of what has been written about early Celtic literature deals with it descriptively as a jumble of literary shards and has little to say about the reading experience of our own (postmodern) age. I doubt that most undergraduates care greatly to pick out the Welsh or Irish threads from Malory's massive tapestry or to debate whether Chrétien's sources were Wace or Geoffrey of Monmouth or anonymous Breton *conteurs*. Furthermore, they tend to be indifferent to the question of the Celtic genealogy of Arthur and of his historicity in general. They know Arthur best as a fantastic character, and they look for a fuller comprehension of the realm of fantasy—which includes what I am calling the Green World. So my approach to the Celtic question has to do with Celtic story, especially as it winds into and out of the Otherworld.

In this realm, Arthur is discovered as a mixture of warlord and elf, existing in "a place that is not a place, and a time that is not a time" (Rees, qtd. in Turner 239), which is to say that he lives in Faërie, the "Perilous Realm" of Enchantment (Tolkien 114). In folklore terms, it is the state of betwixt and between that mortal heroes arrive at as more a condition than a geography, an experience of liminality[1] in which one is suspended from the everyday world, often in a weakened or disadvantaged position, encountering beings from the other side who can seem, confusingly, both enemy and friend. That liminal condition is charged with potency and, as realized in literature, provides a continuing source of power that has touched and disturbed readers from medieval times to the present. I would want to call the place betwixt and between a sacral space, even though I argue its power is preternatural, not supernatural—not a mythical space controlled by the (dimly remembered) ancient gods like Lugh, Maponos, and the Morrigan, nor a space expropriated by Christian allegory. Something in between.

When I urge, then, that Arthurian courses should begin with tales from the Welsh *Mabinogion*—"Of all our ancient traditional prose stories . . . the most essentially Celtic" (Chadwick 289)—I am not proposing source studies or suggesting a developmental sequence from primitive to sophisticated.[2] Rather, I want students to work out for themselves a set of Celtic qualities that are part of the genetic code of the Arthurian character, even as they are rushed downstream through the dynamic rapids and falls of these extraordinary narratives. Such stories, then, will serve to introduce the Celtic question as I believe it most usefully can be asked, and at a primordial level. Thus, for Arthurians, it makes sense to begin with the most archaic, "Culhwch and Olwen," "the most unequivocally Welsh of all the stories in the *Mabinogion*" (Chadwick 291).

In this tale, my students and I meet an Arthur who is the king of Faërie, presiding over a Green World of *hud*, enchantment. Although he has his own wizard, Menw son of Teirgwaedd, one of the "Three Enchanters of the Island of Britain" (Triad 27: Bromwich, *Trioedd* 55), who can cast protective spells "should they come to a heathen land" (Jones and Jones 108), enchantment is so pervasive that one builds up a picture of wizard heroes who perform their deeds extravagantly in the face of extravagant resistance, employing as much magic as is needed. Here are no tournaments or knightly jousts, no courtly dalliance, but rather adventures with shapeshifters, hostile armies, witches, and the monster boar, Twrch Trwyth.

It is most obviously a wondertale (Gwyn Jones, in *Kings, Beasts and Heroes*, can help to identify some of its motifs, such as "Six Go Through the World," "The Grateful Animals," and "The Oldest Animals" 68–71); and *anoetheu*—variously translated "rare and difficult things" or "marvels"—are the key to the extravagance and high spirits of the narrative. To set in relief the tale's archaic features, I recommend the supplementary reading of two brief poetic fragments. First, the "Pa gur" ("What man . . .") from *The Black Book of Carmarthen*, in which Arthur enumerates the exploits of his companions (Bromwich, "Celtic Elements" 45–46). Second, "The Spoils of Annwn," which describes elliptically Arthur's raid on the Otherworld to rescue Gwair and bring back a magic caldron—and from which only seven warriors return (Bollard, "Arthur" 21–23). Kenneth Jackson provides a useful explanation of these fragments in "Arthur in Early Welsh Verse." (Another translation, with extensive notes on the Welsh original and a theory about occasion and provenance, is found in Haycock.) It is this Welsh Arthur of titanic prowess who becomes the enabler for young Culhwch, his nephew, who must achieve a series of tasks before he can win Olwen from her father, Ysbaddaden the Chief Giant.

The presence of Arthur amid so many motifs that predate him, including the central one of "Winning the Giant's Daughter," introduces one major feature of Arthurian story that reorganizes and fuses all these wonders: the imperial extensions of prowess. We may associate this feature with the epic swagger of the style, with its unabashed relish for lists and namings and its self-indulgence in playfully bending the language into new shapes. And the imperial theme explains the geographical hugeness of scope, as in the speech of Arthur's porter invoking a world stretching from Scandinavia to India (Jones and Jones 98). Arthur everywhere overcomes all, including the Otherworld, here displaced from any single location to certain marvelous adventures—ultimate tests along a continuum of tests—so that we find an uncomplicated version of liminality, in which the motif of raids into the Otherworld is transformed into incidents of heroic success. Everyone knows what to do; the world is a puzzle to be unlocked by the brave. And the complications are in the spirals of surface design: no character suffers inward doubts, or needs to prevail over weakness or temptation, or acquires new knowledge or wisdom. Arthur seizes the comb from Twrch Trwyth. Culhwch wins Olwen for his wife.

In the second tale discussed with my students, "Branwen Daughter of Llyr," Celtic story (which Arthur has not yet entered) takes a turn in the opposite direction. Certain places in "Culhwch and Olwen" had had the potential for tragic development, such as Cei's alienation or the Great Boar Hunt and its "mischiefs" (Jones and Jones 128, 135)— glimpses of that archaic motif of terrible losses that prowess must sustain. But these had colored the narrative momentarily without controlling it. In fact, most incidents of murder and mayhem are recounted there with virile good cheer, even with glee; but in "Branwen" the mayhem is never cause for rejoicing: the theme of victory swallowed up in loss gives shape to the whole story.

The imperial challenge is there, in the form of the kingdom of Ireland (again, in a narrative slot filled earlier by the Otherworld); as the Fateful Adversary, Ireland represents a problem never solved. The marriage to bind it to the "Island of the Mighty" fails; the reconciliation that was hoped for between the two kingdoms fails through Irish treachery and the enmity of "fierce, ruthless" Efnisien (Jones and Jones 36). Brân goes over to invade Ireland like an invincible giant, carrying his troops on his back (see Bromwich, *Trioedd*, 284, for euhemerized possibilities); yet although the enemy are slaughtered to a man, Brân is fatally wounded with a poisoned spear and must escape with his surviving band, who number only seven. The tale speaks sadly then of "such victory as there was," which connects to the thematic word *unhappy* as describing the blows given to the calumniated Branwen by the Irish and also the eventual "disclosure" of Brân's head (Jones and Jones 37, 40). And then we must add those places where persons contemplate the events around them and "break their hearts with consternation" (Jones and Jones, with Branwen, 38; with Cradawg, 38–39).

The journey of the seven toward London, under Brân's directive, is to bury his head in London facing France, so that the island may be protected from invaders.[3] But the point of the story is what the travelers do and feel along the way. Here the Otherworld, though not named as such, plays a key role as a locale of pure and unearthly joy during seven years of feasting at Harddlech under the spell of the birds of Rhiannon, and eighty years of feasting at the Assembly of the Wondrous Head at Gwales in Penfro. These are times out of time, purged of the memories of unhappiness. But at last the spell is broken. One of the band opens a fateful door, and they look back over the threshold toward Cornwall. Then "they were as conscious of every loss they had ever sustained, and of every kinsman and friend they had missed, and of every ill that had come upon them, as if it were even then it had befallen them" (39–40). It is, indeed, the power of the sacral liminal space I feel here, for the vision from the Otherworld is a critical act of recognition and knowing, a view back at the life in time lived in blood and loss, that yet leads to a returning and some measure of acceptance.

It seems to me that for the author of this branch, the remembered world of pan-Celtic story—the product of bards and preliterate storytellers nurtured over long centuries innocent of writing—stands in the place of the Green World; for such story is no longer a part of his daily life, and he looks back from the threshold of written literature. Thus Celtic memory becomes his subject, as witness his frequent references to significant threes that are also found in the Welsh Triads, those indices of bardic memory. And he has *composed*—drawing together various motifs and disparate strands—in a way that is different from oral storytelling but appropriate for writing. So he will conclude, "that is what the tale says" (40). We may restate this: not true to a particular story, yet true to "the Tale": *it happens like that*.

The Welsh Triads, as Rachel Bromwich reminds us, illustrate how a pan-Celtic consciousness, indicated by the formula "this island" (as in the title *Trioedd Ynys Prydein*, 'Triads of the Island of Britain'), comes to be centered on the symbolic person of Arthur, with the new formula of place, *llys Arthur*, the "court of Arthur," supplanting the old (lxviii–ix). Likewise, one of the later versions of the Triad of Fortunate Concealments (mentioned in "Branwen" 40) adds a gloss concerning the burial of Brân's head: "And Arthur disclosed the Head of Brân the Blessed from the White Hill, because it did not seem right to him that this Island should be defended by the strength of anyone, but by his own" (Triad 37R, 89).

There is more here than evidence for "the mounting impetus with which the Arthurian material gained in popularity in Wales"(lxix), for the image leads back to "what the Tale says." It says that when Arthur disclosed the Head, recentering the geography of the Green World upon himself, he became at the same time a citizen of that world whose tales would tell *him*, as surely as they told the Blessed Brân. The destiny of those stories now lay upon him; and it would be through the door of his festive castle that subsequent readers would come to look out toward Cornwall and become conscious of every loss they had sustained . . . yet not die of consternation.

Arthurian literature has this peculiarity: that it must cross the threshold into the Green World in order to retain its power to fabulate. The most extraordinary liminal example is surely the legend of the Grail—noncanonical, mysterious, daunting, sacral, Green through and through, teeming with images betwixt and between. But that way leads through other mists, and your guide stops here.[4]

NOTES

[1]*Liminality* (from Latin *limen* 'threshold') is a term first developed by Arnold van Gennep in his discussion of rites of passage; for further definition and applications, see van Gennep 11; Turner 231–32; and MacCana, *Celtic Mythology* 127–28.

[2]My text is Gwyn Jones and Thomas Jones's translation, still admired as the best all-around, though Lady Guest's holds an honored place for its antique charm.

[3]For the archaic motif of the severed head, traceable to notorious Celtic battle practices and to the "cult of the severed head," see Ross, *Pagan Celtic Britain* 61–126.

[4]Those students who want to stray further into Faërie realms apart from Arthur should be directed to K. M. Briggs's delicious *Fairies in Tradition and Literature* and then be left to shift, as it were, for themselves. For background reading in Celtic matters, see Kenneth Hurlstone Jackson's *Celtic Miscellany* and Jeffrey Gantz's *Early Irish Myths and Sagas*. A brief but rich introduction to the early Celts may be found in Myles Dillon and Nora K. Chadwick's *Celtic Realms* (1–17). Two handsome books for the beginner are those by Barry Cunliffe, and Duncan Norton-Taylor. Proinsias MacCana's *Celtic Mythology* also serves as a cultural introduction. Because of the abundance of stimulating writing in their volumes, I also recommend the works of Jan Morris, and Robert O'Driscoll.

Modern Visions and Revisions
of the Matter of Britain

Raymond H. Thompson

For most academics Arthurian literature is predominantly a medieval and, to a lesser extent, nineteenth-century phenomenon. Yet a steady stream of poetry and prose fiction—the latter swollen by the recent surge in popularity of fantasy—offers ample testimony that Arthurian tradition is as vigorous as ever. Increasingly we encounter students whose interest has been aroused not by earlier classroom encounters with Malory or Tennyson but by their leisure reading of modern versions of the Arthurian legend, especially since many of these were written for younger readers. Some may even have discovered Arthur and his knights of the Round Table in films, comics, or role-playing games like Dungeons and Dragons. Clearly it is time to consider how modern visions and revisions of the Matter of Britain can be included in our courses.

I have taught modern Arthurian literature in three different courses: an introduction to English literature, a survey of Arthurian literature through the ages, and a half course on fantasy that focused on Arthurian legend. The first is offered to first-year, the others to upper-level and graduate, students.

The introductory course has room for no more than a couple of Arthurian works. T. S. Eliot's *Waste Land* searchingly probes the problems of modern society, but it is a complex poem that may confuse all but the most talented students at this level. The novels, fortunately, are much more accessible. Mark Twain's *Connecticut Yankee in King Arthur's Court* combines some genuinely humorous writing with a keen satire aimed at the follies of both past and present; and since young people often share Hank Morgan's scornful view of an earlier age, they are more deeply affected when they discover how much damage such insensitivity can cause. Fantasies like Susan Cooper's *Dark Is Rising*, as well as others in that series, and Alan Garner's *Moon of Gomrath* have the advantage of being written for younger readers—and most freshman are, after all, closer to adolescence than adulthood. Both are set in a modern world whose beliefs are challenged by the intrusion of figures like Merlin and Arthur. By contrast, both Rosemary Sutcliff's *Sword at Sunset* and Parke Godwin's *Firelord* present plausible re-creations of fifth-century Britain, involvingly narrated by Arthur himself. In all four novels the protagonists discover that power brings not freedom but responsibility, not privilege but sacrifice, and it is a lesson that all young people struggling toward adulthood need to learn.

The survey of Arthurian literature through the ages offers the chance to include a greater number of modern works and to relate them to earlier tradition. I try to represent a wide range of stories and literary genres to give some idea of the extent of Arthurian literature. Unfortunately, drama has always been the least successful literary form for Arthurian legend, and the twentieth century has not changed this pattern. Two plays that might be taught are Christopher Fry's *Thor, with Angels* and *The Island of the Mighty* by John Arden and Margaretta D'Arcy, but neither represents the authors' best work. I prefer to show John Boorman's film *Excalibur* (1981), which is readily available as a video rental. Although it loses impact on a small screen and the amalgamation of various traditions can be confusing, its use of imagery and music remains powerful.

Arthurian poetry has been much more impressive. Alan Lupack's *"Arthur, the Greatest King": An Anthology of Modern Arthurian Poetry* offers a wide-ranging selection of verse from the nineteenth and twentieth centuries. It can be supplemented by longer poems like *The Waste Land* and Edwin Arlington Robinson's three major Arthurian poems, of which *Tristram* is perhaps the most suitable for teaching.

Since, in the 1950s, fiction replaced poetry as the dominant literary form for dealing with Arthurian legend, a wider choice of novels is available, though publishers have an annoying habit of allowing them to go out of print. As I have argued in my study *The Return from Avalon*, this fiction can be divided into five broad categories: retellings, realistic fiction, historical fiction, science fiction, and fantasy, each distinguished by its attitude toward setting. While shortage of time prevents the classroom study of representative works from each category, essay topics can be set on those excluded. Since retellings translate or modernize medieval works, a comparison with the often conflicting material of their sources reveals much about the process of selection for a modern, often younger, audience. Realistic fiction offers what is intended to be a rational explanation for the Arthurian element that it introduces into a modern setting, and so Walker Percy's *Lancelot* and *Castle Dor* by Arthur Quiller-Couch and Daphne du Maurier present a fresh and intriguing perspective on the Grail quest and the love story of Tristan and Isolde, respectively.

A much larger category than either of the preceding is historical fiction, set either in the Dark Ages or in the High Middle Ages of the romances that were their literary sources. The latter setting has fallen out of favor with historical novelists since the 1950s, but the former is vividly recreated in Rosemary Sutcliff's *Lantern Bearers* and its sequel, *Sword at Sunset*, both of which teach their central hero valuable lessons about life. Alternatives include Mary Stewart's popular Merlin trilogy and her novel about Mordred, *The Wicked Day*.

Science fiction and a related form, science fantasy, which combines science with magic, have rarely been used for the Arthurian legend. Within this narrow selection, the best (apart from *A Connecticut Yankee*, which can just as easily be considered a fantasy) is C. J. Cherryh's intriguing study of role-playing, *Port Eternity*.

The largest category of Arthurian fiction and the one most familiar to students is fantasy. My personal choices for the survey course are T. H. White's *Sword in the Stone*, which poignantly fulfills childhood dreams of a wondrous world, and Thomas Berger's ironic *Arthur Rex*, whose parody of the conventions of Arthurian romance can best be appreciated after just this kind of course. Moreover, the willingness of the knights to risk looking foolish in order to pursue an idealistic dream proves to be self-assertion as heroic as that found in epic or tragedy. This is a lesson that young people today, bound to convention by peer pressure and societal expectations, would do well to heed.

The half course on fantasy allows a fuller exploration of the genre. After a general scrutiny of the field, I examine Arthurian novels from each of the three main groups into which they can be readily divided: mythopoeic, heroic, and ironic.

In mythopoeic fantasy the eternal struggle between good and evil is waged directly between supernatural powers. It usually takes place in a modern setting into which intrude Arthurian relics or characters: thus Merlin provides valuable assistance to the protagonists in C. S. Lewis's *That Hideous Strength*, Garner's *Moon of Gomrath*, and Cooper's series, *The Dark Is Rising*. Sometimes, however, events are set in Arthur's day, as in Gillian Bradshaw's trilogy about Gwalchmai (Gawain). Of her three novels I prefer to teach *Kingdom of Summer*, which reveals the sharp contrast between the idealized image of the Arthurian dream and the harsh reality of the demands it places on those who would follow it.

By contrast, most heroic fantasies are set in Arthur's day, including the type popularly known as sword and sorcery. About half are set in the High Middle Ages, as is White's *Sword in the Stone*; the remainder are set in the Dark Ages, including Godwin's *Firelord* and Marion Zimmer Bradley's best-seller, *The Mists of Avalon*, which adopts the refreshingly different viewpoint of the women associated with Arthur's court. In *The Third Magic* Welwyn Wilton Katz sends a modern teenager on an imaginative journey, first to an alternate world, then to the Dark Ages, to explore the tensions in male-female relationships.

Ironic fantasy is almost invariably set in the High Middle Ages, and it contains three major strands—satire, humor, and affection for the aspirations of high romance—all of which are found in *A Connecticut Yankee*. Satire has grown popular in recent years, producing dark visions of heroic idealism frustrated by human perversity like that

found in John Steinbeck's *Acts of King Arthur and His Noble Knights.*
More typical of the tradition, however, are fantasies like Berger's
Arthur Rex, in which humor is combined with warm affection for the
subject.

The discovery that Arthurian tradition remains as vital today as it
ever was helps students appreciate more fully its inherent adaptability.
Modern authors have used it to explore issues of pressing importance:
the role of women in a society dominated by men, and of young people
in a society dominated by adults; the value of concern for others in a
society in which self-interest is rewarded by material success; and the
reality that lies behind so many illusions. With this discovery grows a
deeper understanding of the legend's enduring fascination: the story of
a leader and his gallant band of followers who strive against all odds to
establish a better world. It is a story with special appeal to young
people, so many of whom share the same dream.

TEACHING THE "HOOLE" TRADITION

Implementing an Interdisciplinary Course

Kathryn L. Lynch

The word *implementing* can be taken in two senses, the institutional and the individual. Readers who want to set up a new course will be interested in the institutional history of similar courses; those who already teach a course in Arthurian literature will want to know how an interdisciplinary approach differs from others and how it works once it has been implemented. My discussion thus falls into two parts.

The Arthurian Legends course I have taught for three years at Wellesley College grew out of an English department seminar first offered in 1973 by a colleague who is now retired, so that its original implementation is something I had to find out about from a visit to the College Archives. The course began to thrive two years later with the establishment of a medieval and Renaissance studies major, which, a year after it had begun, designated the Arthurian Legends course as its recommended seminar, promising for the first time special lectures by members of the art, French, and history departments; in 1977 the course was officially taken out of the English department and adopted by the college as a permanent extradepartmental offering. It has been taught every year since, becoming a kind of tradition itself. One of the course's attractions continues to be the regular appearance of instructors from the art, French, history, German, and music departments, whose presentations frequently bring majors into the medieval and Renaissance studies program. Interestingly, a course entitled Arthurian Romance had an earlier incarnation at Wellesley; it was a regular part of the curriculum from 1904 to 1940. Although this version of the course stayed within the bounds of the English department, catalog descriptions show that even then it offered a more interdisciplinary perspective than other subjects, combining an interest in the Grail, Celtic backgrounds, historical chronicles, and connections between old and modern literatures in several languages. In general, then, its structure has reflected the proposition made to the dean when the course came into the curriculum, that "the field is interdisciplinary by nature" (Lever 2).

What makes my course today interdisciplinary in the most general sense is merely that it employs a variety of pedagogical strategies, both large and small, to get students to respond to the material from more than one viewpoint. Our visiting lecturers, however, probably are most effective in breaking down artificial barriers between disciplines. In a typical semester when we read "Culhwch and Olwen," a long section from Geoffrey of Monmouth's *History of the Kings of Britain*, Chrétien de Troyes's *Lancelot*, Gottfried von Strassburg's *Tristan*, *Sir Gawain and the Green Knight*, an abridged Malory, and selections from Tennyson's *Idylls of the King*, I schedule about four outside lectures. Since my own bias is literary, it is well for me to do this early in the semester in order to get the students used to taking a thoroughly different tack. So when we read Geoffrey, a member of the history department comes, either to discuss the medieval knight and warfare or to provide eleventh- and twelfth-century political backgrounds. In orchestrating each of these outside lectures, the difficulty is to ensure a precise connection between the text we are studying and the background that is supposed to clarify it, yet making these connections is also the most exciting part of the course for me.

Twelfth-century political backgrounds, for instance, easily become relevant to a discussion of Geoffrey through the parallel between Arthur and William of Normandy. Extending this parallel only a bit, one sees that the problems generated by William's distribution of lands among his sons lie behind Geoffrey's absorption with similar questions of ambition, power, and succession—for example, in the Constans-Vortigern-Vortimer episode. Geoffrey's *History*, taken in its full historical context, thus offers a strong king as an antidote to the threat of civil strife, in the same way that Malory's strong Arthur provides a response to the disruption of orderly rule during the Wars of the Roses. Students enjoy seeing how an interest in Arthur's success as leader and conqueror—for example, in his war against Rome—falls in with such periods of civil crisis and frustrated chauvinism, and the historical discussion accordingly helps to illuminate Malory's elegaic tone. If Malory was the Sir Thomas Malory of Newbold Revell in Warwickshire, his service under the earl of Warwick, the "King Maker," would give added biographical point to a larger political concern, as does Geoffrey's dedication of his work to Robert, earl of Gloucester, who Geoffrey must have known would be one of three principal contenders for the throne on the death of Henry I.[1] Thus, both general and specific historical backgrounds help students see the mostly fabulous story of Arthur as rooted in historical conditions.

Even when biographical and general facts are veiled in greater mystery, an interdisciplinary approach can open other avenues. For example, later in the semester, when we read *Sir Gawain and the Green Knight*, a talk on castles and their architecture by a member of the art department reveals the careful mix of real and fantastic that characterizes the Gawain poet's craft. Although many descriptive details link Bercilak's Hautdesert with the otherworld castles of early Irish literature (Whitaker, "Otherworld Castles" 34–38), and make its ornate pinnacles like something out of the Duc de Berry's *Très riches heures*, specific details, like the removal of bedchambers to a "lofte," an area above the ground floor, also show that the Gawain poet had in mind real castles Gawain might have seen in his journey. An example is Beaumaris, in Anglesey, known especially for its concentricity (Anderson 146) and located only a few miles from an ancient burial chamber covered by a green mound. Such juxtapositions of real and otherworldly, human and superhuman, typify this poem and deepen the poignance of Gawain's choices, which themselves bring him up against his own mortal limitations.

In general, students should look beyond a text's surface to what Robert Hanning would call its "vision of history," the way it reflects the assumptions and values of an age and the way those assumptions actively dictate its structure. Such insights may involve seeing something as small as the relation between the abolition of trial by ordeal and Gottfried von Strassburg's tone toward Isolde in her strange ordeal scene or as global as the increasing conflict between public and private realms of experience as we move from Geoffrey to Chrétien to Gottfried. Unfortunately, I do not have room here to discuss every interpretation that the interdisciplinary approach makes possible, but perhaps that limitation, like those Gawain has to face, is just as well, since each coincidence of instructors will no doubt suggest a slightly different construction of the text.

Beyond interpretation, though, a visit from a colleague who reads in the original a work being studied only in translation helps surmount a regrettable defect of many comparative literature courses by vividly reminding the students that a work like the *Lancelot* or *Tristan* was originally poetry, written in verse. Especially with *Tristan*, which we read in A. T. Hatto's excellent Penguin translation, the tight quatrain form and frequent use of chiasmus reinforce meaning at every turn in ways that only an instructor fluent in the original can fully illustrate. Fortunately, this translation includes two pages of the German prologue, so that students can follow along. Another text I have found especially useful from an interdisciplinary standpoint is Michael Senior's abridged translation of Malory's *Tales of King Arthur*, which includes over 125 illustrations, many in color, taken from a variety of illuminated manuscripts. Though I do not always agree with Senior's decisions about when to cut, I have supplemented him in the few instances, like the healing of Sir Urré, when I feel his omissions create serious structural problems. And this text has proved an excellent resource when the class is visited by members of the art department.

Because my course is listed in the catalog as an interdisciplinary or extradepartmental one, students from many different departments with quite varying interests and expectations sign up. I try in response to design assignments that call on their different skills and not to limit written work to the purely literary explications with which I am most comfortable. I begin, then, by asking students to investigate fifth- and sixth-century historical backgrounds, to evaluate some aspect of the legend's basis in fact or, alternatively, as one recent critic suggests, "the power of legend invention" (Shippey). The second assignment asks for a more purely literary discussion, as the students compare selected passages in two or three romances. The third and final paper is a brief review of a modern Arthurian work, modeled on reviews in the journal *Avalon to Camelot*, and the course finishes with a traditional final exam, mixing identification and essay questions.

The texts we study have surprised me by their remarkable coherence as a group and the thoroughness with which they reward interdisciplinary study. Each semester my feelings that the connections I am making become more precise and fruitful have made the course an increasing pleasure to teach. But more than this, I have found that a course in Arthurian literature is an ideal place to focus the spirit of generous cooperation between disciplines that ought to characterize academic life. I am thankful to my colleagues for helping to bring that spirit into my classroom.[2]

NOTES

[1]For a useful discussion of the multiple dedications of this work, see Lewis Thorpe 39–40n7. A second dedication, to the controversial Waleran of Mellent also suggests Geoffrey's embroilment in contemporary affairs. Further general background to the political events of the early and middle twelfth century can be found in R. H. C. Davis.

[2]I very gratefully acknowledge a debt to my colleagues Lillian Armstrong, Eugene Cox, Peter Fergusson, Thomas Hansen, Rachel Jacoff, Owen Jander, Katherine Lever, and Alice Robinson, as well as Matilda Bruckner of Boston College, whose classroom visits and generous conversation have made it possible for me to teach an interdisciplinary course. They should not, however, be held responsible for the details of any of the interpretations offered here, which are my own.

Teaching Individual Characters and Motifs

Joseph McClatchey

My one-semester course Arthurian Literature, which I call Arthurian Romance when I teach it as a half-semester course, is a critical study of the whole cycle of the Matter of Britain, including the subcycles of the Grail legends and Tristan stories, from the Celtic, Breton, and French origins through Geoffrey of Monmouth to Malory and modern versions. I teach the Arthurian tradition as an international literature and seek to impress the students with its complex and fascinating interrelations and intrigues. I want them to feel its grandeur as one of the oldest and largest literatures in the world, spanning some 1,400 years and involving cultures all over the globe. I emphasize the present renaissance in Arthurian scholarship as well as the wealth of imaginative genres so that students may sense the pleasure that we take in living in a golden age of Arthurian studies.

I have designed the course for two major purposes. First, I want students to fall in love with Arthurian literature in general and its major works in particular, to read those works carefully and joyfully as they become acquainted with the several competing critical schools. Second, I offer each student the scholarly pleasure of writing and formally presenting a major paper that investigates an important myth, figure, cycle, or motif from its earliest appearance through its development and modern retellings, interpretations, and adaptations, in order to discover its vital genius.

To achieve these goals, I try, insofar as it is possible, to give the course the integrity of a complete study by carrying the Arthurian literary idea to its logical conclusion. I ask my classes to read this idea both horizontally and vertically. By the *horizontal* reading, I mean the critical tracing of a figure or motif. By the *vertical* reading, I refer to the recognition and criticism of human values, that is, discerning mind, humanity, and poetry in the various works. This process requires asking questions—for example, What is the nature of mind in this work?—that call for further questions: What is the intellectual given that confronts the reader at the start? What evidence of humanity appears? I suggest that this evidence includes profundity of emotion and resiliency of spirit. What is the poetry in this work? By poetry I mean such things as the work's childlike intensity and a given figure's inner vision of the outer world.

I use a variety of classroom procedures, including lectures, slide programs, the reading aloud of modern Arthurian plays, and the showing of Arthurian movies at night. In the semester-long course, the students present and critique their papers. When I teach this course in England for our college's annual summer study program at Oxford, I take the students to the traditional Arthurian sites. To visit Tintagel and Glastonbury while reading Geoffrey and *Perlesvaus: The High History of the Holy Grail* (or even Mary Stewart's *Crystal Cave*) underlines the "romance" in Arthurian romance.

After an introductory series of lectures on story, myth, and Arthurian works as the literature of interlacement, I divide my Arthurian course into three major units—Before Malory, Malory, and Since Malory. My purpose in the opening talks is to present a clear framework for the study of particular figures and motifs and to clarify the kinds of Arthurian literature. I begin with definitions of story and move to myth and its many differing approaches. Then I distinguish myth from monomyth and mythopoeia, making use of the eight components of the monomyth found in David Leeming's *Mythology: The Voyage of the Hero*. Once students grasp the monomyth's place in literary study, they move with ease into literary analysis and especially Arthurian figure delineation. After this accomplishment, it is only a short step to introducing the interlacement pattern of Arthurian romance. That short step involves the distinguishing of Arthurian history, Arthurian legend, Arthurian romance, Arthurian myth, and Arthurian story. When teaching the pattern of romance (see Campbell; Frye 187; Hume), I find it helpful also to explain the difference between interlacement design and interlacement logic (Lewis, *Discarded Image* 193–94; Tuve 363; Vinaver, *Rise* 76, 78). I extend interlacement logic to account for the many and varied Arthurian retellings over the past eight hundred years; for, with each new class, students persist in asking for the one invariable, authorized, and absolutely canonical Arthurian tale.

The unit Before Malory is divided into six subunits: Wales and Arthurian Beginnings, The Arthur Cycle, The Tristan Cycle, When Knighthood Was in Flower, Lancelot, and The Grail Cycle. Within these subunits I teach The Gawain Cycle, The Percival Cycle, and The Galahad Cycle. The unit on Malory, of course, focuses on *Le Morte d'Arthur*. My third unit, Since Malory, is devoted chiefly to nineteenth- and twentieth-century retellings, and it includes The Guinevere Cycle, The Mordred Cycle, and The Taliessin Cycle. Whenever I plan to concentrate on a particular figure or theme, I assign a major text, for instance, Gottfried's *Tristan* or Béroul's *Romance of Tristan* with the Tristan cycle, and Chrétien's *Perceval*, Wolfram's *Parzival*, or "Peredur" (Bollard) with the Percival cycle.

What does teaching a particular figure or motif involve? First, I demonstrate the development of the figure or motif by many writers in diverging texts. I establish the place of a given figure or motif in the tradition by showing its durability and wide handling. I also deepen the students' understanding of its complexity and possible meaning when they encounter it in a particular poem, romance, novel, or film.

Second, in teaching a particular figure or motif I assume a unity or integrity of the Arthurian tradition. Implicit in this assumption is the necessity of teaching both medieval and modern Arthurian literature without slighting either. It raises questions about an Arthurian canon and forces the student to ask why some works are more honored historically than others are. The way a figure or motif is handled in the long traditions enables the student to critically evaluate a particular work in which the figure or motif appears.

Third, my teaching strategy involves a love of Arthurian story that is greater than the impulse or temptation or drive to promulgate a pet theory about, say, Arthurian origins, the meaning of the Grail, or the worthiness of Arthurian literature written after Malory, the Gawain poet, or even Chrétien. It means being willing to read and evaluate both early and recent Arthurian writings to learn how the figure or motif is developing historically, imaginatively, and literarily—even if this endeavor stretches one's love of Arthuriana to its limits.

Fourth, teaching a figure or motif means discovering its genius. By *genius* I am referring to the enduring core or heart of a particular figure or motif—for example, Lancelot. What aspect of Lancelot is always "there" and without which the figure simply is not Lancelot, however he may be named? Tracing him from a Celtic sungod to the latest Arthurian novel should clarify—perhaps surprisingly—that genius. Overruling the objection that everyone already knows the essential elements of a given figure or motif, I suggest that such an investigation, or cycle, reveals more about that figure than a careful reading of an Arthurian classic does. The students' growing interest (even intrigue) as they encounter changes, contradictions, new details and adventures, and perhaps a literary "being" in the figure cannot be equaled in any other way I know of in Arthurian studies.

This realization leads me to a fifth and last consideration, namely that teaching the figure or motif means enjoying the myth or mythicality of it. By *myth* I suggest something more than its genius. Rather, I mean its enduring relation as a part of the great Arthurian myth, as a thing in its own right. Thus, to trace Percival, Tristan, Galahad, Guinevere, and Nimue in their individual cycles is to learn not only what they are and who they are but also to recognize their permanent place in the complex interrelations of all that Arthurian story has given us in the literature of the last millenium and more.

Teaching the "Hoole" Tradition through Parallel Passages

Jay Ruud

The "hoole" tradition of Arthurian literature—spanning the fifteen hundred years from Gildas, in the sixth century, to the likes of Thomas Berger and Marion Zimmer Bradley, in the twentieth—is too vast to be encompassed in a lifetime, let alone a single college semester. Yet ideally the instructor, while concentrating on the peaks of the tradition, like Geoffrey of Monmouth, Chrétien de Troyes, *Sir Gawain and the Green Knight*, and Malory, can give students a sense of the whole range of the tradition and the kind of snowballing effect that occurred as the story passed from one generation to another and as new tellers of the tale added, refined, and filled in the gaps.

One of the simplest and most effective ways of conveying an awareness of the "hoole" tradition is through parallel passages selected from a variety of sources, most of which students would not be reading in their entirety. Thus by concentrating on a single incident in the story, students can see how each author changed, slanted, or adapted a particular incident to fit his or her own purpose or time.

Consider, for example, the crucial incident that marks a turning point in many versions of the legend: the scene in which Arthur learns of Mordred's betrayal. It is a valuable passage because of its importance in establishing the character and motivations of Guinevere.

Geoffrey apparently invented the incident, and his version is brief and direct:

> Arthur spent the following winter in this same locality and found time to subdue the cities of the Allobroges. When summer came, he made ready to set out for Rome, and was already beginning to make his way through the mountains when the news was brought to him that his nephew Mordred, in whose care he had left Britain, had placed the crown upon his own head. What is more, this treacherous tyrant was living adulterously and out of wedlock with Queen Guinevere, who had broken the vows of her earlier marriage.
>
> About this particular matter, most noble Duke, Geoffrey of Monmouth prefers to say nothing. (*History* 257–58)

In Geoffrey's account, Guinevere is clearly culpable: she has broken her marriage vows and is living in adultery. But Geoffrey deliberately refuses to comment or elaborate, giving no motivation for her action and thus opening the door for speculation by subsequent writers.

When Wace retold the story in the Anglo-Norman *Roman de Brut*, twenty years later, he added a passage of foreshadowing when Arthur leaves Britain, in which he describes Mordred as a "marvelously hardy knight . . . a man of high birth, and of many noble virtues, but he was not true" and in which he makes clear Guinevere's motives: "The lady on her side had given her love to a lord of whom much good was spoken" (79).

Wace also alters Geoffrey's later passage in which Guinevere enters the convent. In Geoffrey, we are told that Guinevere "gave way to despair" when she heard of the wars between Arthur and Mordred. She flees and takes the veil "promising to lead a chaste life" (259). But in Wace her repentance seems more sincere, as she enters the convent "by reason of her exceeding sorrow for her trespass, and for the sin that she had wrought" (112–13). Wace, writing when the courtly love ideal was becoming fashionable, puts Guinevere in a more sympathetic light: her sin was love, and therefore she is able to be saved at the end when she repents.

How different she appears in Layamon's *Brut*, some fifty years later! There is no mention of love and no sympathy for Guinevere. Of Mordred and the queen, Layamon says that "they there lost their lives and their souls, and ever afterwards became odious in every land" (235). After a much dramatized scene in which Arthur has a prophetic dream of Mordred and Guinevere tearing down his great hall, he vows vengeance in an angry speech, promising "Mordred I will slay, and burn the queen," to which Sir Gawain, the loyal nephew, adds: "Myself I will him hang, highest of all wretches; the queen I will, with God's law, draw all in pieces with horses" (260).

In the thirteenth-century French Vulgate *Death of King Arthur*, vast changes have taken place. When left in the charge of Mordred, Guinevere "was very angry . . . because she knew such wickedness and disloyalty in him that she was sure that suffering and ill would come of it" (trans. Cable; 156). She resists his plan to marry her and takes refuge in the Tower of London, which Mordred besieges (165–66). And she herself sends the messenger to Arthur telling of Mordred's betrayal, putting the blame on Arthur himself: "My Lord, your wife Queen Guinevere has sent me to you to say that you have betrayed and deceived her, and have not prevented her from being dishonoured. . . . Mordred hates her so mortally that he will defile her body and you will be dishonoured" (191).

When, later, Guinevere enters the convent, she does not take the veil herself but is there for protection and to await the outcome of the battle between Arthur and Mordred. Her motive in entering the nunnery is not repentance (since she is in fact innocent) but fear: "she was frightened of King Arthur and Mordred" (199).

In the fourteenth-century English *Alliterative Morte Arthure* (trans. Krishna), the author follows Layamon's lead in making Mordred's betrayal the central issue and in portraying the queen as culpable. The author of the *Alliterative Morte* adds a scene depicting Guinevere's great woe at Arthur's leaving for the Roman war. She grieves, in lines 699–702:

> I could curse the man who caused this war,
> That denies me the honor of my wedded lord;
> All my life's joy is departing the land
> And I am left in desolation, believe me, forever.

But it is all sham. Granted, when Sir Cradok brings Arthur news of the betrayal, he tells the king merely that Mordred "has wedded Guinevere and calls her his wife" (3550), and Arthur's anger is directed solely at Mordred—gone is the savage threat to tear the queen in pieces. But we see the queen's guilt later in the poem, for when Arthur returns, Mordred writes Guinevere that the king has come back and "bade her fly far off and flee with her children" (3907)—apparently her children by Mordred. She receives the news with great trepidation, and in desperation "she traveled to Caerleon and there took the veil, / Requested the habit in the name of Christ, / But all in falseness and fraud and fear of her Lord" (3916–18).

Ultimately, a look at parallel passages from these sources will reveal that it was the French view that prevailed. Malory used both the *Alliterative Morte* and the Vulgate version but deliberately chose the authority of the latter in his characterization of the queen. He clearly sees Guinevere's love as ennobling, and when he says Guinevere "was a true lover and therefore she had a good end" (ed. Cowen; 426), the statement gains a great deal of effect in the context of previous tradition. Malory's Guinevere, the abbess who dies in true charity and repentance, is the richer when seen against the backdrop of the other Guineveres in the long tradition dating back to Geoffrey of Monmouth.

Using parallel passages, then, can reveal concretely and in easily accessible form a sense of the development of the Arthurian tradition. In a course that would teach Geoffrey of Monmouth and Malory without looking at any full treatments of the legend that occur in between, the parallel passage approach allows students to see what each author gave to the next. Without such understanding, students can only marvel at Malory's variance from Geoffrey, rather than see it in the perspective of the great tradition.

The World of King Arthur: An Interdisciplinary Course

Thomas Kelly and Thomas Ohlgren

For several years we have offered a popular undergraduate course entitled The World of King Arthur. The enrollment in the course has had to be limited to eighty students each time it has been offered. By contrast, previous courses—Viking Age, Medieval Romance, and Gothic Cathedral—attracted only fifteen to twenty students. We were, therefore, somewhat amazed by the response to the new course on King Arthur. The success of the course can be attributed to three essential components: it is interdepartmental, interdisciplinary, and experiential.

Interdepartmental Component

At first glance the mention of interdepartmental involvement in the course may smack of local administrative policies and politics, but we believe the topic deserves mention. While the course could be taught by one teacher from one department, it has benefited by the participation of faculty members from different disciplines. Such participation is facilitated by our crosslisting the course under three numbers: English 230, French 230, and Interdisciplinary Studies 220. These courses have in common that they carry variable titles, which allow thematic experimentation without the bureaucratic need to submit new courses for prior approval; that they are on the sophomore level and thus seem to have targeted the audience most attracted to the topic; and that they focus on composition and development of writing skills. This last point is important for the simple pedagogical reason that students write best on topics that interest them and about which they have something to say. In fact, their interest in topics that are relevant to Arthuriana but are outside the disciplinary expertise of the instructors, has led students to work on research papers with faculty from many departments. The best of these papers have, in turn, contributed to the development of the course by providing both models for students in subsequent semesters and new topics for the course syllabus and lectures. A paper by a talented anthropology major on the Celtic horse goddess Epona, for example, expanded one of the introductory lectures on the Celtic cultural background of the Arthurian legends.

While the course is team-taught by two teachers, who attend every class, a number of visiting speakers are integrated into the schedule of lectures. The local early historian, for example, has presented two classes on the historical backgrounds of fifth- and sixth-century Europe, and a Welsh scholar has introduced the class to the *Mabinogion* and conducted a discussion on the selection in the course textbook (Wilhelm and Gross) from "Culhwch and Olwen." An art historian has presented several slide lectures on the Victorian images of the Arthurian legends, including a survey of the Pre-Raphaelites. The flexible nature of the course provided by the crosslisting has the added feature of allowing us to bring in colleagues from outside the university as well as occasional visitors to campus. A theologian from Notre Dame has discussed the historical context of the church's teachings on love and marriage in relation to courtly love as manifested in Chrétien de Troyes's *Lancelot*, and a visiting Scandinavian scholar has lectured on the reception of Chrétien's courtly romances in Scandinavia. None of the internal visiting lecturers are compensated for their efforts; the classes are given on a voluntary basis. It should be said, however, that, in addition to lending their expertise to the class, the visiting lecturers showcase their talents as teachers, with the result that students often enroll in their classes in a later semester. Cooperation among faculty members in different departments is, then, the first major ingredient in the success of our course.

Interdisciplinary Component

The second ingredient is the firm commitment to examine evidence drawn from different disciplines and media. The course could be taught from the point of view of literature alone, but it would thereby ignore the contributions from archaeology, art history, codicology, film, history, music, myth criticism, psychology, and philosophy. All these fields are vital to a fuller understanding and appreciation of the evolution of the Arthurian legends from Gildas to *Excalibur*.

Because we are not experts in all these fields, we have drawn heavily on a large number of audiovisual materials, including videotapes from the University of Toronto, the films *Perceval, Gawain and the Green Knight, Excalibur, Monty Python and the Holy Grail*, and so on, along with color slides from the extensive holdings in the Purdue Medieval Photographic Archive. Many of these materials are used as visual introductions to concepts highlighted in the course, such as the quest for the historical Arthur (Ashe, *Discovery*), monomyth (Campbell) in the Arthurian legends, the transition from reality to romance, the politicizing of the legends, and the modern return to enchantment (Agena).

From a pedagogical perspective, interdisciplinarity as practiced in this course reflects two different but complementary strategies. Colleagues from different disciplines—history, art history, Celtic studies, theology, and others—are invited in to address specific questions relevant to the themes developed by the two instructors whose academic disciplines are primarily philology and literary studies. At the same time, we examine the phenomenon of Arthur from a broad cultural perspective using an approach similar to Huizínga's investigations of the "play element" of culture. In treating the problems raised, we are "constantly obliged to undertake predatory incursions into provinces not sufficiently explored by the raider himself" (Huizínga ii). To fill in the gaps in our knowledge ahead of time is impossible. Rather than provide all the answers, we challenge students to ask basic questions as they seek to discover the mysteries of the world of King Arthur. The complementary nature of our various interdisciplinary strategies is an effective component of the challenge.

Experiential Component

The experiential nature of the course also accounts for its popularity with students. We openly encourage students to apply their readings to individual projects to be displayed or performed at our annual King Arthur Day, an event that is highly publicized and open to the public both on and off campus. Although some may argue that such projects have no place in a college or university, we believe, by contrast, that the concept of "homo ludens" (Rahner; Huizínga) is a vital component of human development and understanding. While some students opted to create posters showing medieval castles, costumes, or daily life, others seized the opportunity to impersonate their favorite Arthurian character, to re-create a medieval dance or song and perform it, or to reenact a famous battle scene in full armor with rattan weapons. One secret to the success of King Arthur Day is the participation of the Purdue Medieval Society, an undergraduate student organization, along with cosponsorship by a residence hall that has made the day one of its annual events. In course evaluations students have cited the King Arthur Day experience as the most enjoyable part of the course. We evaluate each project carefully and assiduously award extra credit points.

Another opportunity for self-discovery is the requirement of writing two papers. In the first, a research paper, students choose from a wide variety of topics on the historical and cultural backgrounds of the

Arthurian legends. The one limitation is that the cultural topic selected must be related either to the medieval context of the legends or to some later literary or artistic treatment. Suggested medieval topics are alchemy, allegory, architecture, arms and armor, astronomy and astrology, costume, daily life, drama, furniture, foods and feasting, heraldry, and so on. In a second set of research topics, students may examine the modern legacy of Arthur since the Middle Ages; they are asked to analyze their text, artifact, or phenomenon in terms of the use made of the legends of King Arthur. We are assuming that each age or culture reinterprets the legends for its own persuasive goals. In the years we have taught this course, we have received hundreds of papers on such diverse topics as The Symbolism of the Color Green in the Film *Excalibur*, Courtly Love in the Modern World, The Celtic Horse Goddess Epona, The Armor of Gawain in *Gawain and the Green Knight*, A Feminist Retelling of the Legends in *The Mists of Avalon*, Camelot and the Kennedy Years. We schedule the due date of the research paper to coincide with King Arthur Day, thereby encouraging broader participation in the festivities, since the paper can easily be made into a display or performance project.

The second assigned paper comes at the very end of the course and takes the form of a long argumentative essay in which the students are asked: "Why does the fantastic world of King Arthur continue its fascination in an age of science and technology?" This essay is a take-home examination, and, since we expect that the question will guide students throughout the semester in following the historical and thematic content of the readings and lectures, the topic is assigned during the first week of class. More important, however, the question focuses the students' attention on arriving at their own synthesis of the entire course.

While the three course ingredients have contributed to the success of the World of King Arthur, we should not forget that the ultimate appeal is the subject matter itself and its relation to the technological culture in which our students live. Kathleen Agena is probably correct in noting a "return to enchantment" as a response by young people to "the rush of technology which seems to dwarf the significance of the individual" (68).

Teaching the Moderns in an Arthurian Course

Phillip C. Boardman

Arthurian courses have customarily focused on the Middle Ages, studying the origins and development of a tradition leading to Malory's English masterpiece. These courses have usually been taught by medievalists and have perhaps grown out of other studies, such as medieval romance. As such they have appealed mostly to advanced students and English majors.

I think it is fair to say that the proliferation of new versions of the legends, the acceptance of popular culture (including literary forms like murder mysteries, science fiction, and romance novels) as a respectable academic subject, and attempts to enliven the literature offerings for sophomores—all these have led to the establishment of courses that include modern as well as medieval Arthurian works and have as their goal an appreciation of the whole tradition of Arthurian legend and some account of its continuing creativity. In this essay I suggest some ways to incorporate modern works into courses about King Arthur.

A course covering the whole tradition will have time for, at most, three or four modern works. In a course that emphasizes chronological development, the end of the term probably brings Tennyson, Twain, T. H. White, and perhaps one other recent version, say Thomas Berger or a Mary Stewart (this volume contains essays on these writers). The advantage of this organization is its continuing stress on development, showing Victorian romanticism, the reaction to it, the major modern novelistic retelling, and a recent version less closely tied to Malory.

But a course like this virtually suggests itself, and thus it masks some of the capricious creativity of recent writers. Teachers must consciously seek out alternative works and organizations by noting patterns in the recent Arthurian tradition. One set of patterns lies in what I call strategies of invention, those structural and thematic motives that justify retelling an oft-told tale. A second pattern emerges from what used to be called (some time ago) the *forma tractandi*, the form of the treatment. First, the strategies of invention.

The first strategy, the most significant modern development, is the return of Arthur to the sixth century. Because writers are becoming more secure and knowledgable in fifth- and sixth-century materials, it is increasingly strange to pick up a book like White's *Once and Future King* or Berger's *Arthur Rex* and discover a *medieval* king with knights and castles. For almost fifty years, paced by archaeological and historical studies, this new historicist tradition has been taking shape.

In these works the characters' names take an older Welsh or Roman shape, and the knights of the Round Table become a kind of Roman-trained cavalry under their *dux bellorum*, Arthur. Edison Marshall's *Pagan King*, Walter O'Meara's *Duke of War*, and John Gloag's *Artorius Rex* all claim to restore Arthur to his original late-Roman stature. Earlier versions in this tradition focus on Arthur himself; Alfred Duggan's *Conscience of the King*, for instance, is told from the point of view of Artorius's Saxon enemies, so that Guinevere's unfaithfulness and Mordred's revolt are mentioned as rumors and disposed of in a few lines. Arthur himself is the narrator in Rosemary Sutcliff's *Sword at Sunset*, which attempts to strip away all French "innovations," all the trappings of chivalry, to work for a thoroughly *British* Matter of Britain, authentically rooted in the late fifth century, with its culture-rending clash of Roman, Celtic, and Saxon. Sutcliff replaces Lancelot with Bedwyr (Bedivere), who, along with Gwalchmai (Gawain) and Cei (Kay), has become much more important in recent versions. In Gillian Bradshaw's *In Winter's Shadow*, Bedwyr becomes the lover of Gwyn-hwyfar; in Mary Stewart's *Wicked Day*, Bedwyr is simply rumored, falsely, to be the lover. As this new tradition has grown and prospered, it has tried to reintegrate and authentically motivate the discarded French materials into the fifth-century historical frame. Thus Catherine Christian's *Pendragon* restores Lancelot, who returns to his rightful place in Guinevere's bed.

It is important to remind ourselves that when the accurate re-creation of the historical Arthur becomes a main goal of the work, the result is not history but what we now call "historical romance," that natural province of accomplished writers like Elizabeth Jenkins, Mary Stewart, and Mary Renault. Because the value of these works is authenticated not by the internal motives of the Arthurian legend but by historical plausibility, these works yield to a process Maureen Fries calls "rationalization." The novel, as a realistic medium, requires the attempt to subdue the intractable and otherworldly materials that abound in the Arthurian stories. These are, after all, tales of murder, incest, rape, prophecy, magic, miracle, and religious transfiguration. The modern writer must rationalize, or find a natural grounding for, events that stand embarrassingly unexplained in the thirteenth-century Prose Vulgate cycle of Arthurian romances. Malory himself yielded fully to this impulse, placing the Grail castle, so mysteriously evanescent in Chrétien's original, solidly on a street corner in Winchester. T. H. White treats the Grail quest realistically and skeptically by casting it in a series of conflicting reports offered by participants of widely varying gifts.

The second strategy, at the same time, turns the limitations of the novel upside down to exploit a new interest in magic, religion, and pop psychology. A cursory look at the best-seller list shows what a huge market this is, and Arthurian writers have been quick to capitalize on it; their task has been made easier because the Arthurian materials from the beginning have included strands designed to appeal to a fanatic audience. Such materials thrive in the romance tradition that has always existed at the edge of the novel, especially in those works we now call fantasy and science fiction. Partaking of the realistic expectations built into the formal fictional structure of the novel, the marvelous and impossible become real and plausible, almost commonplace. Even in mainstream versions of the legends, the world teems with Celtic bards, sorcerers, and prophets gifted with the sight, and we begin to exult in a generous commerce with occult nature. In an inversion of the classical descent into the underworld, Gwalchmai in Bradshaw's *Hawk of May* visits the eternal world of the light. In a visually stunning ritual, the inhabitants of Marion Zimmer Bradley's Avalon dispel the mists of the lake to reach the sunny island of Avalon, which exists mystically parallel to the shrouded monastery of Glastonbury.

The third strategy, while perhaps the most obvious, is also the most powerful, for it is the structural device that justifies the existence of most recent versions: these works pretend to tell the familiar story from a new point of view. This is a genuine change from the medieval versions of Arthurian romance, which exploit the highly developed, idiosyncratic voice of the omniscient storyteller addressing an audience of his familiars, perhaps even an audience of his patrons (think, for instance, of Chrétien, Gottfried, or Wolfram). Bedivere is the narrator in Christian's *Pendragon*; Guinevere tells her version of events in Bradshaw's *In Winter's Shadow* and in Parke Godwin's *Beloved Exile*; Arthur himself is the teller not only in Sutcliff's *Sword at Sunset* but also in Godwin's *Firelord*. *Hawk of May* is told by the Gawain character, and Pelleas is the narrator of Godfrey Turton's *Emperor Arthur*. Mordred's is the point of view adopted by the narrator in Stewart's *Wicked Day*, just as Sharan Newman's *Guinevere* trilogy is seen through the sensibility of the title character. In a startling tour de force, Bradley's *Mists of Avalon* adopts the point of view, in turn, of all the main women—Igraine, Morgaine, Morgause, and Gwenyfar—with Morgaine as the linking narrator. It is, in fact, hard now to imagine that this strategy is not fully exploited: the National Theater for the Deaf a few years back produced the Percival story, purportedly from the point of view of Percival's horse!

The fourth strategy might be called the boyhood of Hamlet approach. The writing of *enfances* is central to the expansionist impulses of Arthurian romance, and thus Arthur, Percival, Lancelot, and Tristan all found boyhoods within their first century. The *Hawk of May* tells of the childhood of Gwalchmai, and *The Wicked Day* develops a striking background for Mordred. While Bradshaw decides against a full girlhood for Gwynhwyfar in *In Winter's Shadow*, Newman's *Guinevere* is entirely devoted to her life before she meets and marries Arthur. Radically different versions of Merlin's early life are evoked in Stewart's *Crystal Cave* and in Michael de Angelo's *Cyr Myrddin*. The main narrator of *The Mists of Avalon*, Morgaine, casts the entire work as an account of the events of her life, beginning with her mother's loves.

In the final strategy I discuss—certainly not the last one available—writers use the Arthurian materials to establish a cosmic or philosophical position. The thematic energy behind White's "right versus might" argument in *The Once and Future King* is so strong that it assumes almost a motive force in the work, just as C. S. Lewis's contrast between spiritual Britain and "scientistic" England in *That Hideous Strength* underpins that whole book. The *Hawk of May* turns on a dualistic struggle between light, sought by Gwalchmai and Bedwyr, and the forces of darkness, marshaled in Morgawse. Curiously, Bradshaw's decision to see *In Winter's Shadow* through the sensibility of Gwynhwyfar rather than Gwalchmai undercuts the thematic force of their struggle in the last book, for in her brilliant and realistic practicality, and in her sliding morality, Gwynhwyfar cannot be an effective advocate for any cause more supernatural than the expedient Christianity that offers safety in its abbeys. The conflict between pagan and Christian finds a place in most of these books, but nowhere more powerfully than in *The Mists of Avalon*, where the Celtic and druidic worship of the Mother Goddess of nature is forced to yield to the blindly antifeminist and rigidly masculine Christianity. The novel is, in many ways, an epic account of this conflict and its inevitable outcome.

The clearest way to exploit this last strategy in the classroom is to build on thematic links with earlier works in the course. An emphasis on codes of behavior and the interpretation of character in *Sir Gawain and the Green Knight* and Chrétien's *Perceval* can be followed up in Stewart's *Wicked Day*, which attempts a rehabilitation of Mordred and shows the slipperiness of reputation. A number of recent works stand the tradition on its head by examining with a sharp and skeptical eye a worldview or set of values that the medieval works accept. For example, *The Mists of Avalon* looks at the underside of Christianity from the perspective of a vanishing Celtic religion and thus casts an interesting shadow back across the hyper-Christianity of some works in the Grail tradition, like *Perlesvaus* and the French *Queste*. The exquisite refinement of love in Chrétien's *Cligés* or *Sir Gawain and the Green Knight* becomes bawdy and comical in Robert Nye's *Merlin* and Nicholas Seare's *Rude Tales and Glorious*. The chivalric glorification of combat in such works as Wolfram's *Parzival* is cast in an imagery that betrays its violence and expense of spirit in Richard Monaco's version of that story, *Parsival*; savage violence is the main reason for David Drake's military fantasy, *The Dragon Lord*. The wasteland theme from the medieval Grail stories expands its modern implications in T. S. Eliot's long poem, in which modern urban life has lost its sense of rootedness; in Lewis's *That Hideous Strength*, in which the sterility of materialistic and bureaucratic England nearly triumphs over spiritual Britain; and in John Boorman's film *Excalibur* (1981), whose graphically visual wasteland spells the loss of connection between ruler and land. As a capper to any class, students always respond well to the parody of all these themes in the film *Monty Python and the Holy Grail* (1975).

A course might include a variety of these strategies or focus on a single one. Or the different approaches can be topics for discussion in a course that selects books according to the second pattern, as representing different treatments of Arthurian materials. In general, the works seem to me to fall into three large classes, which might be made the basis for selecting readings for a course (Boardman, "Arthur Redivivus"). The first are those that, following an arrested medieval practice, make Arthur a medieval king, presiding over a court of knights and ladies. This group, inheritors of Malory's estate, includes Twain, White, Berger, Monaco, John Steinbeck, and others. The second, contrasting, group includes works that follow the historicist strategy mentioned above. They attempt to place Arthur in an authentically historical sixth-century environment.

The third category is large and diverse, encompassing those works that, unlike works in the first two groups, are not versions of the legends of Arthur but use elements or characters from the legends for other purposes. Many science fiction and fantasy novels, for instance, steal the sword Excalibur or exploit a Merlin-like sorcerer. In *That Hideous Strength* Merlin himself awakes to do battle with a sinister institute of social scientists. In Charles Williams's *War in Heaven* the Grail is found in a small English village, touching off an apocalyptic struggle between good and evil. In Diana Norman's *King of the Last Days*, Arthur's sword is dug up during the reign of Henry II.

Sometimes the characters provide the point of similarity. Nicole St. John's *Guinever's Gift* re-creates the fatal triangle between an archaeologist who discovers Arthur's grave, his assistant, and his wife. Babs Deal's *Grail* takes place at Castle University, where the football hero, named Lance, falls in love with Jenny Hill, the wife of football coach Arthur Hill. The Tristan myth becomes a modern love story in the post–World War II Cornwall, London, and America of Maria

Kuncewicz's *Tristan*. In David Lodge's *Small World* the hero is a naive young Irishman, Persse (Percival), who seeks his ideal woman through the wasteland-world of academic conferences.

In some books, the Arthurian materials are transformed generical-ly—for instance, into a murder story, as in Phyllis Ann Karr's *Idylls of the Queen*; a horror story, as in Philip Michaels's *Grail*; or a spy thriller, as in Anthony Price's *Our Man in Camelot*.

A class that tried to demonstrate the fertility of the modern tradition by selecting from these three patterns would probably choose at least one work from each of the first two and several kinds from the marginal third group, keeping an eye as well on different narrative strategies.

An alternative way to organize the material might prove useful especially for a course that is something other than Arthurian—say, an introduction to literature, a composition course, or a special-topics seminar. A certain character or theme, like Guinevere, the Grail, or chivalry, would be selected and readings chosen, from the entire tradition, on this single topic. Consider, for instance, a course on Merlin. A report on Geoffrey of Monmouth's *Vita Merlini* and a reading of Malory's "Merlin" might be followed by a variety of readings, balanced against the material in Nikolai Tolstoy's recent study of the historical Merlin, *The Quest for Merlin*. Students should be challenged by the diversity of Merlins as they appear in Tennyson's "Merlin and Vivien," Twain's *Connecticut Yankee*, Stewart's Merlin trilogy, Nye's *Merlin*, de Angelo's *Cyr Myrddin*, Drake's *Dragon Lord*, and Lewis's *That Hideous Strength*. Jane Yolen's *Merlin's Booke* offers both short stories and poems, which can be supplemented by short poems such as Edwin Muir's "Merlin," Richard Wilbur's "Merlin Enthralled," Geof-frey Hill's "Merlin," Thomas Good's "End of Merlin," or John Matthews's sequence of poems *Merlin in Calydon*.

I have thrown a number of recent works into the hopper in the hope that teachers might see ways to play them off against one another. There are, of course, a multitude of works that can be assigned to students, many of them traceable through bibliographies (Northrup and Parry; P. A. Brown; Spivack; Boardman, "Recent Arthurian Literature"; Wildman; Reynolds; Taylor and Brewer) and available through libraries. But the problem for teachers is the availability of texts for courses. Most modern Arthurian works belong to that class of mayfly publications that disappear soon after they are hatched. Many of these books are never available in paperback; those that are can be used only briefly. I managed to teach Christian's *Pendragon* twice; the third time it was out of print. I was never successful in getting all three of Bradshaw's or of Newman's trilogies at the same time. This situation (even though I like to begin my Arthurian classes with *The Once and Future King*) probably accounts for our turning inevitably to Tennyson, Twain, White, Stewart, and, now, perhaps, Bradley: we can generally count on their staying at least intermittently in print.

TEACHING MAJOR AUTHORS

Translating *Yvain* and *Sir Gawain and the Green Knight* for Classroom Use

Burton Raffel

I did, as the title of this essay indicates, have classroom readers in mind when I translated the Arthurian poems *Yvain* and *Sir Gawain and the Green Knight*. I wanted to make two beautiful but linguistically formidable texts accessible to those without the necessary skills to read either the Old French of Chrétien de Troyes's *Yvain* or the obscure Middle English dialect in which *Gawain* was composed.

The key words are "beautiful" and "accessible." They sound like perfectly straightforward, even simple, terms. In truth, they lead into thorny and hotly disputed literary and linguistic debates, some of which seem to have been conducted ever since the invention of writing.

No one argues that poems like *Yvain* and *Gawain* are not beautiful. The difficulties occur when we leave the originals and turn to their translations. How do we reproduce a beautiful landscape or painting, a beautiful opera or the face of a beautiful human being for those who have never encountered the original? What standards of beauty must the re-creation adhere to? What responsibilities does the re-creator have?

Let me first illustrate these problems with a brief passage from *Yvain*. Consider the stark beauty of lines 2790–92, describing the hero's misery when he realizes that, unintentionally, he has broken a vow to his absent wife:

> Ne het tant rien con lui meisme,
> Ne ne set, a cui se confort
> De lui, qu'il meismes a mort.

How much of this passage's beauty *can* be translated for students? the octosyllabic meter? the rhyme? the word play? the brutal truthfulness? John Dryden long ago realized that a translation cannot be identical to its original and that the attempt to translate everything all at once is "much like dancing on ropes with fettered legs: a man may shun a fall by using caution; but the gracefulness of motion is not to be expected" (269). Gracefulness of motion, however, is only another way of saying "beauty." What I therefore tried to do, in translating this passage, was to capture as much of that beauty as I could, leaving behind what I could not carry into modern English. I approximated the meter, substituting a three-stress line for the Old French octosyllabics. I abandoned the rhyme, because French is far more rhyme-rich than English and because a poem intended to be read off the page needs rhyme less than it did eight hundred years ago as a poem intended to be read aloud. I worked hard to preserve the word play and the brutal truthfulness—and emerged with these lines:

> There was nothing he hated as much
> As himself, and no one to comfort him
> In the death he'd chosen for himself.
> (Chrétien, *Yvain*)

It is not the Old French, but whoever said it could be? "No poem in translation is the original from which it takes its life; there must be distortion, to a greater or lesser degree, simply by definition. . . . And poetry in translation is either poetry born anew or it is nothing at all" (Raffel, *Forked Tongue* 59, 115). Students are not always as well trained as we would like, nor as sophisticated. But they are entirely capable of distinguishing between what bears some resemblance to beauty and what bears no resemblance whatever. The work of Dryden's "verbal copier" is musty and, above all else, dull. No matter how great our authority, no matter how large the students' respect for our learning, how are we to persuade students that what is being exhibited for them is beauty plain and clear, if we offer them dross in place of gold? Neither pedantic literalism nor dogged prose will or can seem beautiful, and students end by doubting either the original or us—or both.

Which leads me directly to accessibility, the second of my two requirements for successful classroom translation. The translator must not falsify the original or simplify it, presenting it as something easier and more immediately palatable than it truly is. Students must learn to deal with great poetry on its terms, not on theirs. I advocate not the slightest pandering. But I strongly advocate that a translation present itself, as nearly as possible, on the same level, and on the same terms, as the original comes to those who have no difficulties with its language and cultural context. That is, the translator ought not to make complex what is straightforward in the original. Nor should the translator interpose any impediments of his or her own making.

Consider lines 625–630 of *Gawain*, describing the mystic pentangle, and then consider lines 640–665, in which the poet explains what the pentangle meant to Gawain. These are not modern ideas; they need to be presented just as the unknown poet presented them. It is then the students' responsibility (with our help) to deal with what the poet has said. I give only lines 625–630 in the original (orthographically normalized), followed by my translation of both passages:

> Hit is a synge that Salamon set sumquyle
> In byoknyng of trwthe, bi tytle that hit habbez,
> For hit is a figure that haldez fyue poytentz,
> And vche lyne vmbelappez and loukez in other,
> And ayquere hit is endelez; and Englych hit callen
> Oueral, as I here, the endeles knot.

> . . . Solomon shaped that star—
> Triangles blended in triangles—as a symbol
> Of truth, for each of its angles enfolds
> The other, and fastens the other, five
> In all and everywhere endless (and everywhere
> In England called the infinite knot). . . .

> His five senses were free of sin;
> His five fingers never failed him;
> And all his earthly hope was in Christ's
> Five wounds on the cross, as our creed tells us;
> And whenever he stood in battle his mind
> Was fixed, above all things, on the five
> Joys which Mary had of Jesus,
> From which all his courage came—and was why
> This fair knight had her face painted

Inside his shield, to stare at Heaven's
Queen and keep his courage high.
And the fifth of his fives was love and friendship
For other men, and freedom from sin,
And courtesy that never failed, and pity,
Greatest of knightly virtues—and these noble
Five were the firmest of all in his soul.
And all these five met in one man,
Joined to each other, each without end,
Set in five perfect points
Wholly distinct, yet part of one whole
And that whole seamless, each angle open
And closed, wherever it end or begin.
And so the pentangle glowed on his shield,
Bright red gold across bright red stripes,
The holy pentangle, as careful scholars
                              Call it.
                    (Raffel, *Gawain*)

The poet thought this explanation sufficiently important not only to write it, and include it in his poem, but to defend it in advance. "I am in tent yow to telle," he prefaces his discussion, "thof tary hyt me schulde" ("And I'll tell you how, though it hold up this tale"). Students can understand the idea of the pentangle and can learn, from passages like this, a good deal about how the medieval mind worked. But they can acquire these awarenesses only if the translation speaks to them directly and clearly—that is, accessibly.

There is little in *Yvain* that is quite so mystical or even so religiously fervent. But Chrétien too has his lessons to teach, and they should be conveyed to students in language as much like Chrétien's vivid, flowing French as possible:

> Et cil, qui avuec lui estoient,
> Por lui grant hardemant prenoient;
> Que tes a povre cuer et lasche,
> Quant il voit, qu'uns prodon antasche
> Devant lui une grant besoinge,
> Que maintenant honte et vergoingne
> Li cort sus et si giete fors
> Le povre cuer, qu'il a el cors,
> Si li done sodainnemant
> Cuer de prodome et hardemant.
>   (lines 3171–80)

The key words for Chrétien are repeated, and easy to spot: *hardemant* 'courage,' *cuer* 'heart, courage,' *grant* 'eager,' *prodon* and *prodome* 'brave, good knight'; 'gentlemanly.' The translation should similarly feature the ideas represented by these words—though not, as Dryden understood, the words themselves, verbatim. "Since every language is so full of its own proprieties, that what is beautiful in one is often barbarous, nay sometimes nonsense, in another, it would be unreasonable to limit a translator to the narrow compass of his author's words: 'tis enough if he choose out some expression which does not vitiate the sense" (272). Here is my rendering of this passage:

> . . . And those who were with him
> Were suddenly encouraged, and turned
> Into warriors, for many a mean-spirited
> Wretch, and a coward, seeing
> A brave man take on a difficult
> Struggle right in front of his eyes,
> Is attacked by shame, overwhelmed,
> And throws his miserable heart
> Out of his body and acquires
> A true knight's spirit, brave
> And noble and strong.
> (lines 3170–80)

Two of the translator's most severe tests, both as to beauty and as to accessibility, come in passages either bawdy or satirical. Students need to know that what they are reading is neither bowdlerized nor watered down. When Chrétien has a knight respond to Sir Kay's malice in blunt language, students need to read the knight's speech in equally blunt words:

> Sir Kay! You've said such things,
> And often, to better men,
> And wiser, than me. Insulting
> Others is a habit with you.
> Manure will always stink,
> And horse-flies bite, and bees
> Buzz, and bores be boring.
> (Chrétien, *Yvain*, lines 112–18)

Similarly, when the green knight has taunted and teased Gawain and finally nicks him lightly on the neck, and Gawain frantically arms himself and gets ready for combat, students should be shown with absolute clarity both the silliness and the bravery of Gawain's actions:

> The green man stood listening, leaning on his axe
> (It was upside down, he rested on the blade),
> And watching the knight, how bravely he waited,
> How unafraid, armed and ready,
> Standing alert. And he liked what he saw.
> And then he spoke, with a cheerful, booming
> Voice, addressing Gawain: "Warrior,
> Soldier, no need to be fierce, now."
> (Raffel, *Gawain*, lines 2331–38)

Translating for classroom use means translating for untrained but intelligent students, of whom we as teachers have a right to expect careful, close reading. If we give them the tools, they respond well. Bad, dull translations are bad tools, to which students tend to respond with poor classroom performance.

Teaching Gottfried and Wolfram

James A. Schultz

There is a long tradition in Middle High German scholarship that regards Gottfried von Strassburg and Wolfram von Eschenbach as "literary antipodes" and that, in its most elaborate form, imagines Gottfried's *Tristan* and Wolfram's *Parzival* to have been written in polemical opposition to each other. I am pleased to report that my students are of a similar opinion. Although generally unaware of the scholars' views, they also find the two romances quite different: *Tristan* seems relatively accessible and easy, *Parzival* perversely opaque and difficult. Those of us who teach these texts, however, often find ourselves at odds with both the scholars and our students. In courses in which *Tristan* and *Parzival* must serve as exemplars of medieval vernacular textual practice in general, we inevitably draw attention to the features they share. In what follows I have tried to mediate between the scholars, the students, and the teachers by suggesting four headings under which one can make important points about *Tristan* and *Parzival* in particular as well as about medieval narrative in general. I have arranged the topics so that they can be taken up sequentially, as students and teacher make their way through these rather long texts.

Topoi and Tropes

Both Gottfried and Wolfram begin their narratives with the stories of their heroes' parents, and in both cases these stories contain a generous selection of romance topoi in relatively unproblematic, idealized form. One finds exemplary courtliness (Mark's festival), knighthood (Gahmuret, the tournament at Kanvoleis), and feudal virtue (Rual's loyalty), as well as a whole range of love conventions (falling in love, love monologue, court of love). Unless students are familiar with such conventional patterns, they will not be in a position to appreciate what is at stake when, later on, the conventions are undermined.

One can also use the parents' stories to alert students to certain characteristic tropes. When Riwalin and Blanscheflur fall in love, Gottfried gives us antithesis, oxymoron, and chiasmus (883–914/53, 1075/55, 1360–61/58 [verse in Ranke edition/page in Hatto translation]). These frequently employed figures do not merely ornament: they represent rhetorically the intricate relations of "one" and "two" that are essential to Gottfried's dialectics (analysis into opposing abstractions) and to his thematics (love turns two into one). There is hidden meaning as well in names (1994–2022/67) and hidden coherence in acrostics (see Hatto 33). These pages also offer good examples of Gottfried's characteristic stance as commentator: the incidents of the story prompt him to expound general truths and to indulge in abstract analysis (841–74/52, 1331–46/58). In many ways the traditional story functions like a canonical text to which Gottfried attaches a highly rhetorical and pseudodialectical gloss.

One can illustrate some of Wolfram's characteristic tropes in the passage that describes Parzival's birth. It contains a number of circumlocutions, some sufficiently opaque that the narrator must explain them (113, 6–7/66 [verse in Leitzmann edition/page in Hatto translation]), and good examples of his bold metonymic jumps: from the infant's penis, to the adult's sword (metonymy, not phallus!), to his manly heart (113, 23–30/66); from Herzeloide's nipples, to the Virgin's nursing, to a brief catechism (113, 5–26/66). In spite of these jumps, Wolfram never loses sight of the whole, often drawing our attention to events thousands of lines away (112, 28–30/66). Wolfram's rhetoric is distinctive for its willful complexity, its range of registers, and its consciousness of the whole. It is as if he wants to gather all of creation (from body parts to the mysteries of faith) and all of the story (from birth to adulthood) into each moment.

The self-consciousness with which Gottfried and Wolfram deploy their tropes reflects a more general medieval attitude toward narrative art. Contemporary poetic treatises, for example, are devoted not to the ways one might invent a story but rather to the rhetorical means by which an existing story might be elaborated. And skill in elaboration, in the *way* the story is told, is the criterion according to which works are judged: Gottfried attacks Wolfram not for his story but for his style—it is disjointed and incomprehensible without a gloss (4638–90/105–06). Rhetorical stance is also the source of the poet's self-definition: in his dense prologue Wolfram stubbornly asserts his intention to be difficult.

Narrator

When one reaches Tristan's fight with Morolt, two important points can be made about Gottfried's narrator. First, here, as often, he draws attention away from the story itself to the way he tells it: he transforms the fight with Morolt into an elaborate allegory, in explicit contradiction to his source. The same willful bravura is also evident in the literary excursus, in which he pretends to be unable to describe Tristan's armor, then passes judgment on a large number of Middle

High German writers, parades his learning, and finally *does* describe some armor—in the conditional! Second, one can point out that the narrator does not remain altogether consistent: his dismissal of his source before the Morolt fight contradicts the devotion to the source he professes in the prologue (6866–76/133, 115–62/43). These and other contradictions (compare the *sententiae* 15165–68/241 and 16420/257; the relation of the long excursus to the story they interrupt; the different meanings of *triuwe* [loyalty/faithfulness] and *ere* [honor/renown] 177–90/43 and 12507–22/206) are the consequence of a kind of narration that is so focused on elaborating and commenting on the individual moment that it can lose sight of the whole (Christ 117–222).

Wolfram's narrator makes one of his boldest appearances in the so-called *Selbstverteidigung* (114, 5–116, 3/68–69). Here, as elsewhere, he presents himself as a knight, his epic composition as a knightly deed, and his narrative treatment of women as a kind of love service more valuable than that of the *Minnesänger*. This literary-social argument—epic versus lyric, knight versus singer—establishes an analogy between the love service of the knightly narrator and that of the knightly characters (Curschmann 648–62). As usual, Wolfram makes connections. The narrator assumes many other, sometimes contradictory, roles in the course of his narration, and students should be alerted to watch for them.

As idiosyncratic as they are, the narrators in *Tristan* and *Parzival* nevertheless exemplify several general points. The romance narrator is a written representation of a fictional oral performer—which raises the question of orality and literacy in vernacular texts and in medieval society. At the same time, the fictional role of narrator provides the script for the actual oral performer of the romance—which raises the question of the historical modes of performance and reception.

Traditional Structures

When Tristan returns from Ireland the second time, he brings to its conclusion a traditional narrative pattern, the bride quest, or *Brautwerbungsschema*, that forms the structural core of the Tristan story (as of the *Nibelungenlied*): prince lacks bride, councillors suggest a distant princess, messenger is dispatched, performs difficult tasks, returns with bride for the prince. In the Tristan story this is crossed with another traditional pattern, the dragon fight: hero defeats dragon, wins princess. Since the dragon fight is the difficult task by which Tristan accomplishes the bride quest, he (as hero of the dragon fight) in effect wins Isolde for himself at the same time he (as messenger in the bride quest) wins her for Mark: the major tension of the plot is implicit in the combination of traditional structures (Kuhn, *Tristan*). The rest of *Tristan* is a rather loose assortment of common narrative patterns (Mohr): parents, childhood, liberation of (implicitly: winning) the country; later a series of more or less interchangeable adventures. The whole is held together less by a compelling narrative logic than by the continuing presence of the hero and the authority of tradition.

By the end of book 6 of *Parzival* one begins to recognize the contours of a two-part Arthurian pattern (compare *Erec et Enide/Erec* and *Yvain/Iwein*) according to which the episodes of *Parzival* are arranged: in the first part the hero moves from relative anonymity to great renown (certified by Arthur) but then, on account of some failing, is isolated from society; in the second, longer part the hero proves himself again through a series of adventures, reenters society, and ends more renowned than ever. The failing that provokes the crisis (for instance, Parzival's failure to ask the question) always seems inadequate to the ordeal that follows, but the hero accepts his responsibility and entrusts himself to "adventure"—much as the Christian must acknowledge his or her sinfulness and trust in the grace of God; sin, penance, and grace, like the hero's failing, adventures, and rehabilitation, are always incommensurate (Kuhn, "Parzival" 161–74). The Arthurian pattern was already doubled in Wolfram's source, Chrétien de Troyes's *Conte du Graal*, so that the work has two centers, Arthur's court and the Grail castle, each with its own hero (Gawan and Parzival) and each with its own crisis (Cundrie, Kingrimursel). All of *Parzival* from book 3 to the end is embraced by this doubled two-part traditional structure.

Medieval writers often exploit traditional narrative patterns: the venerable Christian scheme is appropriated to "justify" class-specific secular behavior (the knightly search for adventure). Presumably audiences were expected to be familiar with the models and to recognize the way they are transformed. Sometimes these traditional patterns arouse expectations that are frustrated: the *Brautwerbung* in *Tristan* is compromised; book 8 of *Parzival* is a parody of book 7.

Techniques of Amplification

Gottfried elaborates the inherited story by complicating and analyzing each moment. The episode in which Isolde threatens to kill Tristan in the bath is interrupted several times by the arrival of new characters, each with her own opinion of the situation: between their reactions and the narrator's commentary, all the issues involved are set before us. The episode in which Isolde and Mark try to trick each other in bedtime conversation, like the one in which Tristan debates marrying Isolde of the White Hands, shows the same tendency to illuminate all the aspects of a given situation; this kind of elaboration gives Gottfried ample opportunity to display his dialectical rhetoric—but at the same time it leads him to undermine the psychological plausibility of his characters (Christ, 69–77, 118–67). Gottfried's elaborative tour de force is surely the cave of the lovers: what was originally a wretched forest exile has become a full-fledged allegory of love based perhaps on the allegorical exegesis of church buildings (Ranke) or the French tradition of "maisons d'amor" (Kolb). Here, as elsewhere, Gottfried appropriates varieties of religious discourse for his own purposes.

While Gottfried expands by elaborating each individual moment, Wolfram elaborates his inherited story by annexing vast amounts of additional matter. He incorporates large parts of the East: Gahmuret seeks service in Baghdad and has a child by Belacane; this child, Feirefiz, eventually marries Parzival's aunt and Christianizes India. Thus the work offers at the end a vision of a universal Christian empire (Kuhn, "Parzival" 159–61). Wolfram's eagerness to incorporate and synthesize is evident in many other features as well: the work includes 182 characters, of whom 113 are related; fictional time is carefully ordered according to an elaborate chronology based on the liturgical calendar (Groos); the relation of man and woman, of humans and God, of lord and vassal all depend on the same virtue, *triuwe* (loyalty/faithfulness).

By their elaborations romance authors strengthen the connections between various parts of the stories and create new ones, thus heightening the coherence of their narratives. Typological exegesis provides a model for the kinds of connections a medieval audience might have noticed: between Tristan's two trips to Ireland, say, or the three heroes of *Parzival* (Gahmuret, Parzival, Gawan). Just as the Old Testament prefiguration retains its truth even though it is surpassed by the New Testament fulfillment, so Gawan is not discredited even though he is eclipsed by Parzival. These are techniques for multiplying meaning, not suppressing or systematizing it.

The four categories I have offered enable one to study *Tristan* and *Parzival* individually as well as to identify characteristics of medieval narrative in general. While my categories focus on aspects of medieval textual practice, I could just as well have chosen a different perspective: the representation of sexuality, gender, love, and marriage, for instance; or the use of religious rhetoric, concepts, practices, and politics. Regardless of the categories, however, one will want to stress their elaborate, sometimes contradictory relations (Schultz 169–84). Such an emphasis will counter the students' eagerness to reduce texts to a single meaning and will thereby indicate something of the complexity of the individual romance. At the same time it will introduce students to the complex alterity of medieval narrative and thereby indicate something about the historically specific kinds of writing of which the individual romance is but a representative.

Which Malory Should I Teach?

Robert L. Kindrick

Choosing a Malory text has been problematic ever since the publication in 1947 of Eugène Vinaver's edition of Malory's *Works*. There has been a general assumption that the Malory manuscript (British Library Additional 59678) is the "best text." Indeed, a whole generation of scholars has grown up considering the Malory manuscript to be the best and the most original version of what Malory intended the word to be.

For many instructors, especially precollege, the question of which Malory to use as a basis for classroom discussion and review is not debatable. They find themselves saddled with translations, standard textbook selections, or other readily available sources that are specified in curriculum guides. At upper-division and graduate levels, however, the question of which text to teach is indeed critical. Until 1934, Caxton's *Le Morte d'Arthur* was the only version available, but the discovery of the Malory manuscript at Winchester College aroused speculation about the authenticity of Caxton's text and the printer's own role in its transmission (Oakeshott 5–6). That speculation culminated in the widely accepted revisionism of Vinaver when, in 1947, he published a composite of the Malory manuscript and Caxton's text under the title *The Works of Sir Thomas Malory*. Repudiating his own earlier position and breaking sharply with traditional scholarship, Vinaver emphasized Caxton's role not only as "editor" but also as "manipulator" of Malory's text. The arguments that ensue from Vinaver's thesis can be a fruitful source of classroom discussion and student projects.

Caxton, Vinaver contends, made changes in Malory's material that extend far beyond traditional editorial prerogative. Assuming that the early date of the Malory manuscript gives it priority as an expression of the author's intended text, Vinaver argues that Caxton worked from a similar version and made several significant changes (*Works* xxxv–xli; see also Shaw 134–45). First Caxton tried to emphasize the unity of the "hoole book" by actually merging eight tales into a single long romance. Vinaver notes that this could be done only by repressing several of the explicits that appear in the manuscript and by giving the book the unifying title of *Le Morte d'Arthur*. This unity, Vinaver believes, is also related to Caxton's moral emphasis in the work and his admonition to "Doo after the good and leve the evyl and it shal brynge you to good fame and renomee" (3a). Finally, among other charges, Vinaver believes that Caxton was apparently dissatisfied with the length of his book 5 ("The Roman War") and cut and significantly rewrote it. Vinaver's attitude is summarized in his remark that "it is only now that the damage due to Caxton's 'symple connynge' can be partially repaired" (*Works* xxxv).

Obviously these arguments have implications for the classroom. In the wholesale rejection of the Caxton text that followed the second edition of Vinaver's *Malory*, in 1971, many undergraduate and graduate instructors agreed with Vinaver about Caxton's role in the transmission of the "authentic" text. Along with Vinaver, they and their students came to assume the following:

1. that Caxton is not trustworthy in his explanation of editorial procedure;
2. that the revisions in the Caxton *Morte d'Arthur* were made by Caxton from a manuscript closely approaching the Malory manuscript;
3. and therefore that the Malory manuscript is the more reliable reflection of Malory's last revision of the text.

Of these assumptions, 1 and 2 are almost equally condemnatory. The first suggests that Caxton's prologues and epilogues are not reliable guides to his editorial procedure and that Caxton falsified information about his editing purpose for any one of several dubious reasons (Blake, *Caxton and His World* 123–24). The second suggests literary heresy to some modern critics in that the printer dared to tamper with a work of genius, changing incipits and explicits and drastically revising "The Roman War" episode without notifying his readers and our students of the changes.

The first charge has repeatedly involved attacks on the printer's integrity and taste. A careful study of the prologues and epilogues reveals that Caxton did have integrity as an editor. While he may indeed have "followed Burgundian literary taste" (Blake, *Caxton and His World* 68) and may have been arbitrary in his choice of titles, perhaps playing to the court audiences of his time, he often took pains in his prologues and epilogues to inform his reader as precisely as possible about the editorial procedures he followed. Thus there is no reason to believe that he is being false when he explains his editorial procedure for Malory's text. After relating that "many noble and dyvers gentylmen" (2a) had requested that he print a text of the tales of King Arthur and explaining how he himself had to be convinced of Arthur's existence, Caxton states:

> . . . I haue after the symple connynge that god hath sente to me / vnder the fauour and correctyon of al noble lordes and gentylmen enprysed to enprynte a book of the noble hystoryes of the sayd Kynge Arthur / and of certeyn of his knyghtes after a copye vnto

me delyerd / whyche copye Syr Thomas Malorye dyd take oute of
certayn bookes of frensshe and reduced it in to Englysshe / And I
accordyng to my copye haue doon sette it in enprynte / to the
entente that noble men may see and lerne the noble actes of
chiualry. . . .   (3a)

It is important to note that Caxton assures his readers that he printed
the work "accordyng to my copye." Based on his other patterns of
editorial practice, such a statement would not prevent him from taking
minor liberties to modernize spelling and even to eliminate certain
letters, such as thorn and yogh. Certainly it could also permit him to
replace an occasional word that struck him as outmoded or otherwise
inappropriate. He also states:

And for to vnderstonde bryefly the contente of thys volume / I
have deuyded it into xxij bookes / and euery book chapytred.
(3b)

This statement explains the method of organization used by Caxton
himself in the text. His changes of the explicits (if, indeed, *his* changes
they were) are explained by implication in this comment. But his
statements are not indicative of any major revisions, such as those in
book 5. When Caxton makes such substantial revisions, as in the
Polychronicon or his compilation of *The Golden Legend*, he informs his
reader that such changes have been made. His statements are not
always enough to explain the nature of the changes in modern
scholarly terms, but nonetheless the reader is informed that the text
differs in some significant way from Caxton's source or copytext.
    Students find it fascinating to review this evidence about Caxton's
integrity in the light of Vinaver's assertions. They are confronted with
several central cruces in this element alone. They may be asked to
weigh the scholarly arguments amassed by Vinaver based on his
thorough reading of the text. Reference to volume 3 of the *Works* may
take students through some rough textual reading but will help them
gain an understanding of the textual insights of one of the best
medievalists of the last generation. Then they may be confronted with
the textual evidence from Caxton's other works. His general faithful-
ness to his sources and his overall policy of notifying the reader of
significant changes (which we are able to trace with students) clearly
suggest his editorial integrity. Through this kind of evaluation,
students may be led to consider the general problem of literary
creation in the Middle Ages, including the role of sources, the role of
editors, and the general integrity of the editorial process. Many

students will find these to be completely new questions. Having read widely in modern authors, they may be perplexed to find that Caxton could even have played such an important editorial role. However, one has only to cite Thomas Wolfe as an example of another author who relied heavily on his editor. Yet the fact that such editorial assistance was provided through direct exchange indicates an important difference in the relationship of authors and editors in the Middle Ages. Students may then be asked to investigate the issue of the sanctity of an author's work (a more modern notion with which they will undoubtedly be familiar) as distinct from the needs, desires, and proprietary rights of a printer. All these questions can be couched in terms of the process of literary creation.

As a next step it is possible to lead students to a discussion of "The Roman War." Close comparison of the Caxton text, the Malory manuscript, and the sources reveals that Caxton himself would have had to take over the role of author, not editor, to make the necessary changes (Matthews, "Matthews"). It would have been impossible for him to make changes in the Malory manuscript without having an opportunity for firsthand review of the sources himself, a situation that most scholars consider to be impossible. Moreover, students should be made aware that, based on his work with *The Golden Legend* and the *Polychronicon*, we must conclude with N. F. Blake that "comprehensiveness was a principle which often guided his actions" (*Caxton and His World* 119). In short, another interesting question for students to consider emerges from the comparison of the Malory text with other of Caxton's works. Is an editor whose tendency is to provide everything in his source likely to go back to the original source and reduce it? If so, why? Isn't it reasonable to assume, based on the principles found in Caxton's other editorial work, that he would be more likely to include directly what he found in the witness that he received? Given the problems of time that appear in Caxton's other works, how could he have justified a review of the sources, even if he had had access to them? Blake in particular is a good authority to review when trying to direct students to these questions about Caxton's editorial integrity.

Recent evidence about the Malory manuscript itself has provided even more tantalizing possibilities for students to consider. In 1975, Lotte Hellinga, while examining the manuscript, detected traces of fifteenth-century printer's ink. Later and more detailed examination revealed that there were sixty-six traces of printing ink smudges. Other evidence of the printer's workshop began to appear when the manuscript was submitted to examination under ultraviolet and infrared light. Offsets of both lowercase and uppercase examples of Caxton's type 4 and type 2 were revealed. Hellinga believes that the "many offsets and traces of printing ink in the manuscript are a strong indication of its prolonged and intensive use in or near a printer's workshop" (Hellinga and Kelliher 98). She and Hilton Kelliher believe that this additional evidence is supported by the use of an indulgence printed by Caxton in 1489 to mend a tear in leaf 243 (Kelliher 147). While she takes due note of Oakeshott's caution that the fragment's presence proves nothing, Hellinga also believes that it seems far more probable that "the fragment was a piece of waste rather than part of an issued indulgence, and that it was used in or near the workshop." She concludes that while the manuscript was used "intensively in close contact with damp pages of books printed by William Caxton between 1480 and the end of 1483 . . . it must have remained there at least as late as 1489" (Hellinga and Kelliher 99). Hellinga's evidence makes it quite probable that Caxton did indeed have British Library Additional manuscript 59678 in his workshop, very likely at precisely the time he was preparing Malory's work for publication. Hellinga's research helps students explore the fascinating work of paleographical detection, but it poses several other interesting textual questions.

Hellinga's discoveries suggest that Caxton worked from British Library Additional manuscript 59678 and made precisely the revisions that Vinaver indicated. But the revisions in "The Roman War" episode suggest that it would have been virtually impossible for Caxton to use the sources Malory employed. Indeed, Hellinga is persuaded that whatever use Caxton made of the manuscript, he could not have used it for Book 5. She further cautions that "it would seem . . . naive to cast aside all textual evidence hitherto adduced, and to assume that the occurrence of the offsets alone would suffice as proof that Caxton used the Malory manuscript as the basis for his edition" (Hellinga" 137). Where, then, does the Malory manuscript fit into the canon of Malory's works, and, in particular, what was its importance to Caxton when he was in the process of printing Malory's text? Students might or might not accept the conclusion that the Malory manuscript that we now possess is not the prototype for Malory's *Morte d'Arthur* but is instead generally a rejected text.

There is evidence to support this theory from the manuscript itself and from Caxton's editorial procedures. Hellinga notes that there are no marks on the manuscript to indicate that it was a printer's copytext, but she notes that Caxton could not have marked it excessively if it belonged to a noble patron (Hellinga and Kelliher 91–92, 99–100; see also G. Painter 147). Caxton's traditional editorial procedure suggests, however, that there would have been at least some marks if it were his copytext (Blake, *Caxton: England's First Publisher* 55–84). That the Malory manuscript, which is not particularly elaborate by fifteenth-century standards, bears no compositor's marks certainly suggests that it was not Caxton's copytext. Even the possible objection that Caxton intended to return it to a noble patron such as Earl Rivers does not make the lack of compositor's marks any more acceptable. The de Worde *De proprietatibus rerum* was also apparently not the printer's own property, but it shows at least minimal compositor's marks. Moreover, if Caxton had received the manuscript from Earl Rivers or another patron, why did he delay so long in returning it? For him to have kept the manuscript until at least 1489 suggests that it might have been his own copy.

Caxton apparently knew of the Malory manuscript and likely even had it in his possession yet largely rejected it, probably in favor of a more authoritative text. Whether or not one accepts the conclusion that the Caxton version is the "best text," inferences can clearly be drawn about which Malory to teach at the upper-division and graduate level. The answer is both. Recent discoveries by Hellinga and others suggest that many fascinating questions remain to be answered about the relationship between the two texts. Moreover, both are readily available in inexpensive reading texts from the original publisher. Oxford has published the Vinaver edition of the Malory manuscript in a paperback version, which could be supplemented through class use of the three-volume version revised in 1971. The Caxton Malory is readily available through a Penguin edition (ed. Cowen), also inexpensively priced. This version could be supplemented with readings from both the Spisak-Matthews edition of the Caxton text and the Sommer version. Using all these works in conjunction could help to show upper-division and graduate students that the relationship of the Malory manuscript and the Caxton text illustrates some of the most interesting puzzles in medieval literature.

We sometimes forget that the study of sources, analogues, and competing versions of a tale tells us a great deal about essential literary ingredients: setting, characterization, plot, narrative flow, and, insofar as it is respectable to mention such, authorial intention. When we can deal with multiple versions of the "same work," we gain a great deal more insight into the creative process. Insofar as gifted precollege students and lower-division students are prepared to investigate some of the enigmas that develop from such comparisons, they too should be brought gradually into discussion of these issues. However, for upper-division and graduate students, a consideration of these central dilemmas in Malory scholarship is essential.

Teaching Tennyson: *Idylls of the King* as a Serial Poem

Linda K. Hughes

When we seek to recover a historical work for our students, we generally think of reconstructing the social and cultural context in which that work first appeared. Rarely do we also seek to reconstruct the publication or reading format of a work. Yet in the case of Alfred Tennyson's *Idylls of the King* (1859–85), publication format and cultural context were intertwined: the slow building up and issuance of the poem's idylls paralleled the expansion of the Victorian empire itself (Kiernan 138; Hughes and Lund, *Victorian*, ch. 4). If we acknowledge "Morte d'Arthur" (first published in 1842 and later adapted for "The Passing of Arthur") as the starting point of Tennyson's Arthuriad, the poem spanned four decades, during which concepts of national destiny and leadership were as central to Victorian culture as they were to Tennyson's poem.

Mark Girouard and Debra Mancoff give excellent accounts of the gothic and Arthurian revivals and their relation to political and cultural events in England (see also Knight). But even after teachers of Tennyson have assembled the relevant historical material in which the poem can be situated, they face an additional challenge: getting students to read and comprehend a long narrative poem. Ease with blank verse and self-consciously poetic language is hardly a birthright among students, and those who eagerly read Malory or modern Arthurian fiction may be baffled by elliptical or inverted syntax in the *Idylls*. Among students familiar with premodern poetic technique or style, a contrary difficulty can arise: students' impulse to seize symbolic patterns in "The Coming of Arthur" as a sort of key to the poem's mythology and then overread the poem. One solution to these pitfalls is to have students re-create the reading order of Victorian audiences who first received Tennyson's "serial poem" (Tillotson).

The *Idylls'* publication history suggests how much the material format of a work can help create that work's meaning (McGann 189), since the publication order of idylls differed from their order in the completed poem. Elsewhere I have examined in detail the relation among publication format, Victorian reception history, and Victorian culture (Hughes, "Tennyson's Urban Arthurians"). Here I want to focus instead on using the original publication format to enhance students' comprehension of the poem and the Arthurian revival in Victorian England.

I find it useful to begin the sequence on Tennyson with a handout that reproduces the encasing of Tennyson's "Morte d'Arthur" within

"The Epic," as in the original 1842 *Poems.* This starting point helps establish the relative newness of Arthurian legend as a subject for Victorian audiences, as reflected in Tennyson's reliance on a frame and the diffidence of Everard Hall, fictional author of the "Morte." As Walter Nash and others remark, "The Epic" embodies Tennyson's suggested framework for interpreting the "Morte": its references to "Geology and schism" prepare for the lines in the "Morte" on the old order changing and on Bedivere's trial of faith. But the poem also establishes Arthurian legend as an epic subject (line 28) and as an archaic one, a problem Tennyson himself feared might make his "Morte" inaccessible: "For nature brings not back the Mastodon, / Nor we those times; and why should any man / Remodel models?" (36–38).

Seventeen years passed before audiences could read more of the epic that the 1842 poem of the same name teasingly suggested was forthcoming. When Tennyson's 1859 *Idylls of the King* appeared, consisting of "Enid," "Vivien," "Elaine," and "Guinevere," Arthurian materials were still unfamiliar to much of the Victorian reading public (Tillotson 82–85), especially since the stature of Arthurian literature had declined in the seventeenth and eighteenth centuries (Merriman 49–80). Nor did Tennyson's volume enlarge that background. The first edition simply began without preamble, after a modest title page and table of contents, "The brave Geraint, a knight of Arthur's court. . . ." Given the absence of background, the naming of the four idylls after women, and the attention given to their love relationships with men, it is not surprising that Victorian audiences deemphasized mythic or historical themes and lauded these four poems as love stories about recognizable human beings—especially since Tennyson's characters struck reviewers as having a vitality missing from many of Tennyson's earlier works.

The *Athenaeum* immediately pronounced, in July 1859, that "inimitable as this [landscape] painting is, the human figures are still the chief attraction" and maintained that readers follow "the story of [the characters'] passions, their glorious errors, their sublime virtues" until readers enter into "active partnership" with them (74). Two months later the *Eclectic Review* praised Tennyson for abjuring "armorial curiosities with glass beads for eyes" and asserted that "the leading qualities of the poems, artistically, are—the clearness with which humanity is pictured, the reality of the glimpses into outward nature, and the exquisite music of language and rhythm . . ." (288–89).

Students who begin Tennyson's work by reading these four idylls, rather than "The Coming of Arthur" at the head of the completed Arthuriad, are generally more interested and engaged in Tennyson's work, less intimidated by it. The 1859 idylls can stimulate discussion of depictions of love, romance, sexuality, and gender in the Victorian era and our own. And since students must first have comprehended and mastered the poem's contents before they can adequately discuss ideological concerns, this reading format can promote students' involvement in the poetry. The emphasis of these idylls on character and story retains the students' interest and helps them get their bearings before they move on to more demanding readings. In one course I required students to write journal entries after each reading assignment but before class discussion had taken place. After reading the 1859 *Idylls*, most students focused on characterization and the theme of love; many agreed that, in one student's words, "The best part of this book so far is the way Tennyson opens characters up to the reader." (Tennyson's careful attention to the inward lives of female characters was especially striking to the students after they had just read Malory; the contrast in medieval and Victorian texts can also prompt discussion about conceptions of character and consciousness in different historical eras.)

Students' receptivity to Tennyson's characters, as well as Victorian response to the 1859 installment, differs from many twentieth-century assessments based on reading the completed poem in the order assigned by Tennyson. In 1980, Robert B. Martin commented:

> [T]he careful structural unity [Tennyson] imposed upon the poem may be valid on the allegorical level so long as it remains theoretical, but it is hardly to be substantiated by the experience of reading the poem. . . . Too often the allegorical values of the poem remain unexceptionable theories that are unsupported by adequate intensity in the characters and events meant to embody them.   (495)

Students—or critics—who begin with "The Coming of Arthur" could easily reach the same conclusion because of this idyll's overt introduction of the "sense versus soul" theme in the unblemished Arthur's need to be joined with the beautiful flesh of Guinevere if he is to "work my work."

Instructors can point out that the divergent interpretations of Victorian and late-twentieth-century critics are linked to publication format and raise the issue of how reading creates as well as decodes meaning. In any case, asking classes to read the 1859 *Idylls* before going on to the ostensible beginning of the poem in completed versions can help students understand one reason why Tennyson's poem achieved such popularity in its own time. As successive installments of the *Idylls* came out, in 1869, 1871, 1872, and 1885, Victorian reviewers continued to perceive a vital humanity in the poem's characters even after they discerned an emphatic symbolic patterning in the work as well. In reviewing *The Holy Grail and Other Poems*, the 26 February 1870 *Chambers's Journal* noted the "new light . . . thrown [by the 1869 installment] upon the meaning of the story . . . the master-thought which inspired the noble allegory, and it is all the more welcome by reason of its not having been brought too obtrusively before the reader, but kept, as all allegorical signification should be kept, in due subordination to the literal and natural meaning" (138). As late as 1886 the *Edinburgh Review* asserted that in the *Idylls* Tennyson "teaches living lessons by the universality of the humanity he portrays" ("Modern Poetry" 488).

As I remind my students, Victorian readers interpreted the 1869 idylls ("The Coming of Arthur," "The Holy Grail," "Pelleas and Ettarre," "The Passing of Arthur") in the context of the 1859 idylls, rather than (like readers of the completed work) interpreting the 1859 narratives in the context of "The Coming [and Passing] of Arthur." Moreover, Victorian audiences had the opportunity to read, reread, and discuss the 1859 idylls for ten years before encountering a new layer of texts and symbolic patterning. Re-creating the reading order of Tennyson's contemporaries allows students to recover elements of literary history and also, I find, induces them to retain a sense of vitality and interest in their subsequent readings of idylls.

Since Victorian audiences had to pause a decade in between the first and second installments of the *Idylls*, instructors might also pause before going on to the 1869 idylls, using the interval to acquaint students with the course of the Arthurian revival in the 1860s. When the 1859 *Idylls* became popular—ten thousand copies sold in a few weeks (Martin 423)—contemporary Victorian periodicals devoted articles to Arthurian legend to provide missing background for readers (see also Staines, *Tennyson's Camelot* 65–67). Photocopies of actual articles can be distributed to classes. I recommend "La Mort d'Arthur" in the April 1860 *Dublin University Magazine*, "King Arthur and His Round Table" in the September 1860 *Blackwood's Edinburgh Magazine*, and Samuel Cheetham's "Arthurian Legends in Tennyson" in the 1868 *Contemporary Review*. All give full and often sound scholarly rehearsals of the Arthurian tradition, and it seems valuable to me to teach students that intelligent commentaries and thorough scholarship are not late-twentieth-century inventions. Yet these Victorian essays also quite naturally reflect specifically Victorian approaches to the tradition. The first, for example, compares Arthurian heroism to that exhibited during the Napoleonic wars (see Kiernan 133). Pausing between the 1859 and 1869 idylls also provides instructors with the opportunity to review or introduce the Grail legend (and its implications for nineteenth-century theology) before students continue their reading. This pause, finally, gives students time to refine and deepen their interpretations of extant reading.

When the students return to Tennyson's text, their reading schedule itself can help them master the symbolic discourse of the 1869 *Idylls*, an interpretive mode eagerly embraced by Victorian audiences and deliberately offered by Tennyson in the metaphysical themes of the 1869 poems. One of these themes, of course, is the cyclical nature of time; as Arthur says in the 1842 "Morte," "The old order changeth, yielding place to new" (line 240). The *Idylls*, moreover, are structured so that a single episode or passage can echo the past or foreshadow the future while also continuing the narrative, hence suggesting that linear and cyclical time frames coexist and overlap.

The publication of idylls out of the chronological order assumed by the finished *Idylls* reinforced this theme for Tennyson's readers: each installment of the poem inaugurated new cycles of reading and of the realm, since each installment moved from the realm's early to its last days. The 1842 "Morte" began with the end of Arthur. The 1859 idylls reverted to the realm's beginning ("Enid") and halted just before its end ("Guinevere"). The 1869 installment narrated Arthur's "Coming" even before the travails of Geraint and Enid and led to "The Passing of Arthur" (a readaptation—or recycling—of the 1842 "Morte d'Arthur"). The 1872 installment juxtaposed the realm's first jousts ("Gareth and Lynette") with the final ("The Last Tournament," itself first published in the December 1871 *Contemporary Review* before being grouped with "Gareth" in the 1872 volume so that, characteristically, the end preceded the beginning and the beginning adumbrated the end).

As the 22 December 1869 *Guardian* remarked in its review of *The Holy Grail and Other Poems*, "The earliest written of the Arthurian Idylls . . . becomes, in its altered form, the last of the 'Idylls of the King.' . . . our old favourite, which was once the 'Death,' . . . is now the 'Passing,' of Arthur." The 26 October 1872 *Spectator* could interpret Gareth's adventures in the newly published "Gareth and Lynette" as a prefiguring of Arthur's career (1365) because Arthur's coming, reigning, and passing had already been told in previous idylls; and the 30 October 1872 *Guardian* remarked that "Gareth and Lynette" was "in one sense the last idyll, in another sense the second of the series" (1369; Hughes and Lund, "Studying" 243). Just as the publication sequence of the *Idylls* encouraged Victorian perception of the theme of cyclical time, so a reading format modeled on Victorian reception can hasten students' comprehension of Tennyson's symbolic mode.

One student's journal entry, for example, easily connected Gareth's individual challenges to the cyclical element in "Gareth and Lynette":

"Gareth must go through the whole cycle [of battle with Morning-Star, Noon-Sun, and Evening-Star] to become victorious. This one-day cycle is but part of the overall cycle of the story. . . . Out of the old is born the new." Our last reading assignment is "Balin and Balan," the last-published of the idylls (appearing in the 1885 collection entitled *Tiresias and Other Poems*), though its place in the completed *Idylls* is in the middle of the poem. The response of another student to "Balin and Balan"—that it represents an intricate cross-section of themes in the entire *Idylls* (compare Hughes and Lund, "Studying" 235)—would be less likely from a student reading the poem straight through:

> I see this story as a summary of all the books. Most of the themes we have discussed in class are here.
>
> The Holy Grail is tainted. Here are these artifacts stored away in a weird castle by two somewhat unworthy men. Evil and good exist together incongruously. The realm died partly because of the Grail quest and Balan killed by the spear.
>
> Balin shows us the struggle endured by all the knights: how to overcome being just a man and living up to the vows. He fails in his struggle, just as the knights did. . . .
>
> The question of Lancelot and Guinevere as lovers hovers over the story. Are they—aren't they? . . . We see the foreshadowing of Elaine and her love coming between them. Lancelot loves the pure lily (Arthur and Elaine) while Guinevere craves the color (earthly passion).
>
> Balin and Balan are innocents that die. Balin is beset by demons, as is the kingdom, and these demons win. Balan is a little shadowy—reminds me of Arthur. Obviously Balan is good . . . and only kills Balin while upholding his vows.
>
> I see the glory of Camelot when Arthur easily defeats Balin and Balan and then never mentions it. . . . The two brothers kill each other wrongly as the knights in their brotherhood kill each other. So I think all the vows that Arthur adheres to are in the story. All are upheld—to disastrous ends.

Mastering symbolic patterns such as these enables students to understand and recover nineteenth-century symbolic modes that were so important to Victorian writers and audiences and serves as a preliminary step toward students' viewing the *Idylls* from distinctly twentieth-century perspectives. Again, reading *Idylls of the King* according to the publication order that highlighted cycles in the realm and the poem itself enhances such mastery. Moreover, reading the poem one installment at a time introduces successive layers of symbolic patterns instead of forcing students to try decoding several patterns all at once as they begin "The Coming of Arthur." In reading the 1859 idylls, students can focus on the literal story of the kingdom's beginning and end and the theme of love. The 1869 idylls can introduce students (as they did Victorian readers) to overtly metaphysical issues of faith and doubt, the ideal and the real, the grounds for knowing, and the cyclical nature of time, civilization, and experience. The 1872 installment can emphasize the theme of art and language, since "Gareth and Lynette" includes the lines on the city "built / To music, therefore never built at all, / And therefore built for ever" (lines 272–74). "Balin and Balan" can then serve to highlight psychological patterns in the poem, since Tennyson transformed the brothers into twins and treated them as doppelgänger. Ideally, after finishing the serial sequence, students would read the *Idylls* in chronological sequence as well, to expose them to the completed poem as it is known to twentieth-century audiences. Paper assignments or examinations can help ensure this second reading if, as in my own course, time constraints compel us to move on to new work after "Balin and Balan" and one period devoted to the *Idylls* as a whole.

Teaching the *Idylls* serially can work in a number of classrooms. In courses devoted to nineteenth-century literature (such as Victorian poetry, surveys of nineteenth-century British poetry, or nineteenth- and twentieth-century Arthurian literature), students can read one installment of the idylls, turn to other materials, then return to another installment. Indeed, installments could be spaced out during an entire semester, with the passage of time between the "Morte" and "Balin and Balan" suggesting by analogy the effect of passing time on Victorians' four-decades-long reception of Tennyson's Arthuriad. And for advanced students this teaching format can be linked to recent theoretical issues (reception theory, hermeneutics, and textual, gender, and cultural studies) or to intensified acquaintance with historical materials (Arthurian art, the impact of periodicals, the unfolding of Tennyson's reputation and influence, growing concern with imperialism and England's "destiny," the condition of women). No matter how we use this reading and teaching strategy, it can deepen students' awareness of major events in the Arthurian revival and—if my own students' experiences are representative—enhance as well their ability to approach, comprehend, and master Tennyson's poetic discourse in good time.

Teaching White, Stewart, and Berger

Harold J. Herman

How one teaches individual Arthurian works depends on one's overall approach to the course. For my upper-level undergraduate college course on the Arthurian legend, I selected ten works to show the development of the Arthurian tradition from Geoffrey of Monmouth's *Historia* to the present, partly by focusing on individual figures (including Arthur, Guinevere, Merlin, Gawain, Kay, and Tristan), noting differences in the character from work to work and attempting to explain the reason for the changes. This approach, consequently, influences how I teach the Arthurian works of T. H. White, Mary Stewart, and Thomas Berger.

Because Merlin appears in the works of these three writers, I direct my students to examine him as a prophet, a magician, and a human being—Merlin's three roles in the Arthurian legend. Students realize that writers usually stress one of these three roles; in tracing the evolution of Merlin's character, students become aware of a shift in emphasis from one role to another and then can delve into the reasons for the shift.

Before students examine the portrayal of Merlin by the three writers, it is essential to provide some background material. One may, of course, trace the history of Merlin up to White by examining his role especially in Geoffrey, Robert de Boron, and his continuators, Malory and Tennyson. At the least, students must be familiar with *Le Morte d'Arthur*, one of the primary sources of White, Stewart, and Berger. Because my students read Malory's work, I merely review his portrayal of Merlin as a prophet who foretells most of what happens in the work. I ask students to give examples of his prophecies. Of secondary importance are Merlin's magical and human qualities, which are often used to bring about the fulfillment of his prophecies. Students again provide examples, such as the magical transformation of Uther as Gorlois so that Arthur can be conceived that night, his power of hypnotism and invisibility to prevent Pellinore's killing Arthur, and so forth. Examples of his human qualities include placing Arthur in the hands of Ector to provide a safe childhood, acting as Arthur's military adviser to ensure victory over the rebellious kings, serving as Arthur's emissary to arrange the marriage of Arthur and Guinevere, obtaining the Round Table, and selecting some forty knights.

In analyzing Merlin in White's *Once and Future King,* students see that unlike Malory, who portrays Merlin primarily as a prophet, White downplays this role, principally by having Merlin live backward in time

his

and hence recall, however imperfectly, the past rather than tell the future. Moreover, Merlin makes only a few predictions to Arthur, which students can identify—for example, that Arthur will defeat the rebellious kings, that Guinevere will love Lancelot, and that Nimue will lock Merlin away for a few centuries. In the discussion, teachers might note that Merlin forgets to tell Arthur the identity of his mother in order to avert the incestuous relationship with Morgause.

White's Merlin is essentially a magician, specifically a befuddled wizard who is Arthur's tutor. Actually White's Merlin is a combination of two character types: the absentminded professor and the magician. At any rate, by portraying Merlin as Arthur's teacher, White has combined Merlin's roles as a magician and a human being, and because students can distinguish between Merlin's use of magical and nonmagical means of educating his pupil, they have no difficulty analyzing Merlin as a human being.

In discussing Merlin's magic, students should be aware of its two functions. One is humor—the walking mustard pot, dishes that wash themselves, and the "Castor and Pollux blow me to Bermuda" incident (86). White's Disneyesque humor is so prevalent that the original edition of *The Sword in the Stone* can be regarded as a fantasy for juveniles. But some of Merlin's magic, specifically his transformations of Arthur, serve not as humor but as serious lessons in Arthur's education. Because Arthur is the future king, Merlin exposes him to various forms of government—a good topic for classroom discussion. Mr. Pike, swimming in the moat, represents a tyrannical monarch; the hawks, a Spartan military society; the ants, fascism of Nazi Germany or communism; and the wild geese, an ideal form of government. Though some critics, like Maureen Fries ("White" 626), believe that White is advocating that the best rule is the freest, students should also examine the animals, especially the ants, the geese, and the badger, for White's views on Might (war). They can also discuss the effect of Merlin's teaching on the Wart. For example, early in the work Arthur is described by White as a born follower and a hero worshiper; accordingly, Arthur wants to be a knight and fight. In spite of his early magical transformations, to a fish, a bird, and so on, he has not changed, for he is jubilant about winning his first battle, which he describes as " a good battle . . . . a jolly battle, and I won it myself and it was fun" (227). Indeed, it is not until Merlin, as a human teacher, points out that seven hundred kerns were killed that Arthur begins to think for himself; realizing that Might is not Right, he becomes an idealistic leader by instituting the chivalric order of knights of the Round Table as a means of channeling Might. When that plan fails and his knights start to battle each other, in what White calls

Games-Mania, and to revert to family feuds, Arthur subdues Might on behalf of God; when the Grail is achieved, he then tries to suppress Might by establishing common law. At this point, the teacher can discuss White's philosophy of war.

Why White changed Malory's portrayal of Merlin as a prophet to that of a magician who serves as Arthur's tutor is related to each writer's view of tragedy, an important aspect of the Arthuriad. Malory's work is Sophoclean tragedy; White's is Aeschylean (Warner, *White* 129–30; prologue to *Book of Merlyn* xi). Students are often familiar with Sophocles's Oedipus, who is fated to kill his father, marry his mother, and have children by her. Because most of the events in Malory are prophesied by Merlin, one can interpret the theme that fate, rather than free will, determines human destiny. White's work is like Aeschylus's *Oresteia*, for the house of Pendragon is cursed like the house of Atreus. Uther begets Arthur upon the wife of Gorlois, who is killed by Uther's army, an act to be avenged by the Duke of Cornwall's daughters, especially Morgause, whose incestuous relations with Arthur produces Mordred, who destroys his father and the Round Table. And like Aeschylus, White establishes common law to replace tribal justice, which demands that a murdered man's next of kin avenge his death. In White's work, of course, the common-law solution fails and tribal justice (the Orkney feud) prevails again. But fate must be replaced by free will if Arthur (and humankind) is to learn that Might is not Right and that he can try to overcome brute force. For this reason, White changed Malory's portrayal of Merlin as a prophet.

Rather than rely on fate, White provides psychological motivations for the actions of his characters. Here students should examine, for example, the disastrous effect of Morgause on her children. Gawain, as head of the Orkney clan after Lot's death, cannot escape his mother's lessons on the supremacy of the clan. Agravain bears the scars of an Oedipus complex, while Mordred, a product of incest, is warped physically and mentally. The Arthur-Guinevere-Lancelot triangle is another psychological study. Lancelot must sadistically hurt Guinevere before he loves her, and his becoming the greatest knight in the world can be viewed as compensation for his ugliness, which can also partially account for his concern for God. He needs proof, by way of a miracle, that God, who made him ugly, truly loves him. These and other examples of White's motivation should be discussed, for White regarded it as his major contribution to Malory.

Mary Stewart, in her Merlin trilogy, presents a more realistic portrayal of Merlin in fifth-century Britain. Consequently, unlike White, Stewart does not focus on Merlin as a magician. The only magic in *The Crystal Cave* is Merlin's ability to make fire, which he also demonstrates several times in *The Hollow Hills*, especially when he enflames Macsen's sword, though he also magically creates a vision of the chapel altar for the dying priest. Like the prophet of Malory's works, Stewart's Merlin is gifted with sight. Students should consider the nature of these visions, noting that many are of present rather than past or future events and that many are limited (for instance, in *The Crystal Cave* they are primarily of births, deaths, and political outcomes); the source of his sight (immediately from his mother but ultimately from the god); his inability to control the visions, which are triggered by light (though in the later two novels he has some control to see present happenings); and the importance of his virginity (the traditional state of those who have been undone by a woman; note that chastity does not apply to his mother or his beloved in *The Last Enchantment*). An interesting question is which of the religions (Christianity, druidism, Mithras, among others) are most closely associated with his gift, and why.

Stewart's Merlin, though possessing the gift of sight, is essentially a human being; how Stewart creates this complex character is a good topic of discussion, especially if students are knowledgeable about her sources. One way is Stewart's rationalization of supernatural elements in earlier works about Merlin. Unlike Geoffrey's Merlin, who is the son of the devil, Stewart's is the offspring of Niniane and Ambrosius. She also expands Merlin's engineering skills in Geoffrey to account for the self-destructing walls of Vortigern's tower. In Malory, Igerne is duped into bedding Uther because of Merlin's transformation of the king as Gorlois, but in Stewart, there is no magic, only disguise. And unlike Malory's Merlin, who can disappear and reappear, often covering great distances in a matter of seconds, Stewart's Merlin, in various disguises, travels from place to place like any other man. Second, though possessing the gift of sight, Merlin has limited powers. Whereas Malory's Merlin is constantly uttering prophecies, his counterpart in Stewart sees mostly present rather than future events, and there are long periods of time when he has no power but must rely on his own human intelligence. Most important, however, is Stewart's portrayal of Merlin as a human being with human feelings: he gets hungry, cold, seasick, even wounded; he yearns for a father; he is sexually attracted to Keri and Nimue. Incidentally, to humanize Merlin, Stewart altered her sources, and because many of the changes involve her female characters, students can study her treatment of women as strong, ambitious characters (Herman).

Like White, Berger, in *Arthur Rex*, satirizes and pokes fun at the traditional Arthurian legend without belittling its heroic, chivalric idealism (Taylor and Brewer 300). When students examine the various roles of Merlin in this work, they should also note Berger's penchant for the ridiculous and his fondness for irony, especially in the initial scenes with Merlin. For example, Merlin, in the form of a raven, transforms Uther's two knights into frogs and their horses into hounds; he then returns them and himself to their natural forms—a harmless joke, he explains. Learning of Uther's summons, he vanishes and, in a second, materializes at the side of the lovesick Uther, who is transformed into Gorlois and whisked to Tintagel and Igerne. But there really is no need for Merlin's arts, for the wife of Gorlois, a sodomite, is ready and willing to be ravished by Uther.

There are other humorous instances of Merlin's magic, but when Arthur pulls the sword from the stone, Merlin's magic is subordinated to his human role as adviser to the young king. Earlier Merlin berated Uther's conception of monarchy by pointing out that what distinguishes a king from other men is "neither sword nor virile member" but rather a moral superiority. The youthful Arthur is morally superior but to the degree of being pompous. However, with occasional magic and an abundance of sage advice, Merlin aids Arthur to temper his youthful zeal, to exercise prudently his kingly power, to be righteous without being sanctimonious.

Continuing with the analysis of Merlin as a human being, students should note that when the Lady of the Lake (Malory's Nimue) comes to court, Merlin is exposed as a mere mortal. He is the son, not of the devil, but of a mendicant friar and a milkmaid; his magic is debunked as hypnotic spells and sleights of hand; and his inventions of the camera, telephone, and phonograph are dismissed by the Lady of the Lake, who is interested only in the mythic, as childish sports with nature. "But art thou," she asks Merlin, "capable of transforming Envy, Vanity, and Spite into the virtues of Self-Respect, Generosity, and Patience?" (107). Rather than deprecate him, Berger reveals that Nimue does not despise Merlin, for, as she says, he has aided Arthur in his gallant experiment to make noble what has always been mean. In the end, realizing his time has come to leave Arthur, Merlin is content to be locked away in his underground laboratory. In the irony that characterizes human affairs, Berger notes, it is Merlin who is the realist and Arthur who is to become legendary. In such a way, Berger's treatment of Merlin reflects the author's major concerns throughout the novel.

Though I have concentrated on the character of Merlin in the Arthurian works of these three writers, the same approach can be used for other Arthurian figures, especially Gawain, because of Berger's innovative treatment of him, and Mordred, because of Stewart's sympathetic portrayal of him in *The Wicked Day*.

TEACHING STUDENTS AT VARIOUS LEVELS

Teaching Arthur at a Summer Institute for Secondary School Teachers

Ruth E. Hamilton

Although various remedies for the current state of education have been offered by the several commissions that have been studying the matter, two prescriptions have consistently emerged from their reports. To produce significant improvement in the field, secondary school teachers in particular must be better educated in the subjects they teach, rather than in the methods by which to teach them. Furthermore, secondary and postsecondary institutions must begin to work together to formulate coherent philosophies, goals, and policies of education. Several years ago, the Illinois Humanities Council came to the same conclusions and initiated a program of summer institutes for secondary school teachers. The goals of the institutes, as the program guidelines state, include fostering ongoing relationships among colleges, universities, and high schools as well as providing "teachers an opportunity to work with scholars in an examination of important humanistic themes and texts that will engage them in an exploration of the nature, purpose, and value of education in the liberal arts."

During the summer of 1985, I taught a summer institute for secondary school teachers on the Arthurian legend. Sponsored by the Illinois

Humanities Council, the institute consisted of three parts. During the first, fifteen teacher-participants read those Arthurian works that would be the focus of class discussion: *Morte d'Arthur*, *Sir Gawain and the Green Knight*, Tennyson's *Idylls of the King*, Twain's *Connecticut Yankee in King Arthur's Court*, and T. H. White's *Once and Future King*. The four-week on-site seminar, which took place at Northern Illinois University, was the second part of the institute. Continuing education, in the form of interactive classroom visits, research activities, and conferences, formed the third segment. This institute demonstrates how Arthurian literature is useful for a wide variety of pedagogical purposes.

For many reasons Arthurian literature is uniquely appropriate as the topic for an institute devoted to secondary school teachers (and, indirectly, to their students). Various works about Arthur are part of standard high school curricula. Textbooks for surveys of British literature feature excerpts from *Sir Gawain and the Green Knight*, Malory, and Tennyson, while *A Connecticut Yankee* is frequently read in American literature courses. Arthurian material is used in secondary schools not only because it is there but because it fulfills a variety of pedagogical needs. Since it is one of the most enduring and vital legends of Western civilization, teachers can use it to address issues at the very core of humanity: problems of love, loyalty, and duty, questions about war, idealism, and codes of morality.

Yet the legend's value for secondary school teachers goes beyond these basic issues, as I discovered that summer. The Arthurian legend can be used to teach ambiguities to adolescents, who tend to think that everything is wrong or right, black or white. Teenagers trying to form a code of behavior for themselves see others struggling with the same problem. The legend also shows the problem of divided loyalties, a relevant subject to children of divorced parents. And it helps those who think they are immortal begin to contemplate their own mortality.

Another important lesson that Arthurian literature can teach is the interaction between high and low culture. Today's students are likely to encounter the legend first in popular culture, such as the movies *Excalibur* and *Monty Python and the Holy Grail* or novels like those of Mary Stewart. They may even originally experience the stories secondhand, through *Star Wars* or *Dungeons and Dragons*. Once they trace the development of their own interest, students can be encouraged to track the progress of Arthurian literature along both high and low culture lines, by looking at different works as manifestations of particular audiences.

Similarly, because the legend invites discussion at a number of levels, from simple appreciation to complex criticism, it is an appropriate subject for those beginning to enter the world of research, including secondary school teachers. Arthur is a delightful subject for their initiation into scholarship and for their continued research. During the four-week institute, we used Malory for an introduction to research methods and bibliography. As they answer questions about Malory's identity, the Caxton edition, and the Winchester manuscript, teachers become familiar with standard editions, bibliographies, biographical studies, and other research tools.

After this beginning, class discussions introduce major critical questions as well as issues concerning the texts, like the debate over the merit of Caxton's *Morte* versus Malory's *Works*. Through leading questions and by example, the teachers learn to read more carefully and critically. They come to understand the intricacies of each work and ways to teach their students to see them also. Malory sparks debates about violence and about the nature of tragedy. Aided by a historian's guest presentation on feudalism and chivalry, we define courtly love and courtesy with *Sir Gawain*. *The Once and Future King* serves as a springboard for talk about the nature of education and the efficacy of particular teaching methods, especially the "learning by doing" method favored by Merlin and many educators today. The various incarnations of Arthur on film, like *Excalibur*, *Camelot*, and *Monty Python and the Holy Grail*, raise important issues also. As we examine the differences between the literary and the film versions, we focus on the characteristics of each genre; differences between individual movies demonstrate both the history and categories of film. Most important of all, throughout the course teachers explore the changing definition of heroism, shifts in attitudes toward the legend, and varying uses made of it, as well as reasons for Arthur's perennial appeal.

Once they have been introduced to research methods and critical and pedagogical issues, teachers can immerse themselves in primary and secondary material on a single topic. The roles of women in the Middle Ages, Merlin, the origin and development of the character of Galahad, and contemporary visions of Arthur all are fruitful subjects. Creative writers can be encouraged to add to the Arthurian legend, as one of my students did. She wrote a play based on "The Marriage of Sir Gawain and Dame Ragnell," complete with medieval-sounding music, which she planned to have her students produce, as a means of exposing them to several different forms of medieval culture. In addition to traditional research topics, teachers can work on projects aimed specifically at their students. Slide shows are both effective and popular. For example, images of Arthur from different centuries and periods can form the basis of a discussion of changes in illustration over the centuries and from country to country. Slides of sites in Britain can place Arthur in historical and geographical context. Or a slide show can demonstrate the influence of Arthur in contemporary culture. Alternatively, to motivate their students to read further on the subject (and give themselves an excuse for doing the same), teachers can prepare annotated bibliographies of selected Arthurian works.

Once they return to the classroom, teachers apply their enthusiasm about Arthurian literature and their confidence in their knowledge of it in various ways. Some include new works in their syllabi, after petitioning their departments to allow more time for Arthur in the curricula. Others devise new projects, integrating material they learned into other areas of the curriculum. Using as a model incidents in White's book, for example, a teacher can ask the class to write an essay from the perspective of a human transformed into an animal. Another might require the class to write a medieval romance, having made certain that students were well acquainted with the conventions of the genre.

As mentioned previously, Arthur can serve as continuing education for teachers. Our shared interest gives me access to other teachers' classrooms, where we can resume earlier discussions—by comparing applications of material introduced in the institute, for example—and where I can introduce prospective students to medieval studies at the university level. Furthermore, their research on Arthur makes it possible for them to offer seminars to other secondary school teachers, thus disseminating the effects of the institute beyond the original participants.

Teachers can form networks for exchanging ideas, advice, techniques, and research. They may even be inspired to use university libraries for ongoing research, join professional organizations, and deliver papers at conferences, as some of my students did.

Through institutes like mine, secondary school teachers and students become aware that both they and the works they study are part of a much larger world. The world of Arthur opens doors to the world of academe and the world of the humanities.

Lignum Vitae in the Two-Year College

Mary L. Beaudry

In a twentieth-century retelling of the Arthurian legend, *The Once and Future King*, by T. H. White, Arthur prepares to be a squire while his nobly born foster brother Kay trains to be a knight. Mindful of Arthur's destiny, Merlyn waves his staff of lignum vitae over the boy and begins to educate him for life (White 41). By providing educational experiences that delight as well as instruct his student, Merlyn transforms Arthur's naive fascination with winning and losing into leadership qualities rooted in the enduring values of Western culture. Like Merlyn, teachers of literature in a two-year college can transform the attitudes of their students in much the same way.

Two-year-college students perceive the classical tradition as belonging to a more elite group. Many take general education courses only as required and regard their literary heritage with indifference. They wonder, What does all this have to do with me? Even though many feel that their choice of career goals, their economic status, or their past level of academic performance has left them culturally disinherited, they actually hope that the classical tradition does have something to do with them (O'Connell 71). Teaching the Arthurian tradition is an excellent way to encourage these students to claim this heritage for themselves.

Enabling students to perceive the tradition as accessible and relevant to twentieth-century living is a major goal. Although conventional educational principles have maintained that learning takes place deductively, behavioral studies indicate that supplementing theory with practical experience is the ideal approach to learning (Lindgren 229–31). By transferring theoretical knowledge learned from the tradition and applying it to the world of their experience, students can test generalizations against real-world situations.

Since current references to the Arthurian legend are plentiful, inviting students to collect current examples is a good way to elicit student ownership. Common sources include political cartoons, comics, newspaper and magazine articles, films, popular music, and advertising. For students who are unfamiliar with the legend, a written synopsis with a list of characters and terms is helpful to get them started. Group interest increases when discoveries are discussed in class. Some recent finds have included a parking lot layout company using an equestrian knight, Sir Lines A Lot, for its logo; a cartoon depicting an arm brandishing Excalibur caught on the end of a fishing line; an editorial characterizing a mayor's idealistic leadership style as the Sir Galahad approach; and the University of Notre Dame's letterhead showing "Dulac" as the cable address. Students learn that understanding the tradition improves their understanding of the world.

Two-year institutions offer literature and other required liberal arts courses to provide a background of cultural awareness for students whose attention is focused on career preparation. Wherever the Arthurian tradition is included in the curriculum, students can be exposed to a broad cultural perspective while they pursue specific program objectives. Since two-year-college curriculum constraints discourage offering complete courses on the tradition, incorporating an Arthurian unit into the framework of existing general education courses is a practical approach. To plan the unit, instructors need to develop compatible course and unit objectives. Although there are certain pedagogical limitations with this method, they are balanced by the cultural benefits to the student. Many general education courses have broad objectives, such as developing oral and written communication skills, that are compatible with a unit on the tradition. Specifically Arthurian objectives include the following: recognizing and understanding common references to the legend, comprehending and analyzing recent retellings of the legend in comparison with earlier works, identifying the themes and values of the tradition and assessing their impact on twentieth-century life, articulating ways in which the tradition survives in new forms, and presenting orally a written critique, report, or summary related to a contemporary rendition of the legend. Since the tradition survives in so many forms, it is a suitable cultural introduction for two-year-college students—a group noted for its variable levels of academic preparation and ability.

For a successful experience with the tradition, underprepared literature students require a review of (or perhaps an introduction to) basic literary terms, the concept of multilevel meaning, and elementary principles of rhetoric and philology. A class period or two (supported by appropriate study sheets) spent reviewing these ideas and offering clear examples gives students the confidence to work with college-level subject matter. A foundation in these areas provides students with the tools they need to appreciate the tradition. Because students enjoy the challenge of applying their newly acquired knowledge to this respected area of literature, the classroom discussion is more consistently mature.

A unit on the Arthurian tradition can be included in standard courses on drama appreciation, British literature, American literature, and children's literature. For example, in a drama appreciation course a unit—using the script of the Broadway play *Camelot*—can be accomplished in as little as three weeks. By providing a brief synopsis of the play's Arthurian source (White's book), the instructor can help students read for various roles with a deeper understanding of the story. Within the context of this course, activities may include student oral readings of the script (supplemented by recorded songs) and outside assignments to write reviews of selected plays and films treating the Arthurian tradition. Viewing the film *Camelot*, with students required to write reports commenting on direction, casting, acting, costume design, settings, and the like, works well as a culminating activity.

A one-semester survey of British literature offers an excellent format for demonstrating the recurring theme of the Matter of Britain from early times up to the present. Including several different Arthurian works—such as *Sir Gawain and the Green Knight*, some version of the legend based on Malory, Tennyson's *Idylls of the King*, "Lady of Shalott," or other selections—enables students to observe changes in the tradition. *The Once and Future King* is an excellent choice for this level.

A taste of the Arthurian tradition—using, for example, Disney's video or book adaptation of *The Sword in the Stone* or Blanche Winder's *Stories of King Arthur* or some comparable retelling—can be included in a course in children's literature. Students of American literature can be exposed to the tradition if the "Vision of Sir Launfal," Twain's *Connecticut Yankee in King Arthur's Court*, the Mary Stewart books, Catherine Christian's *Pendragon*, Marion Zimmer Bradley's *Mists of Avalon*, and John Steinbeck's *Acts of King Arthur and His Noble Knights* are included as suggested readings. Such choices help students to understand the tradition's influence on American writers.

Although it may not be feasible for students to select the principal work to be studied in a course, they—like other adult students—generally are eager to participate in the selection process. They can be involved, for example, in choosing reading or viewing assignments for individual reports. An excellent resource is a list of various films, books, and other materials that notes their appeal, period, level of difficulty, length, and genre, for students to use in selecting assignments. Audiovisual resources enrich the experience of the tradition and offer varied approaches for a group with differing levels of ability. Students are more likely to enjoy working closely with a piece they have selected for themselves. If they have clear directions and challenging assignments on different levels, the likelihood that students will experience success increases. With these students, affirming individual strengths is far more effective than critically observing their weaknesses.

Whatever courses are used to showcase the tradition, an important aspect of unit preparation is the presentation of background material. Some useful references for a beginning teacher include *The Reader's Companion to World Literature*, Albert C. Baugh's *Literary History of England*, and *The Oxford Companion to English Literature*, and more recent pieces on the subject, such as *Was This Camelot?* by Leslie Alcock; *The Search for King Arthur*, by C. Hibbert and the editors of *Horizon* magazine; *The Quest for Arthur's Britain*, by Geoffrey Ashe; *The Arthurian Legends*, by Richard Barber; and *The Arthurian Encyclopedia*, edited by Norris J. Lacy et al. Background material skillfully presented anticipates the question, What's so great about the tradition? Involving students in the processes of presentation and discovery helps the class and the instructor to feel shared ownership and responsibility for the preservation of the heritage.

When students recognize that the legend is alive and talked about frequently today, they are motivated to learn about it. Students are usually curious about the historicity of the legend, associations with landmarks such as Stonehenge, recent archaeological findings, the reasons for emphasis on the Malory version, the French connection, the addition of Lancelot, the oral tradition, and the feudal system. The challenge for the instructor is to present this material in detail and substance sufficient to capture the interest of the students. Straightforward lists of terms, names, and locations are helpful to those students who lack the time or resources to compile them. Students appreciate an opportunity to discuss the material they understand and to ask questions about what they do not understand.

Helping these students to grasp the importance of the tradition is better than trying to cover too much. One of the most significant outcomes of teaching the Arthurian tradition to two-year-college students is to dispel the notion that classical literature in general and that the Arthurian tradition in particular is elitist and obscure. For the instructor, the most important aspect of planning a successful Arthurian unit is to match the principal work or parts of works to be discussed in class with course demands and student interest and ability. These students balk at obscure texts and archaic language; they are interested in easily accessible material. With simpler texts, these students can more readily accept the challenge of discovering meaning for themselves. By whetting their appetites for Arthurian material and by equipping these students to explore the literature further, instructors encourage long-term involvement with the tradition.

Often ambivalent about higher education and motivated by nonacademic factors, the two-year-college student needs to see in the instructor a demonstrated commitment to the Arthurian tradition. Students look for ways the tradition has influenced people and events; they like to hear personal anecdotes and to learn about related projects and events. Some two-year-college students, skeptical about the value of cultural studies in general, are not easily persuaded by words. They can best be convinced by an instructor who delights in mastery of the subject matter and wants more than anything else to pass it on. As Helen Vendler stated in her Presidential Address to the MLA in 1980, "We owe it to ourselves to show our students, when they first meet us, what we are; we owe their dormant appetites, thwarted for so long in their previous schooling, that deep sustenance that will make them realize that they too, having been taught, love what we love" (350).

The teacher of the Arthurian tradition, like Merlyn with his staff of lignum vitae, can transform the attitudes of today's two-year-college students from a naive fascination with career preparation to an appreciation of culture and a deeper understanding of the meaning of their lives. These students are capable of becoming more than mere employees; like the boy who expected to be a squire but who instead became king of all England, they can become fully human, able to speak and think as civilized beings with the potential to influence the future.

Arthur the Great Equalizer: Teaching a Course for Graduate and Undergraduate Students

Sally K. Slocum

The Seminar in Arthurian Legend for graduate and undergraduate students offered by the English department at my university attracts majors, nonmajors, and sometimes students not regularly enrolled. Since most of our students commute, I am accustomed to a heterogeneous group. Often the class includes students from every rank, some with scant knowledge of meter or the Middle Ages (beyond notions planted by the movies) or of such topics as the alliterative revival. These students sit alongside English majors and graduate students, who may have already studied, say, Chaucer. What equalizes such a class is the Arthurian legend itself, since few people are familiar with the whole scope of the legend. Most are acquainted with some vaguely universal idea of King Arthur and the Round Table, perhaps based on *Camelot*, modern novels, or childhood memories of Merlin the wizard.

My goals for the class, which probably differ from the original goals of individual class members themselves, are simple: I want every student to gain a knowledge of the evolution of the Arthurian legend, to recognize the great achievement of Malory's compilation of the bulk of the developed legend, and to study in detail some particular aspect of the Arthurian world. Mine is not a course specifically in literature, history, genre, or myth, but it embraces these elements and more.

The course is generally divided into two parts: part 1 relies heavily on student reports about the beginnings and expansion of the legend. Part 2 focuses on Malory's *Works* and some other literary contributions, sometimes according to class interest or request.

Since the class is limited to fifteen students, there is time for extensive student participation. During the first class meeting, I circulate a syllabus—really a list of meeting dates accompanied by a chronological list of early Arthurian materials—and require each student to select and sign up for one entry to report on to the class. Because none of the students are knowledgeable about any of the topics (Gildas, Bede, and Nennius are the first subject, Wace is somewhere near the middle, and the Prose *Merlin* near the end), nobody has an advantage. Almost always the last student to get the list is left to make the first report. I comfort that person with the fact that it is a relatively easy report to prepare because there isn't much in the primary sources, and the necessary secondary material is on reserve. I duplicate the assignment sheet to distribute at the next class meeting so that everyone will know who is reporting on what. From the beginning, I make it clear that all will benefit from sharing information, and I urge students to watch for sources another student might need.

The second class meeting is a library tour, with our subject librarian in charge. She assembles major reference works, bibliographies, and several essential books for students to handle, jot call numbers, and note titles, and they learn what kind of information is to be found where. (Books that I expect everyone will need are put on one- or three-day reserve.) After the half hour or so of a brief lecture and "hands on books," we are guided to the reference collection for more bibliographical work, to the "Arthurian shelves," and conclude at the card catalog (and now at the computer). Even if the class were composed totally of graduate students, I would not skip the library tour. Nobody knows enough about libraries; I always learn something. At parting, the librarian offers further help to anyone in need. Surprisingly, only a few seek her help during the term. This course does more to involve students in library research than any other course I teach.

The topics for student reports—about fifteen minutes in length—are based on the chronological development of the legend and follow the order of our text *The Romance of Arthur* (edited by Wilhelm and Gross), supplemented by *Arthur King of Britain* (edited by Brengle). All students are required to study the day's assignment in the text and the parallel material in *Development of the Arthurian Romance* (edited by R. S. Loomis), so that they are prepared for the student reports. There are normally two reports per class meeting, but we are flexible.

I usually confer informally with the students before the report is due, to be sure the relevant information will be included, to give tips, or occasionally to direct a student to a particular source or article. The reports should provide information on biography (if available), sources, the writer's probable purpose, new or different developments, characters, and the like, avoiding manuscript and other editorial problems. I maintain an informal, even casual, atmosphere to keep student nervousness at a minimum. Students are usually excited about their discoveries and are truly interested in the material. If something important is omitted, it is my task to supplement the report without making the reporter feel inadequate or embarrassed in any way. Otherwise, students with future reports to produce would be full of dread. Keeping the class at ease, even jocular, is essential because the reports are central. The reporters may remain seated, use the lectern or board, as they chose. Following the report, class discussion clarifies and focuses the subject at hand. Frequently, a previous reporter is asked for more detail or a review; often students can't wait to supply information. The student is required to submit only a brief outline of the oral report.

With the student reports as a backdrop, it is relatively easy for me to introduce other materials and ideas with lectures and commentary. Approaches to understanding the hero through Lord Raglan's *Hero* or Joseph Campbell's *Hero with a Thousand Faces*, for example, provide an ongoing consideration; Lucy Allen Paton's *Studies in the Fairy Mythology of Arthurian Romance* contributes to the discussions about the intriguing female figures and often leads to Robert Graves's *White Goddess* and Eric Neumann's *Great Mother*. Theories about the Holy Grail, the great popularity of King Arthur in France, the distinction between chronicle and romance, the identity of Merlin, and the bardic tradition fascinate students and lure them to the library for more detail. Courtly love gets continuing attention as it comes up in the literature and as the concept changes. I confess that fays and fairy love receive considerable attention in my course, but probably because they are important. Since there are so many interesting paths to follow, I also confess that I have never taught the same course twice, though the basic pattern is fairly consistent.

Once all the oral reports have been presented, the class meetings concentrate on other literature. Often we study *Sir Gawain and the Green Knight*, but sometimes read "Geraint Son of Erbin" from the *Mabinogion* and Chrétien de Troyes's *Erec and Enide*, or two other cognate stories. Then we turn to Malory, which we read as fast as we can, aiming for about fifty pages per class meeting. (I skip the *Book of Sir Tristram* except for "Lancelot and Elaine.") I order the Vinaver one-volume edition of Malory, but I don't care if students read a translation. Although few of the students are prepared for Malory's spelling, they get used to it quickly and are soon enchanted. Discussion of Malory is guided by class (or my) interest and reflects the emphases of the earlier reports. Students sometimes surprise me by identifying Malory's sources, questioning heroic morality, and making other astute observations. Their sympathies for characters and events are diverse; they are likely to argue about Lancelot's, Guinevere's, or Arthur's loyalty, guilt, or spirituality. Few much like Galahad, but most admire him.

From the beginning of the term, of course, students worry about the final, formal paper, and I prod them to decide on a topic as early as possible. Students have the freedom to research any topic they choose. Some, not many, stay with the topic of their earlier oral report. There are only two conditions: the paper must focus on an Arthurian topic, and they must share their research with others. Cooperation, not competition, is the key. Once again I circulate a sign-up sheet with specified dates for students to fill in with their topics; I distribute this list to the class to encourage them to share sources and information. It is not uncommon for a student to be impatient to deliver a "discovery" of an article to another who is researching the topic. Classes have always been enthusiastic about helping one another, even when two students are working on similar projects. Occasionally I discourage a topic (such as "The Source of the Holy Grail"), and I usually help students to limit a topic, hone a focus, or suggest an interesting area for an undecided student. Free to pursue any Arthurian topic, students have written about subjects such as medieval armor, Japanese Bushido and chivalry, the dwarf at court, Teutonic knights, Morgan le Fay (there is always a paper on fays) as well as more traditional studies of the Arthurian works of such writers as the Gawain poet, Tennyson, Malory, Spenser, T. H. White, John Steinbeck. The final papers are read in class, about two each class meeting, but the final, typed paper is due on the last meeting date, allowing students who draw an early reading date more time to complete the task.

Few can master Arthurian literature, and I do not pretend that I have, but I try to be generous with what I know and to ensure that all my students become familiar with important Arthurian reference works. At the end of the course, a common student reaction is, "Now I'm ready to take this course."

Malory and the Middle English Romance: A Graduate Course

George R. Keiser

While it has long been known that Malory drew on the *Alliterative Morte Arthure* and the *Stanzaic Morte Arthur* as sources, his relation to Continental romance has usually received far more critical attention than his indebtedness to the native tradition. Recently, however, a better understanding of the artistry of Middle English romances and an enhanced respect for them, along with substantial evidence that Malory knew many of these romances, have encouraged closer study of his relation to the English tradition. In *Malory's* Morte Darthur, Larry Benson demonstrated that the reliance on uncomplicated linear narrative, with only limited use of the interlace structure found in the French sources, and the compression of narrative attest that Malory was deeply influenced by English romance. Indeed, P. J. C. Field has argued forcefully that before writing his prose Arthuriad, Malory had experimented in verse romance.

This increased attention to the influence of the native tradition on Malory and my own long-standing interest in the Middle English romance made the decision to offer the seminar Malory and the Middle English Romance almost inevitable when an opportunity to do so came along. The decision was a good one, for reading Malory's *Morte* after looking at a wide range of Middle English verse romances—a very different experience from reading it after a series of mainly continental romances, as I do in an undergraduate Arthurian literature course—yielded as much satisfaction and profit as I had hoped. (The benefits included a subsequent master's report with a surprisingly fresh look at that familiar topic, the love of Lancelot and Guinevere, in the light of the treatment of love in Middle English verse romances.)

The 1986 reprinting of Donald B. Sands's *Middle English Verse Romances* and Benson's *King Arthur's Death* by the University of Exeter Press solves the problem of providing handy and inexpensive editions of an important body of Middle English romances. The one-volume *Malory: Works*, edited by Eugène Vinaver, is ideal for the course, as is Norman Davis's edition of *Sir Gawain and the Green Knight*. Using a modernization of *Sir Gawain*, though not a necessity, can lead to fruitful discussion of the style and diction of the original and of the difficulties facing a poet who attempts to modernize a work of such individuality. For students who have taken creative writing courses (not uncommon these days), the latter point may have particular interest and may, in any case, evoke thought about the challenges medieval English authors, including Malory, encountered when they made their translations and worked their transformations. The many admirable editions of individual romances issued in the past decade or so are too expensive for most student budgets, but consulting the library's copies for comparison with the texts prepared by Sands and Benson reveals some of the problems of editing the romances.

The origins, audience, and dissemination of the romances have been critical concerns at least since the publication of Albert C. Baugh's insightful exploratory studies. While internal evidence can be highly informative, it may, when used without recourse to external evidence, produce dubious interpretations, such as the facile and long-cherished view that the English romances were meant for a "bourgeois" audience. How well and how widely these works were known before Malory, as well as in his time, are questions of significance for the study of Malory's indebtedness to them, as my students soon recognized. In seeking answers to these questions, they found, after learning to read manuscript descriptions, that Gisela Guddat-Figge's *Catalogue of Manuscripts Containing Middle English Romances* and introductions to editions of the romances are prime sources of information concerning readership. From the dating, dialect, and provenance of the manuscripts, the students attempted tentative conclusions about the popularity and longevity of the individual romances, and from the codices they learned about the context in which they were read.

Invaluable for detailed study of these points are the splendid manuscript facsimiles now available. By looking at the *Facsimile of British Library MS. Harley 2253*, the students discovered that, like many of the earliest romances, *King Horn* was written and read in a trilingual (English, Latin, and Anglo-Norman) culture and that its original owners had a strong interest in a related genre, the saints' lives. An examination of the facsimile of Advocates' manuscript 19.2.1, the Auchinleck manuscript, National Library of Scotland, suggests that some readers of *Horn*'s ballad counterpart also enjoyed *Sir Orfeo* and *Floris and Blancheflour*, romances celebrating heroes of native stock (*Richard the Lion-hearted, Bevis of Hamton, Guy of Warwick*), Arthurian literature (*Of Arthoure and of Merlin, Sir Tristrem*), and, like the readers of the Harley 2253, saints' lives. In the facsimile of Lincoln Cathedral Library manuscript 91 (*The Thornton Manuscript*), they learned of one Robert Thornton, a member of the fifteenth-century English gentry who, like Malory, read an Arthurian tale of the Fair Unknown (*Sir Perceval of Galles*), was probably uneasy with the moral failings of Arthur's queen (*The Awntyrs of Arthure*), and knew the *Alliterative Morte Arthure*.

Aware of the manuscript evidence concerning the interests and tastes of readers of vernacular English romances, the students were better prepared to evaluate arguments about the form of the romance and the expectations of readers for works in the form. As a whole, my students favored a comprehensive view of the form, such as that in Dorothy Everett's seminal study, more than the idea of subcategories of romances (for instance, "hagiographical romances") or propositions that works traditionally classified as romances should be excluded. In addition, they were receptive to the variety of forms found in Malory's *Morte*. Finally, examining the romance miscellanies and witnessing the medieval fondness for making compilations provided an informed perspective for probing the vexed question of whether Malory's compilation is one book or eight.

In their presentations and discussions in the seminar and in their papers, knowledge of the English tradition primed the students for a fuller exploration of arguments about Malory's narrative technique. Study of the English writers' episode-by-episode structure and reliance on repetition, parallelism, and contrast for thematic and artistic purposes was helpful in appreciating Malory's narrative art in "The Book of Gareth" and, from a larger perspective, his design in using that book as a contrast to what follows it in his *Morte*. Moreover, familiarity with the characteristic optimism of the earlier romances and the endurance of that optimism, despite the prevalence of tragic themes in later romances, gave sharper focus to a study of Malory's reworking of the Old French *Queste* and *Mort Artu*, especially Malory's determination to set the world in order again after Arthur's death. Also, the respect and affection for the idiomatic style, especially the vigorous dialogue, that developed from their reading of other English romances, came to full flowering when we turned to Malory, whose prose the students delighted in reading aloud.

The facsimile editions of the Winchester manuscript (British Library Additional 59678) and of Caxton's print are useful for the study of Malory's early reception. Having these facsimiles at hand spurred interest in the evidence for Caxton's use of the Winchester manuscript and its potential relevance to the identity of Sir Thomas Malory. Further, the contrast between the two books gave force to the questions of how and why Caxton reshaped the text to make it more accessible, not only by revising Malory's style but also by devising a program of book and chapter divisions that allowed readers to locate specific matter more efficiently than the side glosses in the Winchester manuscript would.

As the increasing (and salutary) interest in studying literature in its historical context is taking hold and as insightful studies of late medieval English culture proliferate, an approach to Malory by way of his native tradition seems an especially accommodating one. Thus, when I offer the seminar again, I hope to make good use of new and important studies in history, such as those on chivalry by Maurice Keen and Nicholas Orme, and in literary history such as Susan Crane's *Insular Romance* and shorter works by Carol Meale and P. R. Coss. Finally, I shall give some attention to the work of other fifteenth-century authors who were attempting to satisfy a new taste for English prose romance and discovering how to adapt the conventions of the verse tradition to this new form, just as Malory was—perhaps, as Field argues, after some experience in writing verse romance.

SPECIFIC APPROACHES

Arthurian Archaeology

Paul E. Szarmach

No matter how text-bound or how "literary" a literature course in Arthuriana may be, it seems inevitable that at some point, generally early on, students ask about the historical accuracy or basis for the myths and legends incorporated in the romances and stories. How real is King Arthur?—a question lurking in the minds of majors and nonmajors alike—arises unexpectedly even in a survey of medieval literature in which Arthuriana is only a fraction of the syllabus. For most generalist teachers the question is a vexation because, while one can always offer a waffling response, there is still the anxiety that out on the library stacks is a mass of texts in history and archaeology that gives complicated answers, already read by the history majors in the group. For those who prefer not to tarry on the matter, David Whitehouse provides a crafty summary of history and archaeology, as does Janice Klein, who also offers eleven illustrations and a brief, useful bibliography. But the best teaching is always based on the knowledge of the primary research as adapted to a particular situation. There are, moreover, broader goals, beyond mere question and answer techniques, that some teachers, especially the card-carrying medievalists, might wish to achieve in presenting an archaeological perspective. These aims include an examination of the following major themes: the relation between "fact" and medieval fiction (or myth and legend), the idea of interdisciplinary study, the ambiguity of evidence in any field, and, finally, the influence that archaeology has had on postwar Arthurian fiction. These are the themes I insinuate, state, or begin to develop in the introductory week in my course on Arthurian myth through a consideration of archaeology and what it can tell us about the kernel facts of Arthurian story.

The content of this first week has varied, over the last decade and more, depending on external factors such as the length of the term and whether I am teaching a "writing emphasis" course and on such internal factors as whether my developing sense of Arthuriana has taken more seriously the "reception" of the medieval versions. Yet the foundation of this introduction has continuously been Leslie Alcock's *Arthur's Britain*. Alcock excavated Cadbury Castle (1966–70), which is sometimes considered the traditional site of Camelot. *Arthur's Britain*, however, is no mere technical report of a dig; rather, it is a broad-based study using every kind of literary evidence, including narrative history, poetry, and other written evidence, such as ecclesiastical records, laws, genealogies, and inscriptions, as well as the material evidence Alcock unearthed at Cadbury. With clarity and precision in setting out fact, inference, and wide interpretation, Alcock presents a full picture of Roman Britain and its plunge into the "Dark Ages." In short, it is a perfect example of a judicious interdisciplinary study that fills out the context for a course in literature. To supplement my own preparation I have at hand Alcock's *Was This Camelot?*, which is a more straightforward and focused account of the archaeological work. Subsequently, Alcock, in "Cadbury-Camelot," offers a fifteen-year perspective on the excavations, wherein he professes an agnostic position on the historicity of Arthur and considers various points, notably the large fortifications on the site, in the context of the advances in research.

During this week of introduction, the work in the classroom and for the student differs from my typical teaching style. Whereas my choice throughout the rest of the course is for discussion (preferred by my department) or modified lecture-discussion, I give slide lectures at the beginning based on materials I have acquired from study trips. Slides are available at various Arthurian sites, but one must be always looking for them, so to speak, and also writing a mental script as one travels, alert for the odd image that might be relevant in a presentation. Some postcards and some British and European publications are not under copyright, thus ready to be turned into slides either at a commercial shop or at the audiovisual facility on the home campus. Photographs from personal visits seem to have an immediacy for student audiences, even when the pilgrim is an amateurish and blurry photographer. Here the light touch can save all from the boredom of "what I did on my summer vacation"; one of my favorites is a slide from a photograph of cows, *cum* their leavings, grazing on Glastonbury tor. Under the present copyright laws it is difficult to turn illustrations and figures in books into slides; it is wise to write for permission in advance.

For those who are unable to work up their own audiovisual backgrounds, the University of Toronto Media Centre offers James P. Carley's twenty-two-minute color film *King Arthur: From Romance to Archaeology*. This still serviceable look at the context of the Arthurian world focuses on Cadbury-Camelot and Glastonbury. The most recent published rental price is $45 ($175 purchase). The Holiday Film Corporation (Whittier, CA 90608) has produced a slide-tape package called *The Story of King Arthur*. The forty color slides include scenes of Cornwall and Tintagel, as well as Cadbury-Camelot and Glastonbury. Special images are the Round Table at Winchester and Arthur's grave within Glastonbury Cathedral. One advances the slide on the tone; a selection from the slides, which might remove some of the more modern images, combined with one's own script or commentary, could produce a more "medieval" presentation.

Student assignments for the week of history-archaeology lectures can indeed vary. In some semesters I have assigned either Geoffrey of Monmouth, Wace, or Layamon to be read as a contrast to the archaeological presentations. Such an assignment can be effective, if there is a period or two available for a follow-up discussion. Good students will seek to engage texts and instructors, some because they want to test their ideas, others because they want to hear more from the teacher. In the last version of my course, which was a writing-emphasis version, in which a significant part of class time throughout the semester was to be devoted to instruction in writing, I decided, in the face of the curricular need, that less is more and thus dispensed with a reading assignment. A library reserve, including the Arthurian Chronicle works, the Alcock books, and Geoffrey Ashe's *Quest for Arthur's Britain* had to serve for those students who wanted more information.

What then can archaeology contribute to the ultimate questions about the Arthurian world? The rivalry, if not the tension, between written and material evidence looms large in the discussion. If Arthur was a major antagonist of the Saxons, then why does he not appear in the *Anglo-Saxon Chronicle?* Before too long students have to consider "higher criticism" of the written record, sorting out dynastic or propagandistic impulses in the anonymous writers. Yet cold, verifiable facts are fewer than a positivist would want. Archaeology is, after all, a discipline that destroys the evidence it seeks to interpret and, as Anglo-Saxonists know too well in the Sutton Hoo controversies, it can introduce new puzzles and questions among the old: where is Mount Badon, finally, and when did the battle occur? Slide images can become the focal point for these issues. The page from [Nennius's?] *Historia Brittonum* describing Arthur's twelve battles, with its blunders and hidden source, reminds us of the fragility of the written word; the aerial shot of Cadbury-Camelot makes Lerner and Loewe's castle seem like puffery; the implements of Romanized Britain suggest that Arthur looked more like Robert Taylor in *Quo Vadis?* than Robert Taylor in *Ivanhoe.*

Still, archaeology and its findings do not so much debunk the Arthurian world as set it in its historical context and, more important, provide a point of reference for Arthurian imagination. Chrétien's mythmaking powers seem beyond human scale in the light of the extant texts that preceded Chrétien and the reality that inspired those texts. The implications for the existence of an oral literature and an unrecorded tradition are immense. It is clear, furthermore, that archaeology is a point of departure for contemporary mythmakers who—like Mary Stewart in, say, *The Wicked Day*—adapt to a grounded universe without loss of imaginative power.

In North America it is difficult to keep up with Romano-British and early medieval archaeology. A firm like Oxbow Books (10 Saint Cross Road, Oxford OX1 3TU, England), which specializes in archaeology, can help the enthusiast, as will such better-known general booksellers as Heffers and Basil Blackwell. To be sure, the many technical reports and studies under way will serve as the basis for future developments, but the more generalist studies now in hand give ample witness, by offering contrastive evidence, to the creative power of the medieval imagination.

Using Nineteenth-Century Visual Arts in the Literature Classroom

Beverly Taylor

As Roger Sherman Loomis and Laura Hibbard Loomis demonstrated long ago, in *Arthurian Legends in Medieval Art*, Arthurian characters and episodes have, from the early Middle Ages, captured the visual as well as the literary imagination. Much as the early twelfth-century mosaic at Otranto, which depicts King Arthur riding a goat, may surprise viewers prepared by Hollywood notions of the mythic king, canvases and drawings from the nineteenth century may awaken students to the variety and complexity in Victorian reflowerings of Arthurian legend. Using limited class time to savor the sumptuous visual feast of the Pre-Raphaelites' brilliant colors or the stark black and white designs of Aubrey Beardsley might seem a luxury for the literature teacher already constrained to fit too much material into the semester. But beyond their intrinsic aesthetic rewards, the pictures serve several important pedagogical ends in the literature class.

Slides depicting scenes associated with their reading can take students from discussion of relationships between the canvases and the literary treatments to consideration of the continuing appeal of Arthurian legend. Visual representations help students isolate what nineteenth-century artists—poets and painters alike—found meaningful in traditional materials, for the intersection of literary and visual interests in the same events and characters points up themes, symbolic meanings, and psychological insights that Victorians discovered or invested in the legends. Besides revealing specifically Victorian concerns, the paintings and illustrations frequently emphasize the enduring qualities of the Arthurian story. The pictures also accentuate the variety of interpretations or applications that painters and poets can generate from a familiar story, attesting to the versatility of the legends.

In addition to demonstrating the topicality, universality, and variety in nineteenth-century reshapings of the traditional story, class discussion of the paintings and drawings yields a more fundamental benefit in the literature class. Most of the Victorian pictures of Arthurian scenes merit careful examination, for the artists—like many of their medieval counterparts—invested scenery, clothing, and gesture with symbolic, even iconographic, significance. Discussions of the thematic implications of the apple trees against which Dante Gabriel Rossetti's Lancelot and Guinevere are juxtaposed as they bid farewell at Arthur's tomb, or of the psychological insight afforded by the details of Isolde's boudoir as she dresses by a rumpled bed in William Morris's easel painting train students to pay close attention to pictorial detail. Having "read" paintings through particulars, students become more alert to writers' imagery, perhaps initially focusing on physical descriptions, but eventually responding to diction, symbols, and larger patterns.

Tennyson's 1832 and 1842 poems—"The Lady of Shalott," "Sir Galahad," and the "Morte d'Arthur"—as well as the enthusiasm for Malory they stimulated, inspired a host of Arthurian drawings and paintings, some prepared as book illustrations and others as oils and watercolors for independent display. The visual arts spurred in the late 1850s by the shared Arthurian interests of Rossetti, Morris, and their artist friends anticipated the continuing series of pictures suggested by Tennyson's *Idylls of the King* after 1859. While it may not be possible to determine how many Arthurian paintings and drawings were produced in the nineteenth century, Richard D. Altick has documented 140 oil paintings alone exhibited between 1860 and 1900; at least 20 derived from Malory and many more were based on Tennyson (345). Among these, the most readily available in book reproductions are those by painters associated with Pre-Raphaelitism—Rossetti, Morris, Edward Burne-Jones, Arthur Hughes. Other important resources include the engravings in Moxon's 1857 collection of Tennyson's poetry, Rossetti's watercolors and drawings produced in the late 1850s (around the time of the ill-fated decoration of the Oxford Union with Arthurian murals), Gustav Doré's 1868 engravings illustrating Tennyson's first four idylls, Julia Margaret Cameron's 1874–75 photographic illustrations of the *Idylls*, and Beardsley's designs for the 1893–94 edition of Caxton's Malory. (And if the course includes American works, Daniel Beard's illustrations of Mark Twain's *Connecticut Yankee in King Arthur's Court*—along with the British George du Maurier's parodic engravings of *A Legend of Camelot* for *Punch* in 1866—demonstrate the satiric capacity of Arthurian material.)

New classroom approaches to the literature arise when students compare treatments of subjects that Victorians painted frequently— the Lady of Shalott and Elaine, usually based on Tennyson, though sometimes derived from Malory's account of Elaine of Astolat; the disastrous loves of Tristran, Lancelot, and Merlin; the quest for the Holy Grail; and the death of Arthur. The related stories of Elaine and the Lady of Shalott offer the greatest single fund of pictures to stimulate reinterpretation of the poetry. (Altick has confirmed at least 35 representations of the Lady of Shalott produced before 1900.) In the Moxon edition of Tennyson's poetry, for example, two diverse illustrations of "The Lady of Shalott," by Rossetti and William Holman

Hunt, may expand student assessments of the poem. Whereas Hunt focuses on the moment when the Lady's web explodes, Rossetti concentrates on her arrival at Camelot. Hunt's artist figure, though entangled by the web of her weaving, is dynamic; Rossetti's damsel poses a tranquil opposition to the hubbub shown behind her. Moreover, contrasts between Hunt's original engraving and his famous oil painting, finished several decades later, differences most notable in the designs decorating the wall behind the lady and her loom, introduced a mystical, specifically religious element into his treatment, fitted to his allegorical explanation of Tennyson's poem. Weighed against Tennyson's objection to Hunt's portrayal of the Lady (see Hunt 2: 124–25) and the poet's explanation of his work's significance, Hunt's comments and pictures amply demonstrate the range of meanings a single story can generate. Class consideration of the amplitude of traditional material will expand profitably if students also examine other artistic depictions of the Lady and Elaine, such as Lizzie Siddall's drawing, Doré's engravings, and the oil paintings of William Maw Edgley, John Atkinson Grimshaw, and John William Waterhouse (who painted the Lady of Shalott three times).

Besides sparking discussion of Tennyson's poems, these various evocations of Elaine and the Lady of Shalott open areas of fruitful exploration. To classes examining the role or representation of women in Arthurian works, for example, the pictures offer an interesting array of depictions, ranging from the fragile, childlike figure in Siddall's drawing of the Lady, whose aspiration toward Camelot and Lancelot is symbolically impeded by a crucifix set before her window, to the powerful artist of Hunt's late painting, whose figure, though bound, is arrestingly colorful and dynamic.

The nature of Camelot in various pictures and poems is another topic that extends students' concern beyond the particulars of a single text to the breadth of meaning available in legendary material. Images in Rossetti's engraving of the Lady of Shalott (a crowd scene that conveys an impression of panic or disaster), his drawing of Lancelot's capture in the queen's chamber (the lovers within a cramped space, menaced by armed men without), and his watercolor of the lovers' meeting at Arthur's garden tomb (the stiff effigy adorned with interior scenes from Camelot intruding between them), along with the architectural designs in Doré's engravings and Grimshaw's oil painting of Elaine, point up significant contrasts in the conception of Camelot that are also found in Victorian poetry. Rossetti's confining, cropped interiors and chaotic crowd scene beyond the tranquil Lady of Shalott contrast significantly with Doré's aspiring Gothic arches and starred ceiling, beneath which dignified, chastened courtiers hear the contents of

Elaine's letter. Similar differences emerge when students review the poets' descriptions of Arthur's court. Whereas Morris, for example, depicts Camelot as blank white roofs and clanging bells that must be excluded from lovers' experience by stone garden walls, Tennyson's Camelot is a delicate balance of weird allegorical images and perplexing symbolic designs, artistically wrought from imagination, yet rendered real—and consequently destructible—in wood and stone. In A. C. Swinburne's poems, Camelot is scarcely described, except as repressive social strictures and gossip, whereas lush nature hospitably houses lovers' trysts and dynamic action. Poets' and painters' depictions of the city raise psychological and symbolic questions: Is it real wood and stone? a product of artful wizardry? a figment of the imagination? Is it expansive or confining? an actual architectural manifestation of the ideal society, or restrictive social codes?

When used to raise such issues as the depiction of women in the Arthurian world or the psychosocial values represented by Camelot, nineteenth-century pictures on Arthurian subjects can take students beyond considering the one poem or episode that originally may have inspired a given canvas to contemplating how various writers of the Victorian period—and of other ages as well—perceived Camelot and its inhabitants, its symbolic meanings and its mythic essence. Seen not only as illustrations and commentaries on the literature that inspired them, moreover, the paintings graphically manifest the continuing richness and vitality of the Arthurian tradition. In the literature classroom, they help students see more intently and ask new kinds of questions.

Teaching Arthurian Film

Kevin J. Harty

Increasingly, undergraduates first learn little of what they know about King Arthur from literature. When they show up for the first day of a semester-long course in Arthurian literature, few have read—and some have never heard of—Chrétien, Wolfram, Malory, Tennyson, Twain, or White. Students do, nonetheless, know something of Arthur, and, more often than not, they have made that acquaintance from film. By including several film treatments of the story of the once and future king, a course in Arthurian literature can afford students an opportunity to appreciate more fully a legend they may have been exposed to only through its more recent cinematic retellings; showing such films can engender, as well, a keener understanding of the examples of cinema Arthuriana they know so well.

My course, now retitled "King Arthur in Literature and Film," begins with a film most of my students have already seen: *Knights of the Round Table, Camelot*, or *Knightriders*. My students then *see* from the start a world with which they are already familiar and which they can then reexamine in the light of their reading as the course moves on to more traditionally taught works: the early Latin and Welsh materials about Arthur as found in translation in Brengle or Wilhelm and Gross, Chrétien's *Yvain* or *Lancelot*, *Sir Gawain and the Green Knight*, and all of Malory. Malory is, I believe, required reading in any course in Arthurian literature, but, even in Keith Baines's abridged rendition, *Le Morte d'Arthur* can overwhelm students.

Having finished Malory, students are ready—they need a break in a heavy schedule of readings and they have acquired a heightened sophistication about Arthur—to appreciate a second film, one of three that bring the quest for the Grail to the screen: *Lancelot du Lac, Perceval le Gallois*, or *Excalibur*. (Our spring term has one more week than the fall term. I often use that extra week to teach two of these three films.) Having caught their breath, thanks to the study of these films, my students are prepared to move on to Twain and White, usually just *The Book of Merlyn*. My course concludes with *Monty Python and the Holy Grail*, a film whose dialogue not a few of my students know by heart.

With more than forty examples of cinema Arthuriana since Edwin Porter's 1904 film *Parsifal* (see Harty, *Cinema*), there is actually sufficient material for a separate course in Arthurian film. Most of us, however, will simply want to use one or more films of the legend of Arthur to supplement the literature we teach. In what follows, I provide an overview of why the films I have mentioned lend themselves to inclusion in a course in Arthurian literature.

For many of our students, the story of Arthur is a story of knightly adventure. This fact undoubtedly contributed to the making of MGM's first film in Cinemascope, *Knights of the Round Table* (1953). The unpaginated souvenir booklet distributed at the film's release claims that researchers for MGM both in Hollywood and in England stuck "close to the facts," basing their script on Malory's "studious work," although what the more learned eye sees on the screen is a bit garbled in terms of the particulars of the legend of Arthur. Infelicities of plot aside, *Knights* is a good example of medievalism à la Hollywood, where the model for movies about knights in armor has long been the western. *Knights* is long on spectacle and adventure, elements our students readily associate with the continuing popularity of the legend of Arthur.

For our students, the story of Arthur is also the story of the conflict between love and friendship. Students more often than not know of this conflict from *Camelot*, either as the Broadway musical (1960) or Joshua Logan's 1967 film version. *Camelot* shares the strengths and weaknesses of its genre—the movie musical—but it does portray, albeit imperfectly, the complex narrative of love and friendship long at the heart of the legend of Arthur.

The story of Arthur is also, for some of our students, the story of a utopian vision. A film somewhat less well known than *Knights* or *Camelot*, George Romero's *Knightriders* (1981) examines the values of Arthurian society as practiced by a group of entertainers in contemporary western Pennsylvania who don medieval garb and mount motorcycles to perform at county fairs and in thrill shows. Romero's film reminds us, often strikingly so, of the utopian thread running through the legend of Arthur. *Knightriders* is an apocalyptic vision of America set in its heartland. Romero's surface debt is to the movie western by way of its subgenre the biker movie, but Romero's deeper debt is to a long tradition that sees Arthur as both once and future king. As such, *Knightriders* makes for a somewhat startling beginning to a course in Arthurian literature, especially one interested in raising the question "Why Arthur?" early on in the semester.

The legend of the Grail will be a less familiar Arthurian theme to students. Having read Malory, they can both reflect on what they have read and better appreciate what they will see in viewing one of three film versions of the quest for the Grail. For the general outlines of its plot, Robert Bresson's *Lancelot du Lac* (1974) owes much to the Vulgate *Mort Artu*. The central focus of the film is on the Grail, although the cup itself appears only twice in the film. Bresson details in gory bleakness the downfall of Camelot because of the continuing adultery of Lancelot and Guinevere. The film, at times distinctly modern in its concerns, is Bresson's meditation on the impossibility of good, of even salvation, in a world gone mad. In Bresson's view, none of us finds salvation; salvation must find us. Salvation finds neither Arthur nor the members of his court—especially not Lancelot, who dies in battle staring heavenward but murmuring Guinevere's name.

Eric Rohmer's *Perceval le Gallois* (1978) offers students an interesting contrast with other examples of cinema Arthuriana. First, as Rohmer stated in an interview, he consciously set out "to rediscover the visions of the Medieval period as it saw itself" (Tesich-Savage 51–52). Second, he carefully followed a medieval text, *Le Conte du Graal* of Chrétien, for his treatment of the story of Perceval. However, Rohmer cut from Chrétien's text the final adventures of Gawain and focused on Perceval by having him take the central role in a medieval Passion Play, in which his spiritual rebirth is shown as a true union with Christ.

John Boorman's *Excalibur* (1981) is in many ways a hybrid. At times, the film's dark vision recalls that of Bresson's *Lancelot*; at times, the film's emphasis on spectacle recalls Logan's *Camelot* and Hollywood's emphasis on the spectacular in films treating medieval themes. Despite his determination "to tell the whole story" of Malory (Kennedy 33), Boorman has been rather free with his source. Since my students have already read all of the *Morte*, they can rather easily see how Boorman has manipulated his sources to contribute another personal vision of the legend of Arthur. Here Arthur is the Grail king, but the Grail is stripped of any Christian associations.

Finally, for something completely different, there is *Monty Python and the Holy Grail* (1975), now—as I indicated earlier—a cult film whose dialogue many students know by heart. There is little in Arthuriana to prepare viewers for the broad satire and farce in this film. What is being lampooned is not, however, the legend of Arthur itself, but rather earlier treatments—film and otherwise—of that legend, a point that becomes abundantly clear to students once they have read widely in the Arthurian tradition. *Monty Python* is then most effectively taught at the end of the term—albeit as a rather nontraditional capstone to a course in Arthurian literature—when students can better appreciate the comic genius that informs this film.

Purists may argue that these and other film versions of the legend of Arthur cheat a generation of students who already read too little. The legend of Arthur has throughout its long history, however, been marked by what Norris J. Lacy calls a "transposability" that both explains and permits its continuing popularity (vii). By incorporating one or several films into a course in Arthurian literature, we enrich, rather than cheat, our students by providing them with insights into one of history's most enduring legends.

APPENDIX

Sample Syllabus

> Weeks 1 and 2: film (*Knights of the Round Table, Camelot,* or *Knightriders*)
> Weeks 3 and 4: Arthur in the early Latin and Welsh traditions
> Week 5: Chrétien, *Yvain* or *Lancelot*
> Week 6: *Sir Gawain and the Green Knight*
> Weeks 7–10: Malory
> Week 11: film (*Lancelot du Lac, Perceval le Gallois,* or *Excalibur*)
> Week 12: Twain, *A Connecticut Yankee* in *King Arthur's Court*
> Week 13: White, *The Book of Merlyn*
> Week 14: film (*Monty Python and the Holy Grail*)

A Note on the Availability of the Films Discussed

Both *Lancelot du Lac* and *Perceval le Gallois* are available for rental from New Yorker Films (161 W. 61st St., New York, NY 10023). All the other films discussed here are available for rental on video tape in Beta or VHS formats. Rohmer's screenplay was published as a special issue of *L'avant-scène du cinéma* in 1979. The screenplay and a number of production-related documents for *Monty Python* were published by Methuen in 1977.

Arthur for Children

Muriel Whitaker

Ever since the Middle Ages, Arthurian literature has been accessible to children (in my definition, young people up to the age of sixteen). In the sixteenth century the royal schoolmaster Roger Ascham complained that *Le Morte d'Arthur* was found in Prince Edward's chamber while God's Bible was banished. Chapbooks about Jack the Giant Killer, ballads about Tom Thumb, and a nursery rhyme about the "bag pudding" king kept Arthur's name alive through the eighteenth century. When James Knowles published, in 1862, the first Malory adapted for juveniles, it was the beginning of an industry. In this century, in addition to adaptations, there have appeared numerous works of fantasy, science fiction, and historical fiction suitable for younger readers. At the high school and university levels this material can be taught in courses on children's literature, fantasy, science fiction, modern Arthurian literature, and popular culture.

Students should first become familiar with the medieval Matter of Britain. As Malory's *Morte d'Arthur* is the chief source of Arthurian story in English, a version of that work should be studied along with a Gawain romance, some form of the poetic *Tristan*, and, possibly, the *Mabinogion*. Finding suitable texts at a reasonable price is a primary problem. If one wants the whole Malory text, the Penguin *Morte* is satisfactory. D. S. Brewer's *Morte d'Arthur* gives parts 7 and 8 of Vinaver's text, along with an excellent critical introduction. Roger Lancelyn Green's *King Arthur and His Knights of the Round Table* supplements Malory with prose versions of "Sir Gawain and the Green Knight," "Sir Gawain and Lady Ragnall," "Geraint and Enid," and "Sir Percevale of Wales." Green obscures the adultery and the Catholicism of the original. Michael Senior's *Sir Thomas Malory's Tales of King Arthur* (1980) is a splendid choice for the illustrations as well as text. For other medieval legends, try Rosemary Sutcliff's *Tristan and Iseult*, Marie Borroff's *Sir Gawain and the Green Knight*, and *The Mabinogion*, translated by Jeffrey Gantz. In modern juvenile fiction, the essential work is T. H. White's *Sword in the Stone*. If time permits, Sutcliff's *Lantern Bearers*, William Mayne's *Earthfasts*, Henry Treece's *Eagles Have Flown*, and Susan Cooper's *Silver on the Tree* are good choices available in paperback.

Instructors might focus on two aspects—the nature of the hero and the ideals of chivalry. The biography of Arthur follows a pattern common to many mythic heroes, such as Perseus, Siegfried, and Cuchulain. As defined by Lord Raglan in *The Hero*, it includes royal ancestry, mysterious conception and birth, protected childhood, supernatural helpers, public recognition, marvelous artifacts, preliminary successes, crucial testing, a victory that benefits society, and apotheosis. (This pattern can be applied also to Lancelot, Tristan, and Galahad.) The literary Arthur is an ideal Christian king, a hero in his own right, the center of a sophisticated court and the founder of the Round Table. Discuss the implications of these attributes in terms of plot development.

While Arthur's greatest knights can be linked to the archetypes of heroic tradition, what defines them specifically is a chivalric code based on loyalty to God, the king, and a lady. These three powers inspire the deeds of prowess, generally arranged in a pattern of quest and combat, that allow the knights to reveal their courtesy, piety, generosity, compassion, and service. Having discussed the ideals of chivalry and courtesy (including courtly love), one may examine the literary implications by considering types of knighthood—the good knight of secular chivalry (for instance, Lancelot, Tristan, Gareth, and the Gawain of metrical romance), the doomed knight (Balan), and the ideal knight of spiritual chivalry (Galahad, Percival). Other topics for discussion include Arthurian women, the uses of magic, the differences between the secular quest and the religious quest, the contrasting values of Camelot and Corbenic, the causes of Arthurian society's downfall, the legends of Arthur's survival in the Otherworld. To assist in sorting out the characters, I provide my students with two family trees—the descendants of Igraine and the ancestors of Galahad.

Modern Arthurian children's literature may be divided into two major categories, fantasy and historical fiction (there are also picture books, to be mentioned later). In fantasy the author creates what J. R. R. Tolkien calls a secondary world of the imagination with its own consistency. Supernatural characters may infiltrate the real world (as in Mayne's *Earthfasts* and Cooper's *Dark Is Rising* series), or characters from the real world may enter the Otherworld (Garner's *Weirdstone of Brisingamen*). Time shift is often utilized to make the connection between medieval and modern (Peter Dickinson's *Weathermonger* and Penelope Lively's *Whispering Knights*). Students can familiarize themselves with the fantasists' objectives and techniques by reading Tolkien's essay "On Fairy-Stories" and essays by Alan Garner et al. in *Children's Literature in Education*. A fantasy that most juveniles will enjoy is White's *Sword in the Stone*. It can be linked to the medieval material through the figure of Arthur, through White's use of Malory, and through the typical romance setting of castle and forest. White's theme is the education of a hero and a king. The Wart is educated in several ways—through formal instruction in the pursuits of a medieval gentleman (archery, jousting, hunting and hawking, swordplay); schoolroom instruction by his tutor, Merlin; and transformations into various animals to teach him about power, courage, evolution, industry, and love of home. As in medieval romance, his heroic qualities are tested during forest adventures. Among questions to consider are these: What use does White make of Malory? Which period of medieval history corresponds to the Age of Uther? From what sources does the author draw his characters? What makes *The Sword in the Stone* so funny? What does it teach the reader about medieval social history? What elements are fantastic?

In studying the second major genre, historical fiction, the instructor should show the relationship between specific texts and the history, geography, and archaeology of Dark Age Britain, the period in which Arthur (if he actually existed) would have lived. Such authors as Sutcliff, Stewart, Treece, and Victor Canning make their stories credible by using the social history and geography appropriate to a particular period and by rationalizing mythic elements.

In the past century, Arthurian children's books have attracted some of the best British and American illustrators, perhaps because the subject allows them to combine a sense of the historical past with an aura of magic and mystery. As several of these books have recently been reissued, it is possible to study them without recourse to a special collections library. See, for example, Henry Gilbert's *King Arthur's Knights*, illustrated by Walter Crane, Howard Pyle's *Story of King Arthur and His Knights*, and Alfred W. Pollard's *Romance of King Arthur and His Knights of the Round Table*. Notable works illustrated by contemporary artists include Errol Le Cain's picture book *King Arthur's Sword*, a comic fantasyland for young readers, Juan Wijngaard's illustrations for Selina Hastings's *Sir Gawain and the Green Knight*, and Victor Ambrus's energetic depictions of chivalric encounters for James Riordan's *Tales of King Arthur*. Though it does not include the Arthurian stories, Gwyn Thomas and Kevin Crossley-Holland's *Tales from the Mabinogion*, illustrated by Margaret Jones, powerfully evokes the magic-imbued Welsh setting of the heroic age. Topics you might discuss and explain include the following: What historical period does the artist choose as the Age of Arthur? How does the artist create a sense of the past? What episodes does the artist choose to illustrate? How do the illustrations affect our perception of character? Does the artist extend the meaning of the text? How does he or she evoke a sense of the supernatural? How important is color in creating a romantic atmosphere?

A number of assignments are suitable for young people. Which you choose depends, among other things, on the age of your students.

Working in groups of two or three, students can do short classroom presentations, using visual materials where possible. This kind of assignment enriches the study of the literature by drawing on history, folklore, art, and other sources; it also promotes camaraderie. Representative topics are the historicity of Arthur, jousts and tournaments, medieval arms and armor, medieval hunting rituals, Arthurian places, castle entertainments, and great illustrators. Older students may be assigned a term paper dealing with Arthurian works not studied in class, to extend their knowledge of the genre:

> Select a work of Arthurian fiction by a contemporary author who uses materials from the Matter of Britain. Briefly summarize the basic myth, legend, or folktale in its traditional form. Show how the author adapts traditional materials in terms of character, setting, plot, and theme. (What is added? What is omitted? What is changed?) Finally, suggest why the author has chosen to use mythic materials in writing for a contemporary audience. Authors whose works might be discussed include Gillian Bradshaw, Victor Canning, Joy Chant, Vera Chapman, Susan Cooper, Alan Garner, Penelope Lively, William Mayne, Andre Norton, Mary Stewart, Rosemary Sutcliff, Henry Treece, and T. H. White.

Movie versions of the Arthur legend have particular appeal for children. Suitable films are Walt Disney's animated *Sword in the Stone*, *Monty Python and the Holy Grail*, and John Boorman's *Excalibur* for the castle and forest settings. A useful slide-tape package is *The Story of King Arthur*.

For teachers seeking background on the subject, there is no shortage of materials. Some particularly useful sources are: Leslie Alcock, *Arthur's Britain*; Geoffrey Ashe, ed., *The Quest for Arthur's Britain*; Richard W. Barber, *King Arthur in Legend and History*; E. K. Chambers, *Arthur of Britain*; Mark Girouard, *The Return to Camelot: Chivalry and the English Gentleman*; Norris Lacy, ed., *The Arthurian Encyclopedia*; Marion Lochhead, *The Renaissance of Wonder in Children's Literature*; James W. Spisak, ed., *Studies in Malory*; Raymond H. Thompson, *The Return from Avalon: A Study of the Arthurian Legend in Modern Fiction*; Tolkien, "On Fairy-Stories"; Grant Uden, *A Dictionary of Chivalry*; and Muriel Whitaker, *The Legends of King Arthur in Art*. Periodicals include *Avalon to Camelot*, *Children's Literature in Education*, *Children's Literature Association Quarterly*, *Signal*, *The Horn Book*. For a bibliography, see Muriel Whitaker, *Children's Literature: A Guide to Criticism*.

Women in Arthurian Literature

Maureen Fries

The exigencies of Arthurian romance invariably affect one's teaching about the women who populate it. Since the stories are not about women but about men, female roles find their context in relation to the male heroic roles they either complement or defy. Early in my course in Arthurian literature, I identify the three prime roles that thus emerge: woman as hero, woman as heroine, and woman as counter-hero.

While "female hero" initially seems a paradox, since a long literary tradition connects the noun with the male, a structural analysis of any plot—Arthurian or otherwise—reveals that the hero is "the man or woman who has been able to battle past his personal and local historical limitations" (Campbell 20) because of superiority in degree to others (Frye 33). Heroes are knowers; heroines are "what can be known" (Campbell 116), the lures that lead the hero to self-realization, their greatest virtue their beauty and marriage the target for which that beauty is aimed. Marriage is either incidental to or absent from the career of the counterhero, who possesses the hero's superior powers of action without any sustained adherence to the dominant culture (Fries, "Malory's Tristram"). Alluring or repelling, or both (as in Chaucer's Arthurian Wife of Bath's Tale), female counterheroes are as capable of destroying the hero's destiny as of completing it.

I begin my analysis of these female categories with Guinevere as she emerges in Geoffrey of Monmouth's *History of the Kings of Britain*. As the most beautiful woman in the land, she is the natural bride for Arthur, and at his recrowning sets a societal example by which the women become "chaste and more virtuous" so that "for their love the knights were ever more daring" (229). Mordred's seizure of her and the kingdom temporarily negates her virtue, but her retirement to the nunnery after the Arthurian catastrophe indicates her ultimate conformation to the Arthurian male hero's values. Guinevere is a heroine, and the prime female instrument around which male action will continue to turn.

Such instrumentality persists in spite of Guinevere's seeming dominance in Chrétien de Troyes's *Lancelot*, which the class studies next. Superficially it is her authority over Lancelot that causes both his shameful actions—mounting the cart, pretending to lose a joust—and his heroic ones—freeing the prisoners of Gorre, besting Meleagant. But she is meanwhile carried off and imprisoned, fought for and defended, freed and returned home and fought for again, not at her own will but at the will of and/or the agreement between the males of the poem. Heroines are predicated by passive verbs; to heroes belong the active ones. Such repeated Arthurian heroinic passivity reaches its epitome in Chrétien's Laudine, who is, in *Yvain*, so bound into patriarchal custom that her patrimony, the magic fountain, depends on a male defender (as a woman she cannot, of course, bear arms). Her supposed imperious rule of her new husband-protector, Yvain, does not enable her ever to leave her fountain; she must send her maid Lunete (of whom I say more later) to rebuke him, and to effect a comparatively easy reconciliation.

Reconciliation is effected differently, I stress to my students, in the case of Chrétien's most interesting female character, Enide. Originally a heroine, even unnamed until her marriage to Erec, she defies her husband's authority with repeated forbidden speech during their quest to restore his honor, saving his life and bringing him glory. Once Erec kisses her in token of her heroic action, however, she resumes her role as heroine, emblemized in the return of the beauty her strenuous effort had altered. Adventures continue, but now only for Erec.

Only women who do not marry seem capable of consistent heroism in Arthurian romance. Virgin in the original sense of the word—living without a man—and connected with the forest and the moon (like their archetype, Diana), Chrétien's Lunete and Malory's Lyonet display the wit and powers of magic that Arthurian female heroes utilize instead of arms to effect change. Chrétien once even calls Lunete *maistre*, a rare designation for a medieval woman; only when condemned for treason does she receive from Yvain return for the aid she has repeatedly given him. That the equally accomplished and helpful Lyonet, whose scolding prompts Gareth to valor and whose supernatural intervention assures his chaste marriage to her sister, is wed at the end of Malory's *Gareth* is a reminder that virgin-heroes may be tamed. As I remind my class, women in medieval literature, as well as life, were hard put to escape male-imposed fate.

Even marriage, however, cannot tame the prime Arthurian female counterhero, Morgan le Fay. Literally wholesome in Geoffrey of Monmouth's *Vita Merlini*, she carries the dying Arthur to Avalon for healing: beautiful, a shapeshifter learned in recondite studies such as astrology as well, she intends her skill for Arthur's good. But this initial heroism is permanently altered in the Prose Vulgate *Lancelot*, in which her liaison with Guinevere's cousin Guiomar leads to the enforced exile of Arthur's sister (as Morgan has now become). Bearing her lover's son, she then seeks out Merlin, who out of love teaches her the arts of enchantment. In the later *Livre d'Artus*, Morgan uses these newfound skills to keep Guiomar in her power and also to foil

Guinevere and Arthur by entrapping Round Table knights-errant in her *val sanz retor*, with its impenetrable magic curtain of air. Morgan's transformation from a beneficent healer to a maleficent sorceress—from a female hero to a female counterhero—coincides with the virulent growth in hatred and fear of women characteristic of the later Middle Ages (see Heer 309–23), which I discuss at this point.

Also transformed are her power and her beauty. Originally self-generated, Morgan's magic now must be learned from Merlin, a man. Although praised for loveliness at times in the Prose Vulgate *Lancelot*, she is also seen as ugly, lecherous, and hot (hypersexual)—to which portrait the Vulgate *Merlin* adds brownness of face. My students have already learned the medieval coefficient of moral goodness with physical beauty (Curry), so they are not surprised that the *Suite de Merlin* shows Morgan's acquiring her ugliness after yielding to intercourse with the devil. Versions influenced by this idea depict her beauty as an enchanted illusion, or a shape she can shift onto another—as in *Sir Gawain and the Green Knight*, in which Morgan is a hag and her double, Bertilak's wife, the lovely lady.

Morgan's own wifehood does nothing to tame her, as it does the virgin-hero. None of her variously named husbands can satisfy her voracious sexual appetite, with its resultant faithlessness. To her postmarital lover Accolon she gives the sword and life-protective sheath of Arthur, which she had promised to keep safe, and Arthur's regaining of these possessions and subsequent slaying of Accolon only produces further dirty tricks. With other sorceress-queens she abducts Lancelot, and alone Alisaunder le Orphelin, and attempts to seduce them both (unsuccessfully). Her plot to kill Urien, most persistently (the name of) her husband, is foiled only by the intervention of their son Yvain. Comparison with actual queenly adultery and its punishment stimulates class discussion of this stage of Morgan's varied career.

That Morgan nevertheless consistently retains her function as Arthur's conductress to Avalon suggests her connection with the concept of the ancient mother goddess (Paton), whose ambivalence toward men she shares. Mother both of life and death (Campbell 202–03), the archetypal Morgan may nurture as well as seek to destroy. One mode by which male authors coped with such frightening (even if only literary) power was to reduce it, and this explains for my students the emergence of the various Ladies of the Lake (whose very name recalls the meaning of Morgan's, "sea-born"). In however many guises (Holbrook), the Lady provides mainly restorative functions—she nurtures the young Lancelot, gives Excalibur to Arthur, and then restores it as he fights Accolon, among other deeds. But her puzzling role in Malory's Balin episode leads to her (apparently) temporary and his permanent destruction. This striking ambivalence has its chief named avatar in Nimue, who in both the Vulgate and Malory's *Morte* besots and shuts up Merlin and then uses the knowledge gained from him to usurp his place as Round Table counselor. Saving both Arthur and Guinevere from plots against them, protecting the knight Pelleas, whom she loves, Nimue finally emerges as one of several queens who bear Arthur to Avalon—a function uniting her with her original, the (now) much less beneficent Morgan. The Ladies all, I tell my students, have been watered down from this powerful original to suit the norms of a medieval and male culture leery of the female counterhero.

While later, especially nineteenth- and twentieth-century, Arthurian works exhibit superficial differences from these medieval models, they continue to deal in all three types of female images: heroines, counterheroes, and (increasingly in our own time) female heroes. Lack of space prohibits citing numerous examples: Tennyson's *Idylls of the King* alone offers fruitful subjects for analysis, especially of the lasting effects of misogyny, and Marion Zimmer Bradley's *Mists of Avalon* is not the only feminist transformation (although it is, so far, the most striking one). No matter which works I choose to end the course, my students continue to exhibit a special and enduring interest in all these fascinating Arthurian women.

Arthuriana and Popular Culture

Mary Alice Grellner

The great variety of themes and tales in the Arthurian tradition of the Middle Ages is being matched, and perhaps exceeded, by the plethora of popular approaches to the old legends today. Since the return of King Arthur to literature, music, and art in the nineteenth century, the comprehensiveness and emotional range of its subject matter have allowed and, indeed, encouraged the exploration and exploitation of offbeat treatments. Such forays, with varying degrees of success, and often from the point of view of a minor or wholly new character, always reflect in myriad ways the concerns and interests of the popular culture.

I have found that a course entitled King Arthur Today, designed as a senior seminar in general studies, attracts a broad cross-section of undergraduates, some of whom come to the course from a childhood addiction to Hal Foster's comic strip *Prince Valiant*, from remembered pleasure in the films *Camelot* or *Excalibur*, or just from a vague curiosity about the title.

The first few weeks of the course are devoted to the historical background of the legend. *These Halls of Camelot*, a filmstrip and record, is excellent as a first-day orientation, covering, as it does, both the archaeological and textual history of the origins of the legend. Slides of modern-day Stonehenge, Cadbury, Glastonbury, and Tintagel, taken by a former student who is a professional photographer, further suggest that though he is a legendary figure, King Arthur has taken root in the geography of England. To establish the framework of the legend as it had developed by Malory's time and also to help students grasp the notion that no one version is the "true" one but that each reflects the vision of its author and its times, I have students look at Elizabeth Jenkins's *Mystery of King Arthur*, Christopher Hibbert's *Search for King Arthur*, Richard W. Barber's *Arthurian Legends*, and Geoffrey Ashe's *All about King Arthur*. Now also available for reference are *The Arthurian Encyclopedia*, edited by Norris Lacy, and *The Return of King Arthur*, by Beverly Taylor and Elisabeth Brewer, both of which have a wealth of bibliographic and evaluative material.

The central portion of the course is devoted to a reading and discussion of key modern novels, such as those by T. H. White, Mary Stewart, and Thomas Berger, discussed elsewhere in this volume. These three writers, taken together, provide a good overview of the basic legend, along with insight into the variety of ways novelists may shape and view the material. Because they are all accessible to the college student, they can be used as a common fund of readings in the class, in much the same way as one would use Geoffrey of Monmouth and Malory in a class focusing on the medieval Arthurian tradition.

In the concluding weeks, we survey novels from the late nineteenth century to the present, each student selecting a work to read and interpret for the rest of the class. Students understand that each novelist has researched, translated, and interpreted a particular strand of the legend, usually taking liberties with it, as did the medieval writers, recasting, rearranging, and reinterpreting characters, incidents, and symbols, reweaving them into an imaginative pattern.

To gain a perspective on what has happened to the legend in the twentieth century, we first look at prose work of the late nineteenth century. The real awakening of the American popular consciousness to the richness of the old tales probably originated in Sidney Lanier's *Boy's King Arthur*, which introduced Malory in a sanitized, idealized form to several generations of readers and writers and provided the basis for a succession of satires and spoofs. Nine years later, for instance, Mark Twain's *Connecticut Yankee in King Arthur's Court* reached the same audience, now grown up and somewhat disillusioned. Hank Morgan taught them to cast a jaundiced eye on a system that could keep a whole population enslaved under the guise of chivalric ideals. In briefer and gentler fashion, both Booth Tarkington in *Penrod* and Heywood Broun in "The Fifty-first Dragon" spoofed the idealization of medieval chivalry. Similarly, John Erskine's *Galahad* and *Tristan and Isolde* poked gentle fun at the Miniver Cheevys of the modern world.

Twain's conceit of time travel to achieve a Janus view of two dissimilar societies had great popular appeal and, in the first half of the twentieth century, reached large audiences in three screen versions. It is unfortunate for students looking at Arthur in popular culture that only the 1949 musical version is still readily available for viewing. The romantic tone of the musical has little in common with the wry spoof in the 1931 Will Rogers version and still less with Twain's black humor and bleak vision of humanity, but it does offer insight into America's post–World War II tendency to see life captured in simple lyrics.

Although dozens of retellings, in both verse and prose, were produced between about 1900 and 1950, it was not until 1938, almost fifty years after Twain's fantasy, that another novelization of Arthurian legend reached an extensive readership and an even larger stage and movie audience. White's series, written over a twenty-year period and brought together as a tetralogy in 1965 under the title *The Once and Future King*, appeals to students because, like Twain, White mixes spoof and satire, juxtaposes criticism of both medieval and contemporary attitudes toward war, and capitalizes on the incongruities without losing sight of the noble and the heroic. After watching *Camelot*, the film based on the Lerner and Loewe stage success, students can analyze the ways in which the adaptation of a complex novel for a mass audience results in the retention of the pretty, the homey, the humorous, and the romantic elements, while White's complexity, anger, ambivalence, and bitterness are lost.

Undergraduates, who see scores of films but seldom if ever critique them, enjoy comparing these novels with their film progeny. They become adept at spotting the differences in tone and attitude, in conception and emphasis, and in speculating, in terms of their perception of the way the world was in the 1940s and 1960s, on why these films spoke to such broad audiences.

Other popular novels based on the legend reflect today's interests in fantasy and science fiction, in magic and the occult, and in the empowerment of women. In *That Hideous Strength*, an allegory of the struggle between good and the secular evil of modern science, with Merlin the object of the struggle, C. S. Lewis shows "how quickly men can be persuaded along the path of evil in the cause of a perverted ideal, and easily come to accept the use of scientific knowledge and technology for evil ends" (Taylor and Brewer 264). In discussing the range of problems raised by the novel, students discover how the symbols in the Arthurian legends have relevance for modern life. A similar set of meanings emerges in Charles Williams's *War in Heaven*, in which the Grail is the object of the struggle, and in John Cowper Powys's *Glastonbury Romance*. More recent fantasy novels set in modern times are Sanders Ann Laubenthal's *Excalibur*, based on a legend of Madoc, a Welsh prince who supposedly reached the New World in the twelfth century; Nicole St. John's *Guinever's Gift*; and Joanne Stang's *Shadows on the Sceptered Isle*. While none of these suffer from an excess of literary merit, they do, like *Castle Dor*, by Arthur Quiller-Couch and Daphne du Maurier, *Lancelot*, by Walker Percy, *The Natural*, by Bernard Malamud, and a number of other novels, attempt to dramatize the relevance of the legend today by reincarnating the stories in modern characters and/or projecting an object of struggle that in the wrong hands can again destroy the kingdom.

Staying more closely with the setting and events of the traditional story, Andre Norton, in *Merlin's Mirror*, has both Merlin and Arthur engendered by Sky Lords from an advanced civilization in outer space, in an effort to restore peace to a race with whom they had once mated. Discussion of the cosmic conflict between forces of good and evil leads students to see the strong element of medieval romance in most science fiction as a way of coming to terms with the complexity of life.

Fantasy and magic, rather than science fiction, figure in Sharan Newman's *Guinevere, The Chessboard Queen*, and *Guinevere Evermore*, in Gillian Bradshaw's trilogy *Hawk of May, Kingdom of Summer*, and *In Winter's Shadow*, and in Marion Zimmer Bradley's sprawling epic *The Mists of Avalon*. These three women novelists have focused on Guinevere—Newman throughout the trilogy, Bradshaw only in the third book. Bradley treats her as one of a group of Arthurian women who hold center stage in this engrossing work. Though all three obviously owe something to the women's movement, Bradley's book is by far the most original and profound, weaving an intricate, psychologically compelling story of the struggle for power of the women behind the throne: Viviane, Igraine, Morgaine, Morgause, Guinevere, Niniane, and Nimue. Beyond this, Avalon becomes an evocative symbol for the loss of power, by the priestesses of the old Celtic religion, to the priests of Christianity, with Arthur fusing the old and the new, effecting the transition from a pagan to a Christian society.

Another strong statement of a woman's role in the passing of power from one ruling group to another is *Beloved Exile*, by Parke Godwin. In this engrossing story, a sequel to *Firelord*, Guinevere is captured by Saxons after Arthur's death and serves as a slave for ten years. During this time of suffering, she learns humility and selflessness and comes to respect her Saxon masters and to perceive in them the qualities that will bring peace to her beloved land.

More recently, Persia Wooley, in *Child of the Northern Spring* and *Queen of the Summer Stars*, the first two novels of a projected trilogy, retells the story with Guinevere as the narrator. Wooley gives us a strong and sympathetic Guinevere, a welcome antidote to Bradley's portrayal.

In selecting a novel to read and interpret for the rest of the class, students are not limited to works mentioned here. Giving them the freedom to experiment often brings interesting and surprising results, such as original poems and short stories, musical productions, and artwork. Occasionally, a student opts to go back to a medieval work, to study it either as the source for a modern novelist or as a work yielding insights about the culture of its time.

As they read and view modern novels and movies based on the Arthurian legends, students confront two related questions: What is it about this particular legend, with its accretions through the centuries, that makes it so appealing to the contemporary writer and reader as a vehicle to explore popular culture and contemporary ideas? And, conversely, what is it about contemporary culture that induces writers to turn to these legendary heroes of a shadowy past to illuminate their vision of the meaning of life?

CONTRIBUTORS AND SURVEY PARTICIPANTS

Mark Allen, Univ. of Texas, San Antonio; Antony Annunziata, State Univ. of New York, Oswego; Heather Arden, Univ. of Cincinnati; Mary L. Beaudry, Univ. of Massachusetts, Lowell; Phillip C. Boardman, Univ. of Nevada, Reno; Gerard J. Brault, Pennsylvania State Univ.; Saul N. Brody, City Univ. of New York; Bradford Broughton, Clarkson Univ.; John Bugge, Emory Univ.; Kathleen Capels, Texas Committee for the Humanities; Douglas Carmichael, St. Lawrence Univ.; Carolyn Collette, Mount Holyoke Coll.; Roger Dahood, Univ. of Arizona; James Dean, Tufts Univ.; Deanna Evans, Bemidji State Univ.; Sandy Feinstein, Southwestern Coll., Kansas; Elizabeth Fishbach, Lafayette High School, Brooklyn, NY; David C. Fowler, Univ. of Washington; Maureen Fries, State Univ. of New York, Fredonia; Ernest Gabrielson, Mingus Union High, Cottonwood, AZ; Alan T. Gaylord, Dartmouth Coll.; Judson Gooding, Bedford, NY; Debi S. Graham, St. Charles West High School, St. Charles, MO; Mary Alice Grellner, Rhode Island Coll.; Margaret Grimes, Michigan State Univ.; Arthur Groos, Cornell Univ.; Sr. Frances Gussenhoven, Loyola Marymount Univ.; Ruth E. Hamilton, Newberry Library, Chicago, IL; Carol Harding, Linfield Coll.; Kevin J. Harty, La Salle Univ.; Geraldine Heng, Cornell Univ.; Harold J. Herman, Univ. of Maryland, College Park; Constance B. Hieatt, Univ. of Western Ontario; Myra Hinman, Univ. of Kansas; Donald L. Hoffman, Northeastern Illinois Univ.; Linda T. Holley, North Carolina State Univ.; Delmar C. Homan, Bethany Coll.; Linda K. Hughes, Texas Christian Univ.; Stanley Kahrl (deceased), Ohio State Univ.; Marianne Kalinke, Univ. of Illinois, Urbana; Noel Harold Kaylor, Univ. of Northern Iowa; George R. Keiser, Kansas State Univ.; Thomas Kelly, Purdue Univ.; Beverly Kennedy, Marianopolis Coll.; Don Kennedy, Univ. of North Carolina, Chapel Hill; William W. Kibler, Univ. of Texas, Austin; Robert L. Kindrick, Eastern Illinois Univ.; Thomas Kinney, Bowling Green State Univ.; Norris J. Lacy, Washington Univ.; Alexander Leupin, Louisiana State Univ., Baton Rouge; Alan Lupack, Rossell Hope Robbins Library, Univ. of Rochester; Kathryn L. Lynch, Wellesley Coll.; Jeanne T. Mathewson, Univ. of Wyoming; Joseph McClatchey (deceased), Wheaton Coll., Illinois; Douglas J. McMillan, East Carolina Univ.; Carolyn M. Melchor, Tidewater Community Coll.; Robert Merrill, Pennsylvania State Univ.; Kathleen Milford, Easton, PA; Don A. Monson, Coll. of William and Mary; N. Morcovescu, Monash Univ.; Sally Mussetter, Univ. of Washington; Marilyn Nellis, Clarkson Univ.; Deborah H. Nelson, Rice Univ.; Thomas Ohlgren, Purdue Univ.; F. Anne Payne, State Univ. of New York, Buffalo; Henry H. Peyton III, Memphis State Univ.; Wendy Pfeffer, Univ. of Louisville; David W. Pitre, Episcopal High School, Baton Rouge, LA; Esther Quinn, Hunter Coll., City Univ. of New York; Burton Raffel, Univ. of Southwest Louisiana; George Reinecke, Univ. of New Orleans; Michael Rewa, Univ. of

Delaware; Mary P. Richards, Univ. of Tennessee, Knoxville; Jeff Rider, Wesleyan Univ.; William Roach, Univ. of Pennsylvania; Lorie Roth, Armstrong State Coll.; Theodore Rupp, Millersville Univ. and York Coll., Pennsylvania; Jay Ruud, Northern State Coll.; James A. Schultz, Univ. of Illinois, Chicago; Harvey L. Sharrer, Univ. of California, Santa Barbara; Martin B. Shichtman, Eastern Michigan Univ; Sally K. Slocum, Univ. of Akron; Patricia Harris Stablein, Folger Shakespeare Library, Washington, DC; Paul E. Szarmach, State Univ. of New York, Binghamton; Ann M. Taylor, Salem State Coll.; Beverly Taylor, Univ. of North Carolina, Chapel Hill; Raymond H. Thompson, Acadia Univ.; Stephanie Cain Van D'Elden, Univ. of Minnesota, Minneapolis; John Michael Walsh, St. Peter's Coll.; Julian Wasserman, Loyola Univ., New Orleans; Jeanie Watson, Southwestern Univ.; Muriel Whitaker, Univ. of Alberta; Robert H. Wilson, Univ. of Texas, Austin; Lenora D. Wolfgang, Lehigh Univ.

WORKS CITED

Primary Sources

Andreas Capellanus. *The Art of Courtly Love*. Trans. John Jay Parry. Ed. Frederick W. Locke. New York: Ungar, 1957.

Arden, John, and Margaretta D'Arcy. *The Island of the Mighty. Plays and Players* (Feb. 1973): 1–32 (Pts. 1 and 2).

———. *The Island of the Mighty. Plays and Players* (Mar. 1973): 1–14 (Pt. 3).

The Auchinleck Manuscript: National Library of Scotland Advocates' MS 19.2.1. Introd. Derek Pearsall and I. C. Cunningham. London: Scolar, 1977.

Augustinus, Aurelius, Saint. *On Christian Doctrine*. Trans. D. W. Robertson, Jr. New York: Liberal Arts, 1958.

Baines, Keith. Le Morte d'Arthur: *King Arthur and the Legends of the Round Table*. New York: Potter, 1962.

Barron, W. R. J., ed. and trans. *Sir Gawain and the Green Knight*. Manchester Medieval Classics. Manchester: U of Manchester P; New York: Barnes, 1974.

Bede, Venerabilis. *Ecclesiastical History of the English Nation*. New York: Dutton, 1958.

Bédier, Joseph. *The Romance of Tristan and Iseut*. Trans. Hilaire Belloc and Paul Rosenfield. New York: Pantheon, 1945.

Bennett, J. A. W., and G. W. Smithers. *Early Middle English Verse and Prose*. New York: Oxford UP, 1968.

Benson, Larry D., ed. *King Arthur's Death: The Middle English* Stanzaic Morte Arthur *and* Alliterative Morte Arthure. Indianapolis: Bobbs, 1974. Exeter: U of Exeter P, 1986.

Berger, Thomas. *Arthur Rex: A Legendary Novel*. New York: Seymour Laurence–Delacorte, 1978.

Boethius. *Consolation of Philosophy*. Trans. V. E. Watts. Harmondsworth, Eng.: Penguin, 1969.

Bollard, John K. "The Story of Peredur, Son of Efrog." Wilhelm, *Romance of Arthur II* 29–61.

Borroff, Marie, trans. Sir Gawain and the Green Knight: *A New Verse Translation*. New York: Norton, 1967.

Bradley, Marion Zimmer. *The Mists of Avalon*. New York: Knopf, 1982.

Bradshaw, Gillian. *Hawk of May*. New York: Simon, 1980.

———. *In Winter's Shadow*. New York: Simon, 1982.

———. *Kingdom of Summer*. New York: Simon, 1981.

Brengle, Richard L., ed. *Arthur King of Britain: History, Romance, Chronicle, and Criticism from Gildas to Malory*. New York: Appleton, 1964.

Brewer, Derek S., ed. *The* Morte d'Arthur: *Parts Seven and Eight*. York Medieval Texts. Evanston: Northwestern UP, 1968.

Bromwich, Rachel, ed. and trans. *Trioedd Ynys Prydein: The Welsh Triads*. Cardiff: U of Wales P, 1978.

Broun, Heywood. "The Fifty-first Dragon." 1921. *Creative Classics Short Stories*. Ed. Ann Redpath. Mankato: Creative Editions, 1985.

Bruce, James Douglas, ed. *The Middle English Stanzaic "Le Morte Arthur."* Harleian ms. 2252. EETS extra series 88, 1903.

Bryant, Nigel, trans. *Percival: The Story of the Grail*. Wolfeboro: Boydell, 1986.

Buescu, Maria Leonor Carvalhao, ed. *Demanda do Graal*. Lisbon: Verbo, 1968.

Burgess, Glyn S., and Keith Busby, trans. *The* Lais *of Marie de France*. New York: Penguin, 1986.

Buridant, Claude, and Jean Trotin, trans. Le chevalier au lion (Yvain): *Roman traduit de l'ancien français par Claude Buridant et Jean Trotin*. Paris: Champion, 1971.

Burrow, J. A., ed. *Sir Gawain and the Green Knight*. 1972. New Haven: Yale UP, 1982.

Cable, James, trans. *The Death of King Arthur* [Prose Vulgate *Mort Artu*]. Harmondsworth, Eng.: Penguin, 1971.

Carmichael, Douglas. *Pendragon: An Historical Novel*. Hicksville: Blackwater, 1977.

Carroll, Carleton W., ed. and trans. *Erec et Enide*. New York: Garland, 1987; New York: Penguin, 1991.

Carter, Henry Hare, ed. *The Portuguese Book of Joseph of Arimathea*. Chapel Hill: U of North Carolina, 1967.

Cawley, A. C., ed. *Pearl, Sir Gawain and the Green Knight*. Everyman's Library. 1962. New York: Dutton, 1972.

Cervantes Saavedra, Miguel de. *Don Quixote*. Trans. John Ormsby. Chicago: Encyclopaedia Britannica, 1952.

Chambers, E[dmund] K. *Arthur of Britain: The Story of King Arthur in History and Legend*. London: Sidgewick, 1927.

Cherryh, C. J. *Port Eternity*. New York: DAW, 1982.

Chrétien de Troyes. *Le Chevalier de la Charrete*. Vol. 3 of *Les romans de Chrétien de Troyes*. Ed. Mario Roques. Classiques Français du Moyen Age 86. Paris: Champion, 1958.

———. *Cligés*. Ed. Alexandre Micha. Paris: Champion, 1975.

———. *Erec et Enide*. Ed. Mario Roques. Paris: Champion, 1973.

———. *Lancelot (Le Chevalier de la Charrete)*. Ed. Mario Roques. Paris: Champion, 1975.

———. *Perceval (Le conte du Graal)*. Ed. Felix Lecoy. Paris: Champion, 1975.

———. *Yvain*. Trans. Burton Raffel. New Haven: Yale UP, 1987.

———. *Yvain (Le chevalier au lion)*. Ed. Mario Roques. Paris: Champion, 1970.

Christian, Catherine. *The Pendragon*. New York: Knopf, 1979. (Published in England as *The Sword and the Flame: Variations on a Theme of Sir Thomas Malory*. London: Macmillan, 1978.)

Cline, Ruth Harwood, trans. *Perceval: Or, The Story of the Grail*. Athens: U of Georgia P, 1985.

Comfort, W. W., trans. *Arthurian Romances, Chrétien de Troyes*. New York: Dutton, 1975.

Cooper, Susan. *The Dark Is Rising*. New York: Atheneum, 1973.

———. *Silver on the Tree*. New York: Atheneum, 1977.

Dante Alighieri. *Dantis Alighieri Epistolae: The Letters of Dante*. 2nd ed. Oxford: Clarendon–Oxford UP, 1966.

———. *Inferno*. Trans. Allan Gilbert. Durham: Duke UP, 1969.

Davis, Norman, ed. *Sir Gawain and the Green Knight*. 2nd ed. Oxford: Clarendon–Oxford UP, 1969.

Deal, Babs. *The Grail*. New York: McKay, 1963.

de Angelo, Michael. *Cyr Myrddin: The Coming of Age of Merlin*. Everett: Gododdin, 1979.

Dickinson, Peter. *The Weathermonger*. London: Gollancz, 1968.

Drake, David. *The Dragon Lord*. New York: Berkley-Putnam, 1979.

Dryden, John. *Of Dramatic Poesy and Other Critical Essays*. Ed. George Watson. Vol. 1. London: Dent, 1962. 2 vols.

Duggan, Alfred. *Conscience of the King*. London: Faber, 1951.

Eliot, T. S. "Tradition and the Individual Talent." *Selected Essays*. London: Faber, 1934. 13–22.

———. *The Waste Land. Poems: 1909–1925*. London: Faber, 1925. 65–85.

Erskine, John. *Galahad: Enough of His Life to Explain His Reputation*. Indianapolis: Grosset, 1926.

———. *Tristan and Isolde: Restoring Palomede*. Indianapolis: Bobbs, 1932.

Facsimile of British Museum MS. Harley 2253. Introd. N. R. Ker. EETS os 255. London: Oxford UP, 1965.

Fedrick, Alan S., trans. *The Romance of Tristan by Béroul and the Tale of Tristan's Madness*. Ed. Ernest Muret. London: Penguin, 1970.

Ferrante, Joan, and Robert Hanning, trans. *The Lais of Marie de France*. New York: Dutton, 1978.

Ford, Patrick K., ed. and trans. *The Mabinogi and Other Medieval Welsh Tales*. Los Angeles: U of California P, 1977.

Frappier, Jean, trans. *Chrétien de Troyes: Le Chevalier de la Charrete: Roman traduit de l'ancien français*. Paris: Champion, 1962.

Fry, Christopher. *Thor, with Angels*. London: Oxford UP, 1948.

Gantz, Jeffrey, ed. and trans. *Early Irish Myths and Sagas*. Harmondsworth, Eng.: Penguin, 1981.

———, ed. and trans. The Mabinogion: *Translated with an Introduction by Jeffrey Gantz*. Harmondsworth, Eng.: Penguin, 1976.

Garbáty, Thomas J. *Medieval English Literature*. Lexington: Heath, 1984.

Gardner, John, ed. and trans. *The Complete Works of the Gawain-Poet in a Modern English Version with a Critical Introduction*. Chicago: U of Chicago P, 1965.

Garner, Alan. *The Moon of Gomrath*. London: Collins, 1963.

———. *The Weirdstone of Brisingamen: A Tale of Alderley*. Rev. ed. Harmondsworth, Eng.: Penguin, 1963; New York: Ballantine, 1981.

Geoffrey of Monmouth. *Historia*. Ed. Jacob Hammer. Cambridge: Mediaeval Academy, 1951.

———. *History of the Kings of Britain*. Trans. Lewis Thorpe. Baltimore: Penguin, 1966.

———. *Vita Merlini*. Ed. and trans. J. J. Parry. Urbana: U of Illinois P, 1925.

Gilbert, Henry. *King Arthur's Knights*. Illus. Walter Crane. 1911. London: Bracken, 1985.

Gildas. *De excidio et conquestu Britanniae*. Trans. Michael Winterbottom. Totowa: Rowan, 1978.

Gloag, John. *Artorius Rex*. London: Cassell, 1977.

Godwin, Parke. *Beloved Exile*. New York: Bantam, 1984.

———. *Firelord*. Garden City: Doubleday, 1980.

———. *The Last Rainbow*. New York: Bantam, 1985.

Good, Thomas. "The End of Merlin." *Selected Poems*. Ed. Michael Hamburger. London: St. George's, 1973. 65.

Goodrich, Peter, ed. *The Romance of Merlin: An Anthology*. New York: Garland, 1990.

Gottfried von Strassburg. *Tristan*. Trans. A. T. Hatto. Harmondsworth, Eng.: Penguin, 1974.

———. *Tristan und Isold*. Ed. Friedrich Ranke. 15th ed. N.p.: Weidmann, 1978.

Green, Roger Lancelyn. *King Arthur and His Knights of the Round Table*. London: Puffin, 1953.

Greenlaw, Edwin A., Charles Grosvener Osgood, et al., eds. *The Works of Edmund Spenser, a Variorum Edition: Faire Queene*. Book 1. F. M. Padelford, special ed. Baltimore: Johns Hopkins UP, 1957.

Guest, Lady Charlotte, trans. *The Mabinogion*. 1877. Ruthin: Spread Eagle, 1981.

Guillaume de Lorris and Jean de Meun. *Roman de la rose*. Trans. Charles Dahlberg. Princeton: Princeton UP, 1971.

Hall, Louis B., trans. *The Knightly Tales of Sir Gawain*. Chicago: Nelson, 1976.

Hastings, Selina. *Sir Gawain and the Green Knight*. Illus. Juan Wijngaard. New York: Lothrop, 1981.

Hill, Geoffrey. "Merlin." *Collected Poems*. Harmondsworth, Eng.: Penguin, 1985. 19.

Jackson, Kenneth Hurlstone. *Celtic Miscellany. Translations from the Celtic Literatures*. Rev. ed. Harmondsworth, Eng.: Penguin, 1971.

Jones, Gwyn, and Thomas Jones, ed. and trans. *The Mabinogion*. Everyman's Library. London: Dent, 1949. Rev. ed. New York: Dutton, 1974.

Jonin, Pierre, trans. *Le roman de Tristan*. Paris: Champion, 1974.

Karr, Phyllis Ann. *The Idylls of the Queen*. New York: Ace, 1982.

Katz, Welwyn Wilton. *The Third Magic*. Vancouver: Douglas, 1988.

Kibler, William W., ed. and trans. *Lancelot: Or, The Knight of the Cart*. New York: Garland, 1981; New York: Penguin, 1991.

Krishna, Valerie, ed. *The* Alliterative Morte Arthure. Pref. Rossell Hope Robbins. New York: Franklin, 1976.

———, trans. *The* Alliterative Morte Arthure: *A New Verse Translation*. Lanham: UP of America, 1983.

———, trans. "The *Alliterative Morte Arthure*: A Verse Translation, with Introduction and Critical Notes." *DA* 23 (1972–73): 1143A. New York U.

Kuncewicz, Maria. *Tristan*. New York: Braziller, 1974.

Lanier, Sidney. *The Boy's King Arthur*. 1880. New York: Macmillan, 1989.

Laubenthal, Sanders Ann. *Excalibur*. New York: Belmary, 1973.

Layamon. *Brut: Arthurian Chronicles*. Trans. Eugene Mason. 1912. New York: Dutton, 1970.

Le Cain, Errol. *King Arthur's Sword*. London: Faber, 1968.

Lerner, Alan Jay, and Friedrich Loewe. *Camelot*. New York: Random, 1961.

Lewis, C. S. *That Hideous Strength: A Modern Fairy-Tale for Grown-ups*. London: Lane, 1945.

Lively, Penelope. *The Whispering Knights*. London: Heinemann, 1971.

Lodge, David. *Small World*. London: Secker, 1984.

Loomis, Roger Sherman, and Laura Hibbard Loomis, eds. *Medieval Romances*. Modern Library 133. New York: Random, 1957.

Loomis, Roger Sherman, and Rudolph Willard, eds. *Medieval English Verse and Prose in Modernized Versions*. New York: Appleton, 1948.

Magne, Augusto, ed. *Demanda do Santo Graal*. 3 vols. Rio de Janeiro: Ministry of Education, National Inst. of Publication, 1944.

Malamud, Bernard. *The Natural*. New York: Farrar, 1952.

Malory, Sir Thomas. *Le Morte d'Arthur*. Ed. Janet Cowen. Vol. 2. Baltimore: Penguin, 1969. 2 vols.

———. *Le Morte d'Arthur*. Ed. H. Oskar Sommer. London: Nult, 1889.

———. Le Morte d'Arthur *Printed by William Caxton, 1485*. Introd. Paul Needham. London: Scolar, 1976.

————. *Tales of King Arthur*. Ed. Michael Senior. New York: Schocken, 1980.

Marie de France. *Les lais*. Ed. Jeanne Lods and Mario Roques. Paris: Champion, 1959.

Marshall, Edison. *The Pagan King*. Garden City: Doubleday, 1959.

Mary, Andre, trans. *Erec et Enide, Le chevalier du lion, traduit de Chrétien de Troyes*. Paris: Bowin, n.d.

Mason, Eugene, ed. and trans. *Arthurian Chronicles (Represented by Wace and Layamon)*. New York: Dutton, 1962.

Matarasso, P. M., trans. *The Quest of the Holy Grail*. Harmondsworth, Eng.: Penguin, 1969.

Matthews, John. *Merlin in Calydon*. Frome, Somerset, Eng: Bran's, 1981.

Mayne, William. *Earthfasts*. London: Hamilton, 1966.

McConeghy, Patrick M., trans. *Iwein*. Ed. Patrick M. McConeghy and James J. Wilhelm. New York: Garland, 1984.

Michaels, Philip. *Grail*. New York: Avon, 1982.

Monaco, Richard. *The Final Quest*. New York: Putnam, 1980.

————. *The Grail War*. New York: Pocket, 1979; London: Sphere, 1981.

————. *Parsival; Or, A Knight's Tale*. New York: Macmillan, 1977.

Monty Python and the Holy Grail. New York: Methuen, 1977. (Screenplay and production materials for the film.)

Morris, William. *The Defence of Guenevere and Other Poems*. 1858. London: Lane, 1904.

Muir, Edwin. "Merlin." *Collected Poems*. London: Faber, 1984. 73–74.

[Nennius?] *Historia Brittonum*. Trans. Edmond Faral. Paris: Champion, 1929.

Newman, Sharan. *The Chessboard Queen*. New York: St. Martin's, 1984.

————. *Guinevere*. New York: St. Martin's, 1981.

————. *Guinevere Evermore*. New York: St. Martin's, 1985.

Nietzsche, Friedrich. The Case of Wagner *and* Nietzsche Contra Wagner. Vol. 8 of *Complete Works of Friedrich Nietzsche*. Ed. Oscar Levy. Edinburgh: Foulis, 1911. 18 vols.

Nitze, William Albert, and T. A. Jenkins, eds. *Perlesvaus: The High History of the Holy Grail*. Vol. 1. Chicago: U of Chicago P, 1932. 2 vols. 1932–37.

Norman, Diana. *King of the Last Days*. London: Hodder, 1981.

Norton, Andre. *Merlin's Mirror*. New York: DAW, 1975.

Nye, Robert. *Merlin*. New York: Putnam, 1979.

O'Meara, Walter. *The Duke of War*. New York: Harcourt, 1966.

Ovid. *The Love Poems of Ovid:* Amores, The Art of Love, The Cures for Love. New York: NAL, 1964.

————. *Metamorphoses*. Trans. Frank Justice Miller. 2nd ed., rev. by G. P. Goold. Cambridge: Harvard UP, 1984.

Owen, Lewis J., and Nancy H. Owen, eds. *Middle English Poetry: An Anthology.* Indianapolis: Bobbs, 1971.

Paris, Gaston, and J. Ulrich, eds. *Suite de Merlin.* 2 vols. Paris, Didot, 1886.

Pensado Tomé, José Luis, ed. *Fragmento de un "Livro de Tristan" galaïco-portuges.* Santiago de Compostela: Consejo Superior de Investigaciones Cientificas, Institute P. Sarmiento de Estudios Gallegos, 1962.

Percy, Walker. *Lancelot.* New York: Farrar, 1978.

Pollard, Alfred W. *The Romance of King Arthur and His Knights of the Round Table.* 1917. New York: Macmillan, 1979.

Powys, John Cowper. *A Glastonbury Romance.* 1932. Woodstock: Overlook, 1987.

Price, Anthony. *Our Man in Camelot.* London: Gollancz, 1975.

Pyle, Howard. *The Story of King Arthur and His Knights.* 1903. New York: Dover, 1965.

Quiller-Couch, Arthur, and Daphne du Maurier. *Castle Dor.* London: Dent, 1961.

Raffel, Burton, trans. *Sir Gawain and the Green Knight.* New York: Mentor, 1970.

Riordan, James. *Tales of King Arthur.* Illus. Victor Ambrus. London: Hamlyn, 1982.

Robinson, Edwin Arlington. "Merlin." *Collected Poems of Edwin Arlington Robinson.* New York: Macmillan, 1929. 235–314.

———. *Tristram.* New York: Macmillan, 1927.

Rohmer, Eric. *Perceval le Gallois. L'avant-scène du cinéma* 221: 1 Feb. 1979. (Screenplay)

Rosenberg, James L., trans. *Sir Gawain and the Green Knight.* Ed. James R. Kreuzer. New York: Holt, 1959.

Rychner, J. Les lais *de Marie de France.* Paris: Champion, 1969.

Sanders, C., and C. E. Ward, eds. *Morte d'Arthur.* New York: Irvington, 1979.

Sands, Donald B. *Middle English Verse Romances.* New York: Holt, 1966; Exeter: U of Exeter P, 1986.

Schach, Paul, trans. *Saga of Tristram and Isond.* Lincoln: U of Nebraska P, 1973.

Seare, Nicholas. *Rude Tales and Glorious: A Retelling of the Arthurian Tales.* New York: Clarkson Potter, 1983.

Sommer, H. Oskar, ed. *Le livre d'Artus.* Vol. 7 of *The Vulgate Version of the Arthurian Romances.* 8 vols. Washington: Carnegie Institution, 1908–16.

Spisak, James W., and William Matthews. *Caxton's Malory: A New Edition of Sir Thomas Malory's* Le Mort d'Arthur, *Based on the Pierpont Morgan Copy of William Caxton's Edition of 1485.* 2 vols. Berkeley: U of California P, 1983.

Stang, Joanne. *Shadows on the Sceptered Isle.* New York: Crown, 1980.

Steinbeck, John. *The Acts of King Arthur and His Noble Knights, from the Winchester MSS of Thomas Malory and Other Sources.* Ed. Chase Horton. New York: Farrar, 1976.

———. *Tortilla Flat.* New York: Grosset, 1935.

Stewart, Mary. *The Crystal Cave.* New York: Morrow, 1970.

———. *The Hollow Hills.* New York: Morrow, 1970.

———. *The Last Enchantment.* New York: Morrow, 1979.

———. *The Wicked Day.* New York: Morrow, 1983.

St. John, Nicole. *Guinever's Gift.* New York: Random, 1977.

Stone, Brian, trans. *Sir Gawain and the Green Knight.* 1959. Rev. ed. Baltimore: Penguin, 1971.

Sutcliff, Rosemary. *The Lantern Bearers.* London: Oxford UP, 1959.

———. *Sword at Sunset.* New York: Coward, 1963.

———. *Tristan and Iseult.* London: Bodley, 1971.

Swinburne, Algernon Charles. *Complete Works.* Ed. E. W. Gosse and T. J. Wise. Bonchurch Edition, 20 vols. London: Heinemann, 1925–27.

Tarkington, Booth. *Penrod.* New York: Doubleday, 1914.

Tennyson, Alfred. *Idylls of the King.* Ed. J. M. Gray. New Haven: Yale UP, 1983.

———. *Poems.* London: Moon, 1857.

———. *The Poems of Tennyson.* Ed. Christopher Ricks. 1969. New York: Norton, 1972.

Terry, Patricia. *Lays of Courtly Love.* Garden City: Anchor-Doubleday, 1963.

Thomas, Gwyn, and Kevin Crossley-Holland. *Tales from the* Mabinogion. Illus. Margaret Jones. New York: Gollancz, 1985.

The Thornton Manuscript (Lincoln Cathedral Library MS 91). Introd. D. S. Brewer and A. E. B. Owen. 2nd ed. London: Scolar, 1978.

Thorpe, Benjamin, ed. and trans. *The Anglo-Saxon Chronicle.* London: Longman, 1861.

Thorpe, Lewis. Introduction. *The History of the Kings of Britain, by Geoffrey of Monmouth.* Harmondsworth, Eng.: Penguin, 1966. 9–47.

Tolkien, J. R. R., and E. V. Gordon, eds. *Sir Gawain and the Green Knight.* 2nd ed. Rev. Norman Davis. New York: Oxford UP, 1968.

Treece, Henry. *The Eagles Have Flown.* London: Allen, 1954.

Turton, Godfrey. *The Emperor Arthur.* Garden City: Doubleday, 1967.

Twain, Mark [Samuel L. Clemens]. *A Connecticut Yankee in King Arthur's Court.* New York: Webster, 1889.

Vinaver, Eugène, ed. *King Arthur and His Knights: Selected Tales by Sir Thomas Malory.* Oxford: Oxford UP, 1975.

———, ed. *Malory: Works.* 2nd ed. London: Oxford UP, 1977.

———, ed. *The Works of Sir Thomas Malory.* 1971. 3 vols. Rev. by P. J. C. Field. London: Oxford UP, 1990.

Wace. *Roman de Brut: Arthurian Chronicles*. Trans. Eugene Mason. 1912. New York: Dutton, 1970.

Wagner, Richard. *Wagner, Richard's Prose Works*. Trans. William Ashton Ellis. 6 vols. 1892. New York: Bronde, 1966.

———. *The Wagner Operas*. New York: Crown, 1938.

White, T. H. *The Book of Merlyn*. Prologue by Sylvia Townsend Warner. Austin: U of Texas P, 1977.

———. *The Once and Future King*. New York: Putnam's, 1958.

———. *The Sword in the Stone*. London: Collins, 1938.

Wilbur, Richard. "Merlin Enthralled." *The Poems of Richard Wilbur*. New York: Harcourt, 1963. 77–78.

Wilhelm, James J., ed. *The Romance of Arthur II*. New York: Garland, 1986.

———. *The Romance of Arthur III: Works from Russia to Spain, Norway to Italy*. New York: Garland, 1988.

Wilhelm, James J., and Laila Zamuelis Gross, eds. *The Romance of Arthur*. New York: Garland, 1984.

Williams, Charles. *Arthurian Torso: Containing the Posthumous Fragment of* The Figure of Arthur. Ed. C. S. Lewis. London: Oxford UP, 1969.

———. *The Region of the Summer Stars*. London: Oxford UP, 1969.

———. *Taliesin through Logres*. London: Oxford UP, 1969.

———. *War in Heaven*. 1930. Grand Rapids: Eerdman's, 1949.

The Winchester Malory. Introd. N. R. Ker. EETS supplementary series 4. London: Oxford UP, 1976.

Wind, Bartina H., ed. *Les fragments du roman de Tristan: Poème du XII siècle*. Edités avec commentaire. Thomas of Britain. Paris: Minard, 1960.

Winder, Blanche. *Stories of King Arthur*. London: Ward, n.d.

Wolfram von Eschenbach. *Parzival*. Trans. A. T. Hatto. Harmondsworth, Eng.: Penguin, 1980.

———. *Parzival*. Ed. Albert Leitzmann and Wilhelm Deinert. Altdeutsche Textbibliothek 12–14. Tübingen: Niemeyer, 1965.

———. *Parzival*. Trans. Helen M. Mustard and Charles E. Passage. New York: Vintage-Random, 1961.

Wooley, Persia. *Child of the Northern Spring*. New York: Poseidon, 1987.

———. *Queen of the Summer Stars*. New York: Poseidon, 1990.

Yolen, Jane. *Merlin's Booke*. New York: Ace, 1986.

Secondary Sources

Abrams, M. H., et al., eds. *Norton Anthology of English Literature*. 2 vols. New York: Norton, 1986.

———. *Norton Anthology of English Literature: Major Authors*. 5th ed. New York: Norton, 1987.

Ackerman, Robert W. *An Index of the Arthurian Names in Middle English*. Stanford: Stanford UP, 1952.

Adams, Henry. *Mont St. Michel and Chartres*. 1905. Princeton: Princeton UP, 1981.

Adams, Robert, ed. *A Tristan Bibliography*. Los Angeles: U of Southern California P, 1943.

Agena, Kathleen. "Return to Enchantment." *New York Times Magazine* 27 Nov. 1983: 66–80.

Alcock, Leslie. *Arthur's Britain: History and Archaeology A.D. 367–634*. 1971. Harmondsworth, Eng.: Penguin, 1973.

———. "Cadbury-Camelot: A Fifteen-Year Perspective." *Proceedings of the British Academy* 68 (1982): 355–88.

———. *Was This Camelot?* New York: Stein, 1972.

Altick, Richard D. *Paintings from Books: Art and Literature in Britain, 1760–1900*. Columbus: Ohio UP, 1985.

Anderson, William. *Castles of Europe from Charlemagne to the Renaissance*. 1970. London: Feindale, 1980.

Ashe, Geoffrey. *All about King Arthur*. London: Carousel, 1969.

———. *Camelot and the Vision of Albion*. London: Heinemann, 1971.

———. "A Certain Very Ancient Book." *Speculum* 56 (1981): 301–23.

———. *The Discovery of King Arthur*. Garden City: Anchor-Doubleday, 1985.

———. *King Arthur's Avalon: The Story of Glastonbury*. London: Collins, 1957.

———, ed. *The Quest for Arthur's Britain*. London: Praeger, 1968.

Auerbach, Erich. *Mimesis: The Representation of Reality in Western Literature*. Trans. W. R. Trask. 1946. Princeton: Princeton UP, 1953.

Barber, Richard W. *Arthur of Albion: An Introduction to the Arthurian Literature and Legends of England*. New York: Barnes, 1961.

———. *The Arthurian Legends*. Totowa: Littlefield, Adams, 1979.

———. *The Figure of Arthur*. London: Longman, 1972.

———. *King Arthur: Hero and Legend*. New York: St. Martin's, 1986.

———. *King Arthur in Legend and History*. London: Cardinal, 1973.

———. *The Knight and Chivalry*. Ipswich: Boydell, 1970.

———. *The Reign of Chivalry*. New York: St. Martin's, 1980.

Baugh, Albert C. "The Authorship of the Middle English Romances." *Modern Humanities Research Association, Annual Bulletin* 22 (1950): 13–28.

————, ed. *A Literary History of England*. 2nd ed. New York: Appleton, 1967.

————. "The Middle English Romance: Some Questions of Creation, Presentation, and Preservation." *Speculum* 42 (1967): 1–31.

Beatie, Bruce A. "Arthurian Films and Arthurian Texts: Problems of Reception and Comprehension." *Arthurian Interpretations* 2.2 (1988): 65–78.

Bennett, J. A. W., ed. *Essays on Malory*. Oxford: Clarendon–Oxford UP, 1963.

Benson, Larry D. *Art and Tradition in* Sir Gawain and the Green Knight. New Brunswick: Rutgers UP, 1965.

————. *Malory's* Morte Darthur. Cambridge: Harvard UP, 1976.

Benson, Larry D., and John Leyerle, eds. *Chivalric Literature: Essays on Relations between Literature and Life in the Later Middle Ages*. Kalamazoo: Medieval Inst., 1980.

Bertau, Karl. *Deutsche Literatur im europaïeschen Mittelalter*. Munich: Beck, 1972.

Bishop, Morris. *A Survey of French Literature*. Vol. 1. San Diego: Harcourt, 1965. 2 vols.

Blair, Peter H. *Roman Britain and Early England, 55 B.C. to A.D. 871*. New York: Norton, 1966.

Blake, N. F. *Caxton and His World*. London: Deutsch, 1969.

————. *Caxton: England's First Publisher*. New York: Barnes, 1976.

Blanch, Robert J., ed. Sir Gawain *and* Pearl: *Critical Essays*. Bloomington: Indiana UP, 1966.

Boardman, Phillip C. "Arthur Redivivus: A Reader's Guide to Recent Arthurian Fiction." *Halcyon* 2 (1980): 41–56.

————. "Recent Arthurian Literature: A Contribution towards a Bibliography." *Chronica* 31 (1982): 15–24.

Boase, Roger. *The Origin and Meaning of Courtly Love: A Critical Study of European Scholarship*. Totowa: Rowan, 1977.

Bollard, J. K. "Arthur in the Early Welsh Tradition." Wilhelm and Gross 13–25.

Bordman, Gerald. *Motif-Index of the English Metrical Romances*. Helsinki: FF Communications, 1972.

Briggs, K. M. *The Fairies in Tradition and Literature*. London: Routledge, 1967.

Bromwich, Rachel, ed. and trans. "Celtic Elements in Arthurian Romance: A General Survey." *The Legend of Arthur in the Middle Ages. Studies Presented to A. H. Diverres*. Ed. P. B. Grout et al. Cambridge: Brewer, 1983. 41–55.

Brooke, Christopher. *The Structure of Medieval Society*. New York: McGraw, 1971.

Brown, Paul A. "The Arthurian Legends: Supplement to Northrup and Parry's Annotated Bibliography (with Further Supplement by John J. Parry)." *JEGP* 49 (1950): 208–16.

Bruce, James Douglas. *The Evolution of Arthurian Romance from the Beginnings down to the Year 1300.* 2 vols. 1928. Gloucester: Smith, 1958.

Bumke, Joachim. *Wolfram von Eschenbach.* 1964. Stuttgart: Metzler, 1976.

Burgess, Glyn S. *Marie de France: An Analytical Bibliography.* London: Grant, 1977.

Campbell, Joseph. *The Hero with a Thousand Faces.* 2nd ed. Princeton: Princeton UP, 1968.

Cavendish, Richard. *King Arthur and the Grail: The Arthurian Legends and Their Meaning.* New York: Taplinger, 1985.

Chadwick, Nora. *The Celts.* Gretna: Pelican, 1982.

Chambers, E[dmund] K. *English Literature at the Close of the Middle Ages.* Oxford History of English Literature. Vol. 2, Pt. 2. Oxford: Clarendon–Oxford UP, 1946.

Cheetham, Samuel. "The Arthurian Legends in Tennyson." *Contemporary Review* 7 (1868): 497–514.

Christ, Winfried. *Rhetorik und Roman: Untersuchungen zu Gottfrieds von Strassburg "Tristan und Isold."* Meisenheim am Glan: Hain, 1977.

Churchill, Winston. *A History of the English-Speaking Peoples.* 4 vols. New York: Dodd, 1983.

Clayton, Peter, ed. *A Companion to Roman Britain.* 1980. New York: Dorset, 1985.

Collingwood, R. G., and J. N. L. Myres. *Roman Britain and the English Settlements.* London: Oxford UP, 1937.

Cosman, Madeline Pelner. *The Education of the Hero in Arthurian Romance.* Chapel Hill: U of North Carolina P, 1966.

———. *Fabulous Feasts: Medieval Cookery and Ceremony.* New York: Braziller, 1976.

Coss, P. R. "Aspects of Cultural Diffusion in Medieval England: The Early Romances, Local Society and Robin Hood." *Past and Present* 108 (1985): 35–79.

Crane, Susan. *Insular Romance.* Berkeley: U of California P, 1986.

Cunliffe, Barry. *The Celtic World.* London: Bodley, 1979.

Curry, Walter Clyde. *The Middle English Ideal of Personal Beauty.* Baltimore: Johns Hopkins UP, 1916.

Curschmann, Michael. "Das Abenteuer des Erzählens: Über den Erzähler in Wolframs 'Parzival.'" *Deutsche Vierteljahrsschrift für Literaturwissenschaft und Geistesgeschichte* 49 (1975): 627–67.

Danker, Frederick E. "Teaching Medieval Literature: Texts, Recordings, and Techniques." *College English* 32 (1970): 340–57.

Davis, R. H. C. *King Stephen: 1135–1154.* Berkeley: U of California P, 1967.

de Rougemont, Denis. *Love in the Western World.* Trans. Montgomery Belgion. New York: Pantheon, 1956.

Derrida, Jacques. *Disseminator*. Trans. Barbara Johnson. Chicago: U of Chicago P, 1983.

———. *The Post Card: From Socrates to Freud and Beyond*. Trans. Alan Bass. Chicago: U of Chicago P, 1987.

Deyermond, A. D. *The Middle Ages*. London: Benn, 1971.

Dillon, Myles, and Nora K. Chadwick. *The Celtic Realms*. London: Weidenfeld, 1967.

Dumézil, Georges. *Mythe et épopée*. Paris: Gallimard, 1968.

Eggers, J. Phillip. *King Arthur's Laureate: A Study of Tennyson's* Idylls of the King. New York: New York UP, 1971.

Everett, Dorothy. *Essays on Middle English Literature*. Ed. P. Kean. Oxford: Clarendon–Oxford UP, 1955.

Faral, Edmond. *La légende arthurienne: Etudes et documents*. Paris: Champion, 1929.

Ferrante, Joan. *The Conflict of Love and Honor: The Medieval Tristan Legend in France, Germany, and Italy*. Paris: Mouton, 1973.

Field, P. J. C. "Malory and *The Wedding of Sir Gawain and Dame Ragnell*." *Archiv* 219 (1982): 374–81.

Fisher, John H., ed. *The Medieval Literature of Western Europe: A Review of Research Mainly 1930–1960*. New York: New York UP, 1966.

Fletcher, Robert Huntington. *The Arthurian Material in the Chronicles, Especially Those of Great Britain and France*. Franklin Bibliographical Series 10. New York: Franklin, 1958.

Fox, Denton J. *Twentieth Century Interpretations of* Sir Gawain and the Green Knight: *A Collection of Critical Essays*. Englewood Cliffs: Prentice, 1968.

Fox, John. *A Literary History of France*. Vol. 1 of *The Middle Ages*. New York: Harper, 1974.

Frappier, Jean. *Amour courtois et table ronde*. Geneva: Droz, 1973.

———. *Chrétien de Troyes: The Man and His Work*. Trans. Raymond Cormier. Athens: Ohio UP, 1982.

———. *Le roman breton. Introduction: Des origines à Chrétien de Troyes*. Paris: Centre de Documentation, 1951.

Frappier, Jean, and Reinhold R. Grimm, eds. *Le roman jusqu'à la fin du xiiie siècle*. Heidelberg: Winter, 1978–84.

Fries, Maureen. "Malory's Tristram as Counter-Hero to the *Morte Darthur*." *Neuphilologische Miteeilungen* 76 (1975): 605–13.

———. "The Rationalization of the Arthurian 'Matter' in T. H. White and Mary Stewart." *PQ* 56 (1977): 258–65.

———. "White, T(erence) H(anbury)." Lacy et al., *Arthurian Encyclopedia*. 626–27.

Frye, Northrop. *The Anatomy of Criticism: Four Essays*. Princeton: Princeton UP, 1971.

Ganim, John. *Style and Consciousness in Middle English Narrative*. Princeton: Princeton UP, 1983.

Rev. of *Gareth and Lynette*. *Guardian* 30 Oct. 1872: 1369–70.

Rev. of *Gareth and Lynette*. *Spectator* 26 Oct. 1872: 1363–65.

Garner, Alan, et al. *Children's Literature in Education*. New York: APS, 1970–.

Girouard, Mark. *The Return to Camelot: Chivalry and the English Gentleman*. New Haven: Yale UP, 1981.

Graves, Robert. *The White Goddess*. Enl. ed. New York: Noonday, 1966.

Green, Dennis H. *Irony in the Medieval Romance*. Cambridge: Cambridge UP, 1979.

Grente, Georges, et al., eds. *Dictionnaire des lettres françaises: Le Moyen Age*. Paris: Fayard, 1971.

Grisward, Joel. *L'archéologie de l'épopée mediévale*. Paris: Payot, 1981.

Groos, Arthur. "Time Reference and the Liturgical Calendar in Wolfram von Eschenbach's *Parzival*." *Deutsche Vierteljahrsschrift für Literaturwissenschaft und Geistesgeschichte* 49 (1975): 43–65.

Guddat-Figge, Gisela. *Catalogue of Manuscripts Containing Middle English Romances*. Munich: Fink, 1976.

Gutman, Robert W. *Richard Wagner: The Man, His Mind, and His Music*. New York: Harcourt, 1968.

Hanning, Robert. *The Individual in Twelfth Century Romance*. New Haven: Yale UP, 1977.

———. *The Vision of History in Early Britain: From Gildas to Geoffrey of Monmouth*. New York: Columbia UP, 1966.

Harty, Kevin J. *Cinema Arthuriana: Essays on Arthurian Film*. New York: Garland, 1991.

———. "Cinema Arthuriana: Translations of the Arthurian Legend to the Screen." *Arthurian Interpretations* 2.1 (1987): 95–113.

Harvey, Paul, ed. *The Oxford Companion to English Literature*. 4th ed. Oxford: Oxford UP, 1967.

Haycock, Marged. "'Preiddeu Annwn' and the Figure of Taliesin." *Studia Celtica* 18–19 (1983–84): 52–78.

Heer, Friedrich. *The Medieval World: Europe 1100–1350*. Trans. Janet Sondheimer. New York: NAL, 1962.

Hellinga, Lotte. "The Malory Manuscript and Caxton." Takamiya and Brewer 127–41.

Hellinga, Lotte, and Hilton Kelliher. "The Malory Manuscript." *British Library Journal* 3 (1977): 91–113.

Herman, Harold J. "The Women in Mary Stewart's Merlin Trilogy." *Arthurian Interpretations* 15.2 (Spring 1984): 101–14.

Hibbert, Christopher. *The Search for King Arthur*. New York: Harper, 1969.

Hieatt, Constance B., and Sharon Butler. *Pleyn Delit: Medieval Cookery for Modern Cooks.* Toronto: U of Toronto P, 1976.

Holbrook, S. E. "Nymue, the Chief Lady of the Lake, in Malory's *Le Morte Darthur.*" *Speculum* 53 (1978): 761–77.

Holmes, Urban Tigner. *Chrétien de Troyes.* New York: Twayne, 1970.

Rev. of *The Holy Grail and Other Poems.* By Tennyson. *Chambers's Journal* 47 (1870): 137–40.

Rev. of *The Holy Grail and Other Poems.* By Tennyson. *Guardian* 22 Dec. 1869: 1439.

Houghton, Walter Edwards, and G. Robert Strange, eds. *Victorian Poetry and Poetics.* Boston: Houghton, 1959.

Howard, Donald R., and Christian Zacher, eds. *Critical Studies of Sir Gawain and the Green Knight.* Notre Dame: U of Notre Dame P, 1969.

Huganir, Gail, ed. *King Arthur Special Issue. British Heritage* 7.4 (June–July 1986): 12–73.

Hughes, Linda K. "Tennyson's Urban Arthurians." Lagorio and Day 2: 39–61.

Hughes, Linda K., and Michael Lund. "Studying Victorian Serials." *Literary Research* 11 (1986): 235–52.

———. *The Victorian Serial.* Charlottesville: UP of Virginia, 1991.

Huizínga, Johan. *Homo Ludens: A Study of the Play Element in Culture.* Boston: Beacon, 1955.

Hume, Kathryn. "Romance: A Perdurable Pattern." *College English* 36 (1974): 129–46.

Hunt, William Holman. *Pre-Raphaelitism and the Pre-Raphaelite Brotherhood.* 2 vols. London: Macmillan, 1905.

Rev. of *Idylls of the King. Athenaeum* 16 July 1859: 73–76.

Rev. of *Idylls of the King. Eclectic Review* ns 2 (July–Dec. 1859): 287–94.

Ihle, Sandra Ness. *Malory's Grail Quest: Invention and Adaptation in Medieval Prose Romance.* Madison: U of Wisconsin P, 1983.

Jackson, Kenneth Hurlstone. "Arthur in Early Welsh Verse." Loomis, *Arthurian Literature* 1–11.

Jackson, W. T. H. *The Anatomy of Love: The Tristan of Gottfried von Strassburg.* New York: Columbia UP, 1971.

———. *Medieval Literature: A History and a Guide.* New York: Collier, 1966.

Jenkins, Elizabeth. *The Mystery of King Arthur.* New York: Coward, 1975.

Jones, Gwyn. *Kings, Beasts and Heroes.* Oxford: Oxford UP, 1972.

Karr, Phyllis A. *The King Arthur Companion.* Privately printed, 1983.

Kato, Tomomi, ed. *A Concordance to the Works of Sir Thomas Malory.* Tokyo: U of Tokyo P, 1974.

Keen, Maurice. *Chivalry.* New Haven: Yale UP, 1984.

Kelliher, Hilton. "The Early History of the Malory Manuscript." Takamiya and Brewer 143–58.

Kelly, Douglas, ed. *Chrétien de Troyes: An Analytic Bibliography*. London: Grant, 1976.

Kennedy, Beverly. *Knighthood in Malory's* Morte Darthur. Dover: Brewer, 1985.

Kennedy, Harlan. "The World of King Arthur according to John Boorman." *American Film* 6 (March 1981): 30–37.

Ker, W. P. *Epic and Romance*. 1908. New York: Dover, 1957.

Kermode, Frank, John Hollander, et al., eds. *The Oxford Anthology of English Literature*. 2 vols. New York: Oxford UP, 1973.

Kiernan, Victor. "Tennyson, King Arthur, and Imperialism." *Culture, Ideology and Politics: Essays for Eric Hobsbawm*. Ed. Raphael Samuel and Gareth Stedman Jones. London: Routledge, 1982. 126–48.

"King Arthur and His Round Table." *Blackwood's Edinburgh Magazine* 88 (1860): 311–37.

Klein, Janice. "The Life and Times of King Arthur." *Expedition* 29 (1987): 48–55.

Knight, Stephen. *Arthurian Literature and Society*. New York: St. Martin's, 1983.

The Knights of the Round Table. New York: Greenstone, 1954. (Unpaginated souvenir booklet for MGM's 1953 film.)

Köhler, Erich. *Ideal und Wirklichkeit in der höfischen Epik: Studien zur Form der furhen Artus- und Graldichtung*. Tübingen: Niemeyer, 1970.

Kolb, Herbert. "Der Minnen hus: Zur Allegorie der Minnegrotte in Gottfrieds *Tristan*." *Euphorion* 56 (1962): 229–47.

Kuhn, Hugo. "Parzival: Ein Versuch über Mythos, Glaube und Dichtung im Mittelalter." *Deutsche Vierteljahrsschrift für Literaturwissenschaft und Geistesgeschichte* 30 (1956): 161–98. Rpt. in *Dichtung und Welt im Mittelalter*. By Kuhn. Stuttgart: Metzler, 1959. 151–80.

———. *Tristan, Niebelungenlied, Artusstruktur*. Munich: Akademie der Wissenschaften, 1973.

Lacy, Norris J. *The Craft of Chrétien de Troyes: An Essay in Narrative Technique*. Leiden: Brill, 1980.

Lacy, Norris J., and Geoffrey Ashe. *The Arthurian Handbook*. New York: Garland, 1988.

Lacy, Norris J., with Geoffrey Ashe, Sandra Ness Ihle, Marianne Kalinke, and Raymond H. Thompson, eds. *The Arthurian Encyclopedia*. 2nd ed. New York: Garland, 1991.

Lagorio, Valerie M., and Mildred Leake Day, eds. *King Arthur through the Ages*. 2 vols. New York: Garland, 1990.

Lambert, Mark. *Style and Vision in "Le Morte Darthur."* New Haven: Yale UP, 1975.

Large, David C. "Wagner's Bayreuth Disciples." *Wagnerism in European Culture and Politics.* Ed. David C. Large and William Weber. Ithaca: Cornell UP, 1984. 72–133.

Leeming, David Adams. *Mythology: The Voyage of the Hero.* 2nd ed. New York: Harper, 1981.

Le Gentil, Pierre. *Littérature française du Moyen Age.* Paris: Colin, 1975.

Legge, M. Domenica. *Anglo-Norman Literature and Its Background.* Clarendon–Oxford UP, 1963.

Lever, Katherine. "Letter to Alice S. Ilchman." 26 Jan. 1977. Curriculum Committee, Extradepartmental Folder. Records of the Dean of the College. Wellesley College Archives, Wellesley, MA.

Levy, Bernard S., and Paul E. Szarmach, eds. *The Alliterative Tradition of the Fourteenth Century.* Kent: Kent State UP, 1981.

Lewis, C. S. *The Allegory of Love: A Study in Medieval Tradition.* Oxford: Clarendon–Oxford UP, 1936.

———. *The Discarded Image: An Introduction to Medieval and Renaissance Literature.* Cambridge: Cambridge UP, 1964.

Lindgren, Henry Clay. *Educational Psychology in the Classroom.* 3rd ed. New York: Wiley, 1967.

Lindsay, Jack. *Arthur and His Times: Britain in the Dark Ages.* London: Muller, 1958.

Littleton, C. Scott, and Ann C. Thomas. "The Sarmatian Connection." *Journal of American Folklore* 91 (1978): 513–27.

Lochhead, Marion. *The Renaissance of Wonder in Children's Literature.* Edinburgh: Canongate, 1977.

Loomis, Roger S[herman], ed. *Arthurian Literature in the Middle Ages: A Collaborative History.* Oxford: Clarendon–Oxford UP, 1959.

———. *Arthurian Tradition and Chrétien de Troyes.* New York: Columbia UP, 1949.

———. *Celtic Myth and Arthurian Romance.* New York: Columbia UP, 1927.

———. *The Development of the Arthurian Romance.* New York: Norton, 1963.

———. *Wales and the Arthurian Legend.* Cardiff: U of Wales P, 1956.

Loomis, Roger Sherman, and Laura Hibbard Loomis. *Arthurian Legends in Medieval Art.* 1938. New York: Kraus, 1970.

Lumiansky, Robert M., ed. *Malory's Originality: A Critical Study of* La Morte Darthur. Baltimore: Johns Hopkins UP, 1964.

Lupack, Alan, ed. *"Arthur, the Greatest King": An Anthology of Modern Arthurian Poetry.* New York: Garland, 1988.

MacCana, Proinsias. *Celtic Mythology.* Library of the World's Myths and Legends. Rev. ed. Feltham: Newnes, 1983.

Mancoff, Debra. *The Arthurian Revival in Victorian Art.* New York: Garland, 1990.

Manlove, C. N. *Impulse of Fantasy Literature*. Kent: Kent State UP, 1983.

Markale, Jean. *King Arthur: King of Kings*. London: Gordon, 1977.

Martin, Robert Bernard. *Tennyson: The Unquiet Heart*. Oxford: Oxford UP, 1980.

Matthews, William. "Matthews on Malory." Unpublished ms., courtesy of Mrs. Lois Matthews.

———. *Old and Middle English Literature*. New York: Appleton, 1968.

Maynardier, G. H. *The Arthur of the English Poets*. 1907. New York: Houghton, n.d.

McGann, Jerome J. "The Monks and the Giants: Textual and Bibliographical Studies and the Interpretation of Literary Works." *Textual Criticism and Literary Interpretation*. Ed. Jerome J. McGann. Chicago: U of Chicago P, 1985. 180–99.

Meale, Carol. "Manuscripts, Readers and Patrons in Fifteenth-Century England: Sir Thomas Malory and Arthurian Romance." *Arthurian Literature* 4 (1985): 993–1026.

Mehl, Dieter. *The Middle English Romances of the Thirteenth and Fourteenth Centuries*. London: Routledge, 1969.

Merriman, James Douglas. *The Flower of Kings: A Study of the Arthurian Legend in England between 1485 and 1835*. Lawrence: U of Kansas P, 1973.

Mickel, Emmanuel J., Jr. *Marie de France*. New York: Twayne, 1974.

Miller, Miriam Youngerman, and Jane Chance. *Approaches to Teaching* Sir Gawain and the Green Knight. New York: MLA, 1986.

"Modern Poetry." *Edinburgh Review*. 163 (1886): 466-98.

Mohr, Wolfgang. "Tristan und Isolde." *Germanisch-romanische Monatsschrift*. 57 NF 26 (1976): 54–83.

Moore, John C. *Love in Twelfth-Century France*. Philadelphia: U of Pennsylvania P, 1972.

Moorman, Charles. *Arthurian Triptych: Mythic Materials in Charles Williams, C. S. Lewis, and T. S. Eliot*. Perspectives in Criticism 5. Los Angeles: U of California P, 1960.

———. *A Knyght There Was: The Evolution of the Knight in Literature*. Lexington: U of Kentucky P, 1967.

Moorman, Charles, and Ruth Moorman. *An Arthurian Dictionary*. Jackson: U of Mississippi P, 1978.

Morris, Colin. *The Discovery of the Individual, 1050-1200*. London: SPCK, 1972.

Morris, Jan. *The Matter of Wales: Epic Views of a Small Country*. Oxford: Oxford UP, 1984.

Morris, John. *The Age of Arthur: A History of the British Isles from 350–650*. New York: Scribner's, 1973.

Morris, Rosemary. *The Character of King Arthur in Medieval Literature.* Wolfeboro: Longwood, 1982.

"La Mort d'Arthur." *Dublin University Magazine* 55 (1860): 497–512.

Myers, Alec R. *England in the Late Middle Ages (1307–1536).* New York: Penguin, 1952.

Nash, Walter. "Tennyson: 'The Epic' and 'The Old "Morte."'" *Cambridge Quarterly* 6 (1975): 326–49.

Neumann, Eric. *The Great Mother.* Trans. Ralph Manheim. Bollingen Series 47. Princeton: Princeton UP, 1972.

Newman, F. X. *The Meaning of Courtly Love.* Albany: State U of New York P, 1968.

Newstead, Helaine. "Arthurian Legends." *Romances.* Vol. 1 of *A Manual of the Writings in Middle English, 1050–1500.* Ed. J. Burke Severs. New Haven: Academy of Arts and Science, 1967. 38–79. 2 vols.

Northrup, Clark S., and John J. Parry, eds. "The Arthurian Legends: Modern Retelling of the Old Stories. An Annotated Bibliography." *JEGP* 43 (1944): 173–221.

Norton-Taylor, Duncan, et al., eds. *The Celts.* New York: Time-Life International, 1974.

Oakeshott, Walter. "The Finding of the Manuscript." Bennett 1–6.

O'Connell, Barry. "Where Does Harvard Lead Us?" *Toward the Restoration of the Liberal Arts Curriculum.* New York: Rockefeller Foundation, 1979. 59–76.

O'Driscoll, Robert, ed. *The Celtic Consciousness.* Portlaoise: Dolmen, 1981.

Orme, Nicholas. *From Childhood to Chivalry.* London: Methuen, 1984.

Owen, D. D. R. *Noble Lovers.* New York: New York UP, 1975.

Painter, George D. *William Caxton.* London: Chatto, 1976.

Painter, Sidney. *French Chivalry: Chivalric Ideas and Practices in Mediaeval France.* Baltimore: Johns Hopkins UP, 1940.

Parry, John J., ed. *A Bibliography of Critical Arthurian Literature for the Years 1922–29.* New York: MLA, 1931.

Parry, John J., and Margaret Schlauch, eds. *A Bibliography of Arthurian Critical Literature for the Years 1930–35.* New York: MLA, 1936.

Paton, Lucy Allen. *Studies in the Fairy Mythology of Arthurian Romance.* 1903. New York: Franklin, 1960.

Pickford, Cedric E., Rex Last, and C. R. Barker, eds. *The Arthurian Bibliography.* Totowa: Biblio, 1983.

Pochoda, Elizabeth T. *Arthurian Propaganda: "Le Morte Darthur" as an Historical Ideal of Life.* London: Oxford UP, 1971.

Pound, Ezra. *The Spirit of Romance.* New York: New Directions, 1968.

Raffel, Burton. *The Forked Tongue: A Study of the Translation Process.* Hague: Mouton, 1971.

Raglan, Lord. *The Hero*. London: Watts, 1949.

Rahner, Hugo. *Man at Play*. New York: Herder, 1972.

Ranke, Friedrich. "Die Allegorie der Minnegrotte in Gottfrieds Tristan." *Schriften der Königsberger Gelehrten Gesellschaft*. Geisteswissenschaft-liche Klasse 2 (1925): 21–38.

Reed, John R. *Perception and Design in Tennyson's* Idylls. Athens: Ohio UP, 1970.

Rees, Alwyn D. "Modern Evaluations of Celtic Narrative Tradition." *Proceedings of the Second International Congress of Celtic Studies*. Cardiff: U of Wales P, 1966. 31–61.

Reid, Margaret J. C. *The Arthurian Legend: Comparison of Treatment in Modern and Medieval Literature*. London: Edinburgh and Boyd, 1960.

Reiss, Edmund E., Louise Horner Reiss, and Beverly Taylor. *Arthurian Legend and Literature: An Annotated Bibliography*. 2 vols. New York: Garland, 1984.

Reynolds, William D. "Arthuriana: A Bibliography of Published Treatments of the Arthurian Legend, 1951–1983." *Studies in Medievalism* 2 (1983): 89–106.

Rhys, John. "Preface." *Le Morte d'Arthur*. 2 vols. London: Everyman, 1906.

———. *Studies in the Arthurian Legend*. Oxford: Clarendon–Oxford UP, 1891.

Robertson, D. W., Jr., ed. *The Literature of Medieval England*. New York: McGraw, 1970.

Rosenberg, John D. *The Fall of Camelot: A Study of Tennyson's* Idylls of the King. Cambridge: Harvard UP, 1973.

Ross, Anne. *Pagan Celtic Britain: Studies in Iconography and Tradition*. London: Routledge, 1967.

———. *Pagan Celts: The Creators of Europe*. Totowa: B & N, 1986.

Ryding, William W. *Structure in Medieval Narrative*. Paris: Mouton, 1971.

Schultz, James A. *The Shape of the Round Table: Structures of Middle High German Arthurian Romance*. Toronto: U of Toronto P, 1983.

Sharrer, Harvey L. *A Critical Bibliography of Hispanic Arthurian Materials: The Prose Romance Cycles*. Wolfeboro: Grant, 1977.

Shaw, Sally. "Caxton and Malory." Bennett 114–45.

Shippey, T. A. "Ancient British Inventions." *TLS* 30 May 1986: 583.

Shirt, David J. *The Old French Tristan Poems: A Bibliographical Guide*. Wolfeboro: Grant, 1980.

Sienaert, Edgar. Les lais *de Marie de France: Du conte merveilleux à la nouvelle psychologie*. Paris: Champion, 1977.

Silver, Carole. *The Romance of William Morris*. Athens: Ohio UP, 1982.

Smith, Henry Nash. *Mark Twain's Fable of Progress: Political and Economic Ideas in* A Connecticut Yankee. New Brunswick: Rutgers UP, 1964.

Southern, R. W. *The Making of the Middle Ages*. New Haven: Yale UP, 1953.

Spearing, A. C. *The Gawain-Poet: A Critical Study*. Cambridge: Cambridge UP, 1970.

Spiers, John. *Medieval English Poetry: The Non-Chaucerian Tradition*. London: Faber, 1957.

Spisak, James W., ed. *Studies in Malory*. Kalamazoo: Medieval Inst., 1985.

Spivack, Charlotte. "Merlin Redivivus: The Celtic Wizard in Modern Literature." *Centennial Review* 22 (1978): 164–79.

Staines, David. *Tennyson's Camelot: The Idylls of the King and Its Medieval Sources*. Atlantic Highlands: Humanities, 1982.

Starr, Nathan Comfort. *King Arthur Today: The Arthurian Legend in English and American Literature, 1901–1953*. Gainesville: U of Florida P, 1954.

Stenton, Doris. *English Society in the Early Middle Ages, 1066–1307*. 1965. Harmondsworth, Eng.: Penguin, 1971.

Stevens, John. *Medieval Romance: Themes and Approaches*. London: Hutcheson U Library, 1973.

Takamiya, Toshiyuki, and Derek Brewer, eds. *Aspects of Malory*. Wolfeboro: Longwood, 1986.

Tatlock, J. S. P. *The Legendary History of Britain: Geoffrey of Monmouth's Historia regum Britanniae and Its Early Vernacular Versions*. Los Angeles: U of California P, 1950.

Taylor, Beverly, and Elisabeth Brewer. *The Return of King Arthur: British and American Arthurian Literature since 1900* [misprint for 1800]. Woodbridge, Eng.: Boydell, 1983; New York: Barnes, 1983.

Taylor, Henry Osborne. *The Medieval Mind: A History of Development of Thought and Emotion in the Middle Ages*. Cambridge: Harvard UP, 1962.

Tesich-Savage, Nadja. "Rehearsing the Middle Ages." *Film Comment* 14 (Sept.–Oct. 1978): 50–56.

Thompson, Raymond H. *The Return from Avalon: A Study of the Arthurian Legend in Modern Fiction*. Westport: Greenwood, 1985.

Thompson, Stith. *Motif Index of Folk Literature*. 6 vols. Bloomington: Indiana UP, 1955–58.

Tillotson, Kathleen. "Tennyson's Serial Poem." *Mid-Victorian Studies*. Ed. Geoffrey Tillotson and Kathleen Tillotson. London: Athlone, 1965. 80–109.

Tolkien, J. R. R. "On Fairy-Stories." *The Monsters and the Critics and Other Essays*. Ed. Christopher Tolkien. Boston: Houghton, 1984. 109–61.

Tolstoy, Nikolai. *The Quest for Merlin*. London: Hamish Hamilton, 1985.

Tomkieff, Olive G. *Life in Norman England*. New York: Putnam, 1966.

Topsfield, L. T. *Chrétien de Troyes: A Study of the Arthurian Romances*. Cambridge, MA: Cambridge UP, 1981.

Treharne, R. F. *The Glastonbury Legends: Joseph of Arimathea, The Holy Grail and King Arthur*. London: Cresset, 1967.

Turner, Victor. *Dramas, Fields, and Metaphors: Symbolic Action in Human Society.* Ithaca: Cornell UP, 1974.

Tuve, Rosemond. *Allegorical Imagery: Some Medieval Books and Their Posterity.* Princeton: Princeton UP, 1966.

Uden, Grant. *A Dictionary of Chivalry.* London: Longman, 1968.

Uitti, Karl D. *Story, Myth, and Celebration in Old French Narrative Poetry.* Princeton: Princeton UP, 1973.

van Gennep, Arnold. *The Rites of Passage.* Trans. Monika B. Vizedom and Gabrielle L. Caffee. 1908. London: Routledge, 1960.

Vendler, Helen. "Presidential Address 1980." *PMLA* 96 (1981): 344–50.

Vinaver, Eugène. *The Rise of Romance.* New York: Clarendon–Oxford UP, 1971.

———. "The Shaping Spirit in Medieval Verse and Prose." *Sewanee Medieval Colloquium Occasional Papers* 1 (1982): 9–18.

Warner, Sylvia Townsend. Prologue. *The Book of Merlyn.* By T. H. White. Austin: U of Texas P, 1977.

———. *T. H. White: A Biography.* London: Chatto, 1967.

Watson, Jeanie, and Maureen Fries, eds. *The Figure of Merlin in the Nineteenth and Twentieth Centuries.* Lewiston: Mellen, 1989.

Wellesley College. *Catalogue Issue of the 1976-77 Bulletin.* Wellesley: Wellesley Coll., 1976.

West, G. D. *French Arthurian Prose Romances: An Index of Proper Names.* Toronto: U of Toronto P, 1978.

———. *French Arthurian Verse Romances, 1150–1300: An Index of Proper Names.* Toronto: U of Toronto P, 1969.

Weston, Jessie L. *From Ritual to Romance.* 1920. Garden City: Doubleday–Anchor, 1957.

Whitaker, Muriel. *Arthur's Kingdom of Adventure: The World of Malory's "Morte Darthur."* Totowa: B & N, 1984.

———. *Children's Literature: A Guide to Criticism.* Edmonton: U of Alberta P, 1976.

———. *The Legends of King Arthur in Art.* Woodbridge, Eng.: Boydell, 1990.

———. "Otherworld Castles in Middle English Arthurian Romance." *The Medieval Castle: Romance and Reality.* Ed. Kathryn Reyerson and Faye Powe. Medieval Studies at Minnesota 1. Dubuque: Kendall, 1984. 27–45.

Whitehouse, David. "The Real Arthur." *Humanities* 7 (June 1986): 22–24.

Whitelock, Dorothy. *The Beginnings of English Society.* Harmondsworth, Eng.: Penguin, 1950.

Wiegand, Herbert E. *Studien zur Minne und Ehe in Wolframs* Parzival *und Hartmanns Artusepik.* Berlin: De Gruyter, 1972.

Wildman, Mary. "A Supplementary Bibliography of Twentieth-Century Arthurian Literature." *Arthurian Literature* 3 (1983): 129–36.

——. "Twentieth-Century Arthurian Literature: An Annotated Bibliography." *Arthurian Literature* 2 (1982): 127–62.

Wilson, Anne. *Traditional Romance and Tale: How Stories Mean.* Ipswich: Brewer, 1976.

Wilson, Colin. *The Search for the Real Arthur.* Bodmin, Eng.: Bossiney, 1979.

Zumthor, Paul. *Essai de poétique médiévale.* Paris: Seuil, 1972.

Films and Recordings

Items marked (V) are available in video.

The Black Knight. Dir. Tay Garnett. Columbia, 1954.

Camelot. Dir. Joshua Logan. Warner Brothers, 1967. (V)

A Connecticut Yankee in King Arthur's Court. Dir. Tay Garnett. Paramount, 1949 (Films, Inc., 733 Wilmette Ave., Suite 202, Wilmette, IL 60091).

Excalibur. Dir. John Boorman. Orion, 1981. (V)

Gawain and the Green Knight. Dir. Stephen Weeks. United Artists, 1973.

King Arthur: From Romance to Archaeology. James P. Carley. Univ. of Toronto Centre for Media Studies, 1975.

Knightriders. Dir. George Romero. United Film, 1981. (V)

Knights of the Round Table. Dir. Richard Thorpe. MGM, 1953. (V)

Lancelot du Lac. Dir. Robert Bresson. Mara Films, 1974 (New Yorker Films, 161 W. 61st St., New York, NY 10023).

Monty Python and the Holy Grail. Dir. Terry Gilliam and Terry Jones. Python Pictures, 1975. (V)

Parsifal, by Richard Wagner. With George London, Arnold Van Mill, Ludwig Weber, Wolfgang Windgassen, Hermann Uhde, and Martha Modl. Cond. Hans Knappertsbusch. Bayreuth Festival Chorus and Orchestra. London Records, RS65001, 1951.

Perceval, le Gallois. Dir. Eric Rohmer. Gaumont–New Yorker Films, 1978 (New Yorker Films, 161 W. 61st St., New York, NY 10023).

Prince Valiant. Dir. Henry Hathaway. Fox, 1954.

The Spaceman and King Arthur. Dir. Russ Mayberry. Disney, 1979. Cartoon.

The Story of King Arthur. Slide-tape package. Holiday Film Corp., Whittier, CA, n.d.

The Sword in the Stone. Dir. Wolfgang Reitherman. Disney, 1963. (V)

These Halls of Camelot. Filmstrip and record. Thomas Wettengel, 1972 (Scott, Foresman, Glenview, IL).

Journals and Newsletters

Arthurian Interpretations. 1984–90. Ed. Henry Hall Peyton III. See *Quondam et Futurus: A Journal of Arthurian Interpretations.*

Avalon to Camelot. Ceased publication in 1990; some back issues available. Publ. Freya Reeves Lambides (PO Box 6326, Evanston, IL 60204).

Bibliographical Bulletin of the International Arthurian Society. 1949–present. c/o Hans R. Runte (Dept. of French, Dalhousie Univ., Halifax, NS, Canada B3H 3J5).

Encomia: Bibliographical Bulletin of the International Courtly Literature Society. Ed. Maria Dobozy (Dept. of Languages and Literatures, Univ. of Utah, Salt Lake City, UT 84112).

International Arthurian Society North American Branch Newsletter. Ed. Hans R. Runte (Dept. of French, Dalhousie Univ., Halifax, NS, Canada B3H 3J5).

Quondam et Futurus: A Journal of Arthurian Interpretations. 1991–present. Ed. Henry Hall Peyton III (Dept. of English, Memphis State Univ., Memphis, TN 38152). Formerly two journals, *Arthurian Interpretations* and *Quondam et Futurus: Newsletter for Arthurian Studies.*

Quondam et Futurus: Newsletter for Arthurian Studies. 1980–87. Subtitled *Quarterly for Arthurian Studies,* 1988–90. Ed. Mildred Leake Day. See *Quondam et Futurus: A Journal of Arthurian Interpretation.*

Tristania. Ed. Pedro Campa (Edwin Mellen Press, 240 Portage Rd., Lewiston, NY 14092).

INDEX